The Theory of Oral Composition

Folkloristics
Alan Dundes, General Editor

THE THEORY OF ORAL COMPOSITION

History and Methodology

JOHN MILES FOLEY

INDIANA UNIVERSITY PRESS
Bloomington and Indianapolis

Manufactured in the United States of America

Library cf Congress Cataloging-in-Publication Data
Foley, John Miles.
The theory of oral composition.
(Folkloristics)
Bibliography: p.
Includes index.
1. Oral history.   I. Title.   II. Series.
D16.14.F65   1988   901   87–45402
ISBN   0–253–34260–0
ISBN   0–253–20465–8 (pbk.)
1 2 3 4 5 92 91 90 89 88

This book is for
ROBERT PAYSON CREED
scholar, mentor, wilgesith

CONTENTS

EDITOR'S FOREWORD

The Oral-Formulaic Theory is one of the relatively few theories of folklore that have developed in the twentieth century. The majority of folkloristic theories and methods began in the nineteenth century. The Oral-Formulaic Theory, which was inspired originally by Homeric scholars trying to determine the extent to which the *Iliad* and *Odyssey* were the results of an oral poetic process, may be seen in the larger context of a formalist and structuralist intellectual paradigm.

Whereas the nineteenth-century theories of folklore were essentially diachronic and primarily concerned with the historical reconstruction of the past, twentieth-century theories tended to be synchronic and more involved with investigating the functions and forms of folklore. Russian formalism, the so-called Prague school of linguistics, the search for basic structural units in folkloristic genres, and the Oral-Formulaic Theory are all examples of the same basic tendency. The key questions asked were not how old a particular item was or where or when it might have originated, questions that intrigued nineteenth-century scholars. Instead, twentieth-century folklorists became interested in the actual performances of folkloristic phenomena, their compositional elements, and eventually their impact upon the audience. What a folklore item is and how it behaves replaced the earlier speculations about its possible origin.

The fundamental issue that stimulated the development of the Oral-Formulaic Theory was whether an epic was memorized verbatim or composed anew each time an epic singer recited it. Although the initial interest centered on the Homeric epic, the fieldwork to test the theory was carried out in Yugoslavia rather than Greece since it was in the former country that an ongoing, live epic tradition could be observed in situ. The fieldwork of Milman Parry and later that of his star pupil, Albert Lord, led to the theory that epic singers composed anew each time they sang, utilizing a selection from a host of traditional formulas to fill in each critical slot in the overall sequence of thematic slots.

The technique of re-eliciting the "same" epic from the same epic singer (as well as from other singers) confirmed for Parry and Lord the validity of what has come to be termed the oral-formulaic approach to epic composition. Once the Theory had been formulated by Parry and Lord, they sought to apply it to Homer's epics to demonstrate the oral nature of the process that led to the creation of the *Iliad* and *Odyssey*. (In one sense, the nineteenth-century bias in favor of seeking the historical reconstruction of the past continued.) Not only did the Theory, based upon extensive field-work in Yugoslavia, revolutionize thinking about Homeric epos, but also scholars working with other "literary" traditions that had probable oral connections—the Bible, for example—were quick to comprehend the possible implications of the Theory for their special literary domains. Accordingly, the Oral-Formulaic Theory has been applied to the Old Testament, the four Gospels of the New Testament, the *Song of Roland, Beowulf,* and many, many other important works of "literary" art.

Folklorists can recognize the kinship between the Oral-Formulaic Theory and such breakthroughs as Vladimir Propp's *Morphology of the Folktale* (first published in Russian in 1928). Just as an epic singer can draw upon a choice of allo-formulas to fill a particular slot in his or her narrative sequence, so a Russian tale-teller, according to Propp's analysis, may choose a particular motif to fulfill one of the thirty-one functions contained in a standard Russian fairy tale. (Of course, it may be that whereas epics allow for improvisation, fairy tales as a genre are less hospitable to free choice by their narrators.) The Oral-Formulaic Theory and Propp's celebrated *Morphology* share a common notion of a structural slot filled by one of a set of possible slot-fillers. Historically, it may also be of interest that both Lord and Propp were partial to a myth-ritual approach. Propp believed that his fairy tale structural sequence reflected some kind of adolescent initiation ritual, while Lord contended that what he called the Return Song story pattern (Absence, Devastation, Return, Retribution, and Wedding) was related to some vegetation generation ritual. (Both Propp's and Lord's schemes begin with "absence" and end with "wedding.") To be sure, the Myth-Ritual Theory is a separate and distinct theory. One can accept Propp's *Morphology* and the Oral-Formulaic Theory as empirically valid without necessarily granting credence to the proposed myth-ritual basis of a given formalistic pattern.

Folklorists can also see that Parry and Lord's pioneering fieldwork in the 1930s in Yugoslavia was in some ways a precursor of what is termed for lack of a more apt label "performance theory." In this theory, or rather approach, the emphasis is upon performance rather than text. Performance involves both performer and audience and it is the very interaction of these two that results in a given text. Studying such a text divorced from its interactional context is considered methodologically inappropriate. The Oral-Formulaic Theory, however, does tend to emphasize text rather than context. It is, in fact, through meticulous comparative examinations of texts of the "same" epic that one is able to identify formulas and themes. So, although Parry and Lord did encourage the study of epic performances in the field as opposed to limiting themselves to perusing epic texts in the library, they continued to be primarily interested in texts, not contexts. (We

get little sense of the audience's reactions to epic elements or their interpretations of the possible meanings of such elements in most discussions
of Oral-Formulaic Theory. And certainly most of the applications of Oral-
Formulaic Theory have been to contextless literary epics.)

One of the principal objections to the Oral-Formulaic Theory is that it
can give the appearance of being an all too mechanistic process of picking
out traditional formulas from an epic. The very same criticism can be applied to any of the formalistic approaches to folklore. Propp defines the
structure of the generic Russian fairy tale but tells us little or nothing of
the possible social or psychological significance of the schema he has so
carefully delineated.

There is one other matter that should be raised in connection with the
Oral-Formulaic Theory. Its champions proclaim it as one of the more important approaches to the serious study of oral tradition. Yet it is by no
means clear whether or not the Theory applies to many genres of oral
tradition. There can be no question that it does apply to the epic genre,
though there is dispute about whether (1) epic is a worldwide genre and
(2) the Theory applies to all those epics reported thus far. But it is doubtful
to say the least whether Oral-Formulaic Theory can be applied to any of
the many fixed-phrase genres of folklore—for example, proverb or riddle.
Proverbs are not composed anew each time they are uttered. Without the
possibility of improvisation, it would appear that the Oral-Formulaic
Theory would not be applicable. To the extent that general oral tradition
includes a fair number of fixed-phrase genres and to the extent that Oral-
Formulaic Theory cannot be deemed applicable to such genres, one cannot
really maintain that Oral-Formulaic Theory is a general theory of oral
tradition. It is one thing to propose a theory of epic composition; it is quite
another to argue that such a theory is a valid approach for all of oral
tradition. Still, even if Oral-Formulaic Theory were valid only for the epic
genre, it would be of importance. The epic is unquestionably a major genre
of folklore, and thus any theory proposed to deal with such a major genre
would be significant.

In this volume of the Indiana Folkloristics Series, the history and development of the Oral-Formulaic Theory is deftly surveyed. After a preliminary chapter treating the beginnings and forerunners of the Theory,
John Miles Foley skillfully summarizes the achievements of Milman Parry
and Albert Lord in successive chapters. Thereafter he reviews how Oral-
Formulaic Theory has been applied and modified in an impressive number
of branches of literary scholarship, involving a considerable array of language traditions. In a final chapter, he indicates the possible future directions of this innovative and important theory.

Professor Foley is admirably qualified to write the definitive overview of the Oral-Formulaic Theory. Through his own many publications—especially his superb annotated bibliography devoted to the totality of oral-formulaic scholarship, *Oral-Formulaic Theory and Research* (1985), and his imaginative editorship of *Oral Tradition*, a journal he founded in 1986—he has established himself as a master of the Theory. Professor of English and William H. Byler Chair in the Humanities at the University of Missouri, John Foley has written an erudite, vivid account of the rise of Oral-Formulaic Theory.

ALAN DUNDES

PREFACE

This is a concise history of the Oral-Formulaic Theory, that is, a book that follows the evolution of one particular approach to the study of oral tradition in its many forms and in its influence on the world of literate and literary works. Specifically, this study treats the field of scholarship created by Milman Parry and Albert Lord—and thus also known as the Parry-Lord theory—and carried by them and other scholars into more than one hundred separate language areas. Since Parry began his work with Homer, a sizable percentage of the books and articles in the discipline of Oral Theory have been concerned with ancient Greek oral tradition. Likewise, because Parry's and Lord's groundbreaking fieldwork on oral epic took place among the South Slavic *guslari* in various parts of Yugoslavia, a fair number of contributions touch on Serbo-Croatian. Other areas have also received significant attention, among them Old English, Old French, the Hispanic traditions, medieval German, African, Turkish, Chinese, Japanese, Irish, Russian, Native American, and numerous others. For a sense of the enormous spread of Oral Theory, one need only consult *Oral-Formulaic Theory and Research* (Foley 1985), an annotated list of relevant scholarship through 1982 (with annual updates in the journal *Oral Tradition*); fully fifteen hundred of the more than eighteen hundred entries in that bibliography stem directly from the work of Parry and Lord.

Having said something about what the present book attempts to do, I may also be allowed a few words about what it does not try to accomplish. First, the Indiana Folkloristics Series format, which very sensibly encourages brevity of presentation, does not allow for an extended rehearsal of bibliography; thus I have included in these pages only those works that I consider most important to the development of the Theory. In general, the most significant works are discussed in the text, with some additional references in the footnotes to each chapter. I refer the reader to *Oral-Formulaic Theory and Research* for further relevant citations, and also note that, as explained in chapter 5 of the present volume, *Oral Tradition* will be publishing a series of survey essays on many of the areas most affected by Oral Theory. Apologies are due those who detect one or more lacunae in the discussions below, and I would respond only that, in addition to the inevitable oversights, every scholar must construe a shared discipline slightly differently.

Second, this volume, like the bibliography, makes no pretense of treating approaches to oral tradition that fall outside the Theory. Occasionally a related book or article that does not proceed directly out of Parry-Lord scholarship has been mentioned, but this is a rare practice and one intended only to offer a window into other research that may prove helpful to the reader. Nor, I trust, do I serve as an apologist for the Oral Theory in this book. At every point I have endeavored to avoid the polemics that have too often intruded upon scholarly writings in this field (and too often deflected concern from issues that need to be addressed calmly and fairly). Of course, there would be no point in undertaking a history of an approach I find unrewarding, but in recounting how Oral Theory came to be I hope to have succeeded in telling the tale *pravo* (straightforwardly) and not *krivo* (crookedly, falsely), as the South Slavic *guslari* would say.

Thus the opening chapter has to do with the origins of the Theory in philology, anthropology, and the Homeric Question. Here we can distinguish between simple anticipation of certain of Parry's findings and real influence; as might be expected, cases of the former outnumber cases of the latter, but we can detect some true influences that had an important effect on his thinking and therefore on the formation of the field. Chapters 2 and 3 document the achievements of, respectively, Milman Parry and Albert Lord, starting with Parry's theses and papers on Homer and continuing through their joint fieldwork in Yugoslavia and Lord's comparative extensions to other fields. The bibliography at the end of this volume contains a complete list of their writings. Chapter 4 surveys what Parry and Lord made possible: the establishment of a new discipline that has now spread widely throughout the study of world literature. The chapter's first two sections cover ancient Greek and Old English, the two most active areas, in some detail, while the third section looks much more briefly and selectively at other traditions. Discussion of the major objections to the Theory, as well as of suggestions for its modification, is interwoven throughout the fourth chapter. The fifth and final chapter considers some of the most promising new directions in Oral Theory over the past twenty years, and includes some observations about the tasks ahead if the field is to meet the challenges of the enormous expansion and complication it has undergone in its sixty years of existence.

This book is intended to serve as an introductory history, and for that reason it is best read from beginning to end, after which more intensive investigation of individual areas can proceed with some knowledge of parallel activities in research on other traditions. I stress this point because the Oral Theory has not seldom suffered from confusion and "reinvention of the wheel" engendered by a lack of awareness of parallel research. Readers who wish to locate discussion of works by a particular author or in a given language area should consult the index.

Parts of the third chapter draw from the introduction to the Lord Fest-schrift (Foley 1981b), and parts of the fourth and fifth to a lesser extent from the introduction to the annotated bibliography (1985). Other technical matters include the practice of referring to Milman Parry as "Parry" and to Adam Parry as "A. Parry"; Adam's wife, Anne Amory Parry, is cited as "Amory Parry." Similarly, "Lord" designates Albert Lord, while his wife, Mary Louise Lord, is referred to as "M. Lord."

I would like to thank those who have helped with this project, but despair of remembering all those people and institutions that have contributed in one way or another. I am very grateful to the Research Council and the Provost of the University of Missouri for a research leave during the 1985–86 academic year, during part of which this manuscript was written, and to Deans Milton Glick and Theodore Tarkow and Provost Gerald Brouder for establishing a Center for Studies in Oral Tradition that will help to focus work on Oral Theory and other approaches to oral tradition. Missouri's Ellis Library and its staff have been extremely helpful throughout my search for exotic materials, and Harvard University's Widener and Houghton Libraries were treasure-hoards of rare sources for chapter 1. The manuscript was reviewed by Alan Dundes and Albert Lord, both of whom made numerous excellent suggestions for its improvement. Among colleagues who shared their expertise and time were Patrick Gonder, Joseph Harris, Gregory Nagy, Joseph Nagy, Walter Ong, Alain Renoir, Edgar Tyler, and Ruth Webber. It was, of course, Alan Dundes who first suggested this project to me, and I hope the product has in some way justified the invitation.

Finally, my thanks and love to Anne-Marie, big Joshua, and little Lizzie for their encouragement and patience during the sometimes trying period during which this book took shape. The dedication speaks for itself, although it does not, indeed cannot, say nearly enough.

Center for Studies in Oral Tradition
University of Missouri/Columbia

I.

PHILOLOGY, ANTHROPOLOGY, AND THE HOMERIC QUESTION

In tracking the development of the Oral-Formulaic Theory from its origins in the writings of Milman Parry and Albert Lord through its contemporary influence on more than one hundred language traditions, it is well to recall what preceded the famous research initiated by Parry and carried to fulfillment by Lord. Just as no intellectual movement springs quite full-grown from the minds of its most immediate creators, so the Theory was built in part on the scholarship and opinions of earlier thinkers.[1]

One aspect of this prior work may conveniently be categorized as the history of responses to the ages-old Homeric Question, that is, to the question of who Homer was, when he composed the poems we conventionally attribute to him, and what implications the answers to these queries have for the edition and interpretation of the *Iliad* and *Odyssey*. A second area of significance is the contribution of philology, in particular that brand of nineteenth-century German philology that helped to formulate answers to the Homeric Question by documenting and attempting to explain the repetitive, formulaic nature of the poetic diction. The third prominent stream in the confluence of disciplines that assisted in shaping the Theory was what we would today call anthropology or ethnography. Here Parry found a model for his comparative investigations, and especially for the fieldwork expeditions undertaken in Yugoslavia.

Although we shall be concerned in this opening chapter with the ways in which each area helped to create the overall context in which Parry and Lord formulated the opening statement of the Theory, it will soon become apparent that in order to gain a real sense of the history and evolution of the field we must distinguish between anticipation and influence. For many of the premises of the Oral Theory were advocated by one or more scholars or laymen long before, even centuries before, their inclusion as part of a comprehensive and unified explanation. Mere anticipation of this or that point, particularly when it occurs apart from any comprehensive, overarching theory and without the benefit of rigorous argumentation or submitted proof, cannot be given much relative weight in the chronicle of the evolution of Oral Theory. Nor can such simple position-taking, which often amounts to disembodied speculation, be considered an influential part of the process which led to the Theory. On the other hand, we can detect a handful of important influences on Parry as he began his work, and it is to these scholars and their writings that we shall devote the major part of our attention.

The Homeric Question

Perhaps the earliest scholarly anticipation of Homer's orality can be attributed to Flavius Josephus (born A.D. 37/38), a Jewish priest, Pharisee, and ardent champion of Jewish religion and culture. In the first book of *Contra Apionem*, his final work and an apologia for Judaism, he takes to task the revered classical culture of the ancient Greeks for its initial illiteracy:

> Even of that date [of the Greeks' acquisition of literacy] no record, preserved either in temples or on public monuments, could now be produced; seeing that it is a highly controversial and disputed question whether even those who took part in the Trojan campaign so many years later made use of letters, and the true and prevalent view is rather that they were ignorant of the present-day mode of writing. Throughout the whole range of Greek literature no undisputed work is found more ancient than the poetry of Homer. His date, however, is clearly later than the Trojan war; and even he, they say, did not leave his poems in writing. (I.11–12; Thackeray 1926: 167)[2]

To this general retort to Greek anti-Semitism he then adds a startlingly modern remark on the composition of the Homeric poems:

> but [they say] that the poems (lit., poetic work) were put together just as they were remembered distinctly from songs, and that through this process their many inconsistencies arose.

As early as the first century, then, Josephus anticipates the causal link between oral composition and narrative inconsistency that was to exercise so many later generations of Homerists.[3]

The seventeenth and eighteenth centuries saw the emergence of a large number of anticipatory writings, the first of which was by François Hédelin, the Abbé d'Aubignac: *Conjectures académiques ou Dissertation sur l'Iliade* (1715; Magnien 1925).[4] Basing his argument on Josephus, Hédelin contended that

> since this Homer left in writing no works that bear his name, one must
> conclude that he never composed them, and if he never composed them
> one must conclude that he did not exist. (40)

His major interest in the poems was in what he viewed as their literary
shortcomings, and as an explanation for these perceived deficiencies he
offered the *conjecture académique* that the works we have are not unified
literary compositions but rather the compilations of redactors for whom
history has supplied the convenient fiction of "Homer."[5]

Unlike the Abbé d'Aubignac, whom Magnien has shown had no Greek,
Richard Bentley, another who anticipated certain aspects of the Oral
Theory, was the most accomplished classicist of his day. In addition to the
remarkable discovery of the letter (and sound) digamma that had vanished
from the surviving Homeric texts, Bentley undertook in 1714 to respond
to A. Collins's treatise of a year earlier. The title given the response, *Remarks
Upon a Late Discourse of Free-Thinking*, indicates the general subject of the
debate: Bentley was seeking to demolish logically (and often satirically) the
so-called doctrine of freethinking, which advocated doing away with learning and tradition in favor of the individual's unencumbered pursuit of
truth. Bentley the philologist, to whom learning and tradition are all,[6] reacts
vigorously against Collins's claim that Homer had carefully designed his
poems for the ages:

> Take my word for it, poor *Homer* in those circumstances and early times
> had never such aspiring thoughts. He wrote a sequel of Songs and Rhap-
> sodies, to be sung by himself for small earnings and good cheer, at Festivals
> and other days of Merriment; the *Ilias* he made for the Men, and the *Odysseis*
> for the other Sex. These loose Songs were not collected together in the form
> of an Epic Poem, till *Pisastratus*'s time about 500 years after. (19)

While he assumes a literate composer even of the "loose songs and rhap-
sodies," Bentley is not far from Josephus and Hédelin in his idea of the
gradual (and post-Homeric) accretion of the poems.[7]

The next important opinion on Homer's literacy or lack of it came from
Robert Wood, an amateur classicist and politician who traveled the Homeric
lands in search of the one-time haunts of Achaean and Trojan heroes. On
the testimony of history and of the poems themselves, Wood denies possible
literacy for Homer and spends a good deal of *An Essay on the Original Genius
of Homer* (1767)[8] making the case for an oral bard:

> As to the difficulty of conceiving how Homer could acquire, retain, and
> communicate, all he knew, without the aid of letters; it is, I own, very striking.
> And yet, I think, it will not appear insurmountable, if, upon comparing the

fidelity of oral tradition, and the powers of memory, with the Poet's knowledge, we find the two first much greater, and the latter much less, than we
are apt to imagine. (259)

In addition to emphasizing the mnemonic power of verse and song and
projecting the importance of the oral medium when the written mode of
recording history is unavailable, he also calls as witness the oral traditions
of Central America and medieval Ireland, among others. Although Wood
does not have much to say on the actual methods by which such feats of
memory are accomplished, he does anticipate some of Parry's central tenets.

In 1795 Friedrich Wolf published a treatise, *Prolegomena ad Homerum*,[9]
that was to serve as a catalyst for the nineteenth-century battles between
Analysts and Unitarians, and which therefore may be seen as a true and
important influence on the genesis of the Oral Theory. Wolf proposed,
and for the first time summoned historical and archaeological proof to bear
out the contention, that writing could not have been available to Homer;
from this assertion he went on to argue that the Homeric texts had necessarily to be the creation of later redactors who joined together the primi-
tive oral songs into the works we celebrate for their unity of design. He
attributed the incongruities noted as early as antiquity to this process of
conglomeration, viewing the composite songs as expressions of "folk-
memory" handed down through schools of professional reciters. The co-
herence of his theory, ballasted as it was with scholarly evidence, set the
stage for the literary archaeology—the search for textual strata—that constituted the Homeric Question during much of the nineteenth century.

Because it was precisely the last stages of the Analyst-Unitarian controversy that Parry encountered as he was coming to terms with the Homeric
texts, Joachim Latacz was later to argue that *traditionelle Homerforschung*
from Wolf onward was not only an anticipation of and an influence on the
Theory but in general also its unacknowledged predecessor.[10] To an extent,
he is quite correct; Wolf had furnished what seemed to be a solid case for
Homer's orality, and Gottfried Hermann connected what would later be
defined as formulaic style with oral composition:

> Because of (1) the structure and combination typical of the composition, (2)
> the adaptation of diction to meter, (3) the addition of ornamental words,
> and (4) the paratactic method [*additive Art*] of joining attributive expressions
> to already completed concepts—all of this together inclines toward and
> forces one to the conclusion that these poems were made not for reading,
> but rather for hearing. (1840: 47)[11]

But neither scholar integrated his brilliant insights into a comprehensive
and exacting theory of poetic composition of the sort Parry was to offer
the classical world, and the same may be said for their contemporary and

later comrades. Once again, the seeds of the Theory may be found in many places, early and late, but the full-grown expatiation that has matured into a discipline of its own had yet to be born.

As mentioned above, the Analyst-Unitarian issue, the argument over one or many Homers, was the form taken by the Homeric Question throughout most of the nineteenth century. One scholar whose writings helped to focus the work of the Analysts by providing a theoretical base for the dismemberment of the poems into their constituent parts was Karl Lachmann. In the spirit of the then-current romantic interest in the collection of oral lays and their identification with national ethos, he proposed in 1816 a "lay-theory" (*Liedertheorie*) for the Middle High German *Nibelungenlied* and, twenty years later, for the *Iliad*.[12] In concert with his and others' examples, a new science of ferreting out the supposed contributions of this or that poet or redactor flourished in the latter part of the nineteenth century. To its credit, this was a methodology grounded firmly in philology: the Analysts proceeded from observation of linguistic and narrative anomalies to an explanation in terms of different poets and editors, so that the composite text of Homer was understood as the product of many centuries of reworkings. This brand of scholarship reached its apogee with the *Homerische Untersuchungen* (1884) of Ulrich von Wilamowitz-Moellendorff, with its minute and thoroughgoing dissection of the *Odyssey* that combines the flower of Analytic technique with a command of the possibilities for the history and transmission of the poem.

The opposing faction, composed of those who championed the hypothesis of a single genius author to whom we owe both the *Iliad* and the *Odyssey* in their surviving forms, were not nearly so many in number or so careful in their philology. These Unitarians never developed the kind of school or methodological sophistication that characterized the activities of the Analysts, being mostly content merely to assert their views and to offer opinions based on subjective apprehensions. An exception to this rule occasionally appeared, as in this observation by John A. Scott on the tradition with which he reasoned Homer must have been in contact:

> Homer and his predecessors must have had a great store of similes, descriptions, and narratives from which they freely drew; the original passage may be incorporated in many parts of Homer, e.g., the description of a headlong plunge from the deck and the comparison with a diver may well be repeated in the original form in the passage in the Odyssey . . . , since such a description so natural must have originated long before Homer. (1911: 321)[13]

As might be expected, the school of Analysis continued to develop,[14] taking many different and complex forms, while Unitarianism became virtually a historical curiosity. This differential evolution was due in part to the advent of Oral Theory, which disenfranchised the Unitarians and to which the Analysts and Neoanalysts have usually paid little attention.[15]

Philology

While earlier and contemporary answers to the Homeric Question created the context for Milman Parry's demonstration of Homer's oral tradition, the German classical linguists provided the methodology which he adapted to the task. As Parry's heavy citation of the philologists throughout his published works indicates, they were true influences on his thinking, and particularly on the precise kind of analysis for which his work is admired. As illustration of the influence of these scholars' ideas, I shall discuss the most important aspects of writings by the three philologists whom he most frequently cites—Johann Ernst Ellendt, Heinrich Düntzer, and Kurt Witte—and by his mentor Antoine Meillet.

In *Über den Einfluss des Metrums auf den Gebrauch von Wortformen und Wortverbindungen*, an essay published in 1861, Ellendt notes that Immanuel Bekker had already offered evidence of word-forms in the Homeric poems that seemed to be caused by the demands of the meter, and "which otherwise would perhaps have been unnecessary" (60). He now wishes to extend Bekker's situation-specific citations to a more general rule, if only by example.[16] The headings under which he presents his data are themselves telling: (1) change of gender of a noun, (2) change of number, especially of the dual and plural, (3) the influence of meter on the use of both the active and middle moods of verbs, and (4) the influence of meter on the use of other unusual word-forms. Although Ellendt was interested only in pointing out some of the ways in which meter helped to determine phraseology for poets "who do not write" ("die nicht schrieben," 79), he registers his belief that a complete collection of examples would explain the Homeric characteristic of repeating whole- and half-line phrases.[17] In his work Parry found the seeds of his own discussion of the role of meter in the formation of traditional formulaic diction.

Heinrich Düntzer, a contemporary of Ellendt, was also concerned with the influence of the hexameter on Homer's diction, and produced many studies on the subject, a number of them cited by Parry. In "Über den Einfluss des Metrums auf den homerischen Ausdruck" (1864), Düntzer looked at the metrical determination of personal pronouns, numerals, adjectives, verbs, and word-formation in general, with a major interest in the specific kinds of deflection in morphology caused by the interaction of phraseology and meter. His conclusions were more far-reaching that those of Ellendt; for example, he argued from his evidence that metrical convenience left the poet to select now this, now that form. Without doubt, only one of these forms was in use in the contemporary language, but the epic mode of expression had assumed for itself a certain privilege, even to employ earlier forms, in order to ease the flow of the verse. (88–89)

Here we see described not simply a special poetic language (or *Kunstsprache*) evolved to serve the needs of the epic poet, but more specifically a poetic language that took shape and continues to operate in symbiosis with the demands of the Homeric hexameter. Düntzer is not far from Parry's requirement that a formulaic phrase must occur "under the same metrical conditions" (1930: 272).[18]

It was particularly in the area of fixed epithets (*stehende Beiwörter*) that Düntzer exerted a telling influence on the early formation of the Oral Theory. In the case of such phrases, he contended, the principle of selection was not aesthetic but rather metrical; after a lengthy list of illustrations, he summarizes:

This selection of examples will fully suffice to show the poet's craft, how he influenced the selection and formation of his fixed epithets, and especially how in this respect the metrical requirement was of first importance and only extremely rarely did regard for sense have any bearing. (1864: 107)

To this clearly stated premise he then added a word on the nature of the craft of epic verse-making and its continuing role in later poetic composition:

This method depends wholly on the manipulation of synonymous phrases and on the extraordinary plasticity of a language rich in its manifold forms and expressions, through which the epos also exerted a significant force on later poets and even on prose usage. (ibid)

The extent of Parry's attention to Düntzer's theories can be appreciated directly by his quotation from the latter's "Zur Beurtheilung der stehenden homerischen Beiwörter" (1872: 510), which emphasizes the independence of Homer's choice of epithets from the usual artistic criteria employed by literate, post-traditional poets (Parry 1928a: 124). At the same time, another passage from the same essay will illustrate the shortcomings of Düntzer's ideas about Homeric composition; in discussing a selection of epithets, Düntzer remarks:

The alternation of these same two epithets has come about only through the requirement of the verse. And this is the second point, which I can touch

> on only briefly. The epic singer, to whose [actual] songs we can lay claim to
> an important extent, saw for himself that he enjoyed various privileges which
> eased the flow of the onrushing singing for him with a natural abundance
> of possibilities [*in natürlicher Fülle*]. What shortening and lengthening of
> quantity, elimination and introduction of vowels, what multiplicity of coex-
> istent forms side by side, what alternation in number, case, tense, and mood
> had the epic poetic art permitted itself in accordance with metrical conve-
> nience! (513)

Notwithstanding such pathbreaking observations, which were either cas-
tigated or ignored by contemporary scholars much in the same way that
Parry's work has often been maligned for its supposed preference for a
mechanistic rather than an aesthetic explanation, Düntzer never penetrated
beyond a largely synchronic view of Homeric phraseology. And even where
he assumed a later influence on post-Homeric poetry and prose, we find
no precise notion of an entire traditional diction, composed not only of
repetitions modulating under the influence of meter but also of larger,
integrative systems of phraseology or of the diachrony that underlies the
diction. Once again we glimpse a verifiable influence, and a crucially significant one, but without the comprehensive theory of composition Parry
would provide.

Witte's particular focus was likewise on the morphology of Homeric
words and compounds, especially those which occurred after the bucolic
diaeresis, that is, in the last two feet of the hexameter. In "Zur Flexion
homerischer Formeln" (1912a), Witte argued that scholars had not taken
sufficient account of the regularity of caesura, or word-break, between the
fourth and fifth feet, and that examination of this section of the line revealed a great many lexical items that occurred only or principally at that
point because of the fit between their metrical pattern and the favored
adonean rhythm of dactyl plus the sixth-foot anceps, __ u u __ __u.[19] Witte
also had a sense of the chronological development of the poetic language
in association with the hexameter, an aspect of his work that may well have
influenced Parry's ideas about the tradition behind Homeric diction:

> The oldest Greek literary language is bound by the dactylic hexameter; thus
> it appears only natural that in that case the verse structure [*Versgebilde*] was
> a determining influence on the external shape of its linguistic forms. Never-
> theless, the relatively later origin of the greater number of these forms proves
> and consequently illustrates that at every stage of the epos the verse had
> allowed creation of compounds of the shape __ uu __ __u. (1912b: 120–21)

In Witte's writings we can see the beginnings of a realization of the importance of the system of caesuras for the structure of Homeric diction,
an aspect which Parry would later enlarge upon and incorporate into his
demonstration of the formulaic and traditional nature of the phraseology.

We should not leave the philologists without briefly considering the role of Parry's own mentor at the Sorbonne, Antoine Meillet. In *Les Origines indo-européennes des mètres grecs* (1923), a volume which unconvincingly posited a foreign source for the Homeric hexameter, Meillet nonetheless made some telling, if telegraphic, remarks about Homer's formulaic traditional style:

> The Homeric epic is made up entirely of formulas which are transmitted by the poets. If one takes a sample passage, he can quickly recognize that it is composed of verses or parts of verses that are found again in the same textual form in one or more other passages. Even those verses whose constituents one does not find in another passage also have the character of formulas, and no doubt it is only by chance that they are not preserved elsewhere. (61)

Meillet's study was of course devoted in part to establishing a non-Hellenic origin for the hexameter, and so his comments on the language of Homer must be taken in that perspective. But, even given that slant, his description of the traditional idiom is very close to the characterization Parry was to offer in the Harvard essays of 1930 and 1932:

> [The hexameter] is verse wherein all is artificial and traditional: the vocabulary, full of archaic words; the grammar, in which the old forms are maintained alongside the new ones, and in which one encounters Aeolic beside Ionian forms; the phonology, a mixture of forms of various dates and from various dialects. (61)

When one considers the fact that Parry not only refers to this study in his published writings but also wrote his two doctoral theses under Meillet's direction, these remarks become particularly suggestive.

The German and French linguists thus influenced, and not simply anticipated, Parry's Oral Theory in a number of significant ways. From Ellendt, Parry learned of the shaping force of the hexameter and of the various kinds of changes called for by the strictures of the verse-form. In the work of Düntzer, perhaps the most farsighted and important of the four, Parry read not only of the role of meter but also of the special poetic language thus formed and, most critically, of the real possibility that Homer's fixed epithets were chosen not for their finely honed aesthetic appeal but rather on the basis of their metrical suitability for a particular position in the line. From Witte came an emphasis on the metrical divisions in the hexameter and on their effect on morphology and perhaps an incipient notion of the historical and continuing symbiosis of meter and diction that was lacking in the writings of Ellendt and Düntzer. In the work of his mentor Meillet he met with the opinion that Homeric epic was entirely formulaic, and further that the language in which the poems were composed was traditional and artificial, a *Kunstsprache* that had evolved for a specific function. With these solid scholarly contributions in hand, and with a knowledge of the Homeric Question as it was then being posed, Parry was ready to propose the first phase of the overarching theory that would harmonize the various new findings with what he had himself discovered about the kind of poet Homer must have been. But the full flower of Oral Theory, the journey from tradition to orality, still lacked one precious contribution: that of anthropology.

Anthropology

As we shall discover in the next chapter, Parry's first step—the demonstration of a poetic *tradition* underlying Homer's epics—was taken with the 1928 doctoral theses. He reached this stage in his developing Oral Theory in the context of contemporary opinion on the Homeric Question, with the aid of current linguistic contributions, and by the creative insight and philological rigor he brought to the investigation. But one more crucially important influence remained before Parry was to posit an *oral* Homer, and that was the perspective from ethnography, or anthropology.

Throughout his published work from 1930 onward, and especially in the groundbreaking essays of 1930 and 1932, Parry made frequent reference to the writings of Vasilii V. Radlov, whose firsthand account of fieldwork among the Turkic peoples of Central Asia seems to have influenced the evolution of Parry's ideas more than scholars have realized. In the foreword to *Der Dialect der Kara-Kirgisen* (1885), the fifth volume of Radlov's five-part publication of his collections, *Proben der Volkslitteratur der nördlichen türkischen Stämme,* we find a rich and detailed introduction to the performance of oral poetry among the Kara-Kirghiz, with references to the question of improvisation versus memorization, the units of oral traditional composition (especially narrative units), the role of the audience, the multiformity of tales and their parts, and the mixture of old and new in the oral poem; discussion of the significance of narrative inconsistencies; and continuing comparison with the Homeric poems. As Parry read through this brief but dense introduction, he must have found welcome reason to believe that many of the characteristics that he and others had studied in the Homeric poems were imaged in the living oral poetry reported by Radlov.

As a historical point, it is important to realize that, although there were other accounts of oral poetry that no doubt also impinged on Parry's developing notions of Homer as an oral bard,[20] this expert and focused study was the earliest scholarly source that offered an inside look at an extant oral culture. Radlov's work illustrated that theories could be buttressed not only by textual analysis but by direct observation, that hypotheses could arise not simply in response to problems that lacked explanation but as empirical measurements of real phenomena that were within the investigator's own sphere of experience. Along with the even more influential testimony given by Matija Murko on the South Slavic oral epic tradition, Radlov's writings on the Kara-Kirghiz suggested both specific avenues for investigation outside of the textual analysis to which classical learning had necessarily been obliged to devote itself and the more general and far-reaching possibility for anthropological verification and expansion of textual research.

Some examples of Radlov's observations and explanations will illustrate both dimensions of the importance of this kind of analogy for the evolution of the Oral Theory. As a careful fieldworker who made a practice of listening to many versions of the same narrative, Radlov noticed that a singer's rendition of a given song was neither purely memorized nor created wholly anew with each performance, but that bards practiced an art that allowed variation within limits, without realizing, of course, that they were not reciting a song "word for word."[21] Thus he notes that

> every capable singer always improvises his songs for the presentation of the moment, so that he is never in the situation of reciting a song in precisely the same way twice. They do not believe that this improvisation constitutes an actual new composition. (1885: xvi)

By means of a thoughtful comparison to a piano recital, Radlov goes on to characterize the oral performance as a recalling of traditional material in a momentary or nominal form, as the joining together of the old and the known with the new and the unfamiliar. Such a performance is made possible by the singer's idiomatic control over the commonplaces of his narrative tradition:

> By virtue of extensive practice in recitation, he has in readiness entire sets of "recitation-parts" [*Vortragstheilen*], if I may use the expression, which he joins together in fitting ways during the course of his narration. Such "recitation-parts" consist of descriptions of certain occurrences and situations, like the birth of a hero, his coming of age, praise of weapons, preparation for battle, the sounds of battle, a hero's speech before battle, the description of individuals or of horses, the characteristics of renowned heroes, praise for a betrothed's beauty, portrayal of one's home, the law, a banquet, invitation to a feast, a hero's death, a funeral lament, description of a landscape, the onset of night and the break of day, and many others. (xvi–xvii)

Although Parry will not confront such commonplaces in his published works until his famous response (1936a) to Walter Arend's 1933 study of *typischen Scenen* in Homer, the fact that Radlov had suggested such typical scenes or motifs so early must have had its effect on Parry's evolving ideas about comparative research and the Homeric poems.

What makes this influence more likely is Radlov's explicit conception of these "idea-parts" (*Bildtheile*) as plastic, multiform entities. He defines the singer's art in terms of how idiomatically and even artistically he handles the "recitation-parts":

> The art of the singer consists only in arranging all of these ready-made "idea-parts" coherently, as the course of events requires, and in joining them together through newly composed verses. The singer is thus able to sing all of the previously mentioned "idea-parts" in very different ways. He knows how to sketch one and the same idea in a few short strokes, or describe it in detail, or enter into an extremely detailed description in epic breadth. The more adaptable to various situations the "idea-parts" are for a singer, the more diverse his song becomes and the longer he can sing without wearying his audience by the monotony of his images. The inventory of "idea-parts" and the skill in their manipulation are the measure of a singer's ability. (xvii)

Of course, as an adherent of then-current *Liedertheorie*, Radlov saw the origin of these traditional units, these building blocks (*die Bausteine*), in the folk as a whole as opposed to the individual, but this opinion, if somewhat romantic and inexact, did serve to emphasize their traditional origin and dynamics. And, given such a dynamics, he warned against interpreting narrative inconsistencies as interpolations, that is, as the epic shards used by the Analysts to pry open the strata of the Homeric poems:

> We must guard against taking all inconsistencies [*Widersprüche*] as later in-terpolations, since such inconsistencies are precisely the characteristic of every true folk poetry. (xxvi)

In sum, although Radlov wrote at a time when certain universally ac-cepted premises, such as the evolutionary progression from folk song to composite epic, somewhat qualified his views, his contribution to Parry's thought was quite real.[22] Both by illustrating a comparative method that juxtaposed a living oral tradition and the manuscript poems of Homer and by offering a number of specific analytical insights about oral narrative composition, he set before Parry a general method and particular results that were to be refined in themselves as well as combined with the contributions of the philologists.

Likewise, Friedrich Krauss—with reference to the oral poetry of the Yugoslav *guslari*, the very epic tradition Parry and Lord were to experience for themselves some years later—offered some similar observations based on his fieldwork with more than one hundred singers. In "Vom wunderbaren Guslarengedächtnis" (1908), he described the singers' remarkable memories partially in terms of the units of composition employed to make their songs; in addition to simple repetitions, "it appears that the *guslar* also manipulates stereotyped portrayals and descriptions whereby he considerably compresses his actual [memorized] store of narrative material" (183). By using these *"Klichés"* the singer is able to compose fluently and to add material to his repertoire with ease:

> The *guslar* invents nothing more of importance, since the fixed formulas, from which he neither can nor wishes to vary, are available to fulfill his needs through the centuries-old bequest of the old tradition. To make a new song his own, that is, a song which is until that point composed of unfamiliar subject-matter, requires a practiced *guslar* who so thoroughly knows suitable *Klichés* that he need only listen attentively [to determine] in what order the *Klichés* follow and whether in longer or shorter form, or in what connection they present themselves in the new set of circumstances. (184)

But, although he goes on to describe other aspects of a tradition of verse-making, Krauss emphasizes near-memorization over traditional composition by means of these multiforms.[23] This tendency in turn ascribes much more importance to the individual poet and the individual oeuvre than to the poetic tradition at large.

Arnold van Gennep, to whom Parry also refers quite frequently, attempted in his little book *La Question d'Homère* (1909) to explain further the remarkable feats of memory in which Krauss had been so interested. For van Gennep the phenomenon was also explicable in terms of "clichés":

> the poems of the guslars consist of a juxtaposition of clichés, relatively few in number and with which it suffices merely to be conversant. The unfolding of each of these clichés proceeds automatically, following fixed rules. Only their order can vary. A fine guslar is one who handles these clichés as we play with cards, who orders them differently according to the use he wishes to make of them. (52)

Although he feels that recent archaeological discoveries have made the possibility that Homer himself was a preliterate oral bard unlikely, he does acknowledge the role of comparative studies in oral tradition in understanding the roots of Homeric epic. In addition to van Gennep, Parry cites Marcel Jousse (*Le Style oral rythmique et mnémotechnique chez les Verbo-moteurs*, 1925) for his attempt at a psychological theory behind oral style. It is, however, difficult to point to any particular insight by Jousse that might have triggered a response in Parry's thinking; since the monograph is an idiosyncratic synthesis of philosophy, psychology, and secondhand field-work reports, one would probably do well to consider it a general influence that made Parry more aware of the cultural institution of oral tradition and the highly organized system of unwritten communication it provided.[24]

Of the ethnographers who reported on living oral traditions, the most dependable in Parry's own opinion (1933–35: 440) were Radlov on the Kirghiz and Gerhard Gesemann and Matija Murko on South Slavic. Gesemann acknowledged his and others' debts to Murko:[25]

> Today we know, especially since the praiseworthy accounts by Murko, that the Serbo-Croatian singer is also an improviser, who by virtue of an entirely fixed technical method presents a new improvisation each time he sings a song. (1926: 65)

Fully in control of the technical aspects of verse-making, from the intricacies of the heroic decasyllable to the associated phraseology, dialect mixture, fixed epithets, and instrumental accompaniment (69–70), Gesemann advanced the study of South Slavic oral poetics by defining and illustrating the "composition-scheme" (*Kompositionsschema*), a multiform traditional unit as large as the entire tale:[26]

> The improviser has yet another "means," one which allows him not to compose only single verses and to string them one after another, but on the contrary to give an overall pattern to the whole [story or scene] that he wishes to perform, an "arrangement," as we say in academic terms, with "beginning, middle, and end," a narrative structure [*Erzählungsstruktur*] in a pattern according to which the action can be told, in short, a *Kompositionsschema*. (69)

Gesemann goes on to describe two categories of composition-schemes, one involving constituent epic actions such as duels or larger battles and the other independent of the overall action of the particular story. He follows this taxonomy with illustrations of recurrent patterns in South Slavic, and we may be justified in viewing his ideas as at least suggestive for Parry as the latter grappled with the *typische Scenen* that Walter Arend (1933) described in the Homeric poems.[27] But another aspect of Gesemann's contribution may be as important as any for the fieldwork that Parry and Lord were to undertake. As part of his proof of the significance of the composition-scheme, Gesemann describes an experiment he conducted in the summer of 1914 at a military hospital in Kragujevac. The investigator saw that a singer there heard a new song about the heroic death of the son of a physician in the hospital. On request

> the singer immediately sang [the song] freely, the very first time character-istically shaping the entire story in one of the most frequently recurring composition-schemes. Naturally, he was of course not present when the young man fell. But he stylized the event in such a way that he was able to sing some hundred verses and to satisfy the experiment. . . . (66)

This kind of in situ testing practiced by Gesemann and others may well have influenced Parry and Lord in their own experimentation.[28]

Of all prior investigations, however, none so influenced Parry's evolution from conceiving of Homer as a traditional poet to understanding that this poet also had to be an oral bard as did the works of Matija Murko.[29] Parry himself recalled the sequence of events some years later:

> It happened that a week or so before I defended my theses [1928a, b] for the doctorate at the Sorbonne Professor Mathias Murko of the University of Prague delivered in Paris the series of conferences which later appeared as his book *La Poésie populaire épique en Yougoslavie au début du XXe siècle*. I had seen the poster for these lectures but at the time I saw in them no great meaning for myself. However, Professor Murko, doubtless due to some remark of M. Meillet, was present at my *soutenance* and at that time M. Meillet pointed out with his usual ease and clarity this failing [to see that Homer must also be oral] in my two books. It was the writings of Professor Murko more than those of any other which in the following years led me to the study of oral poetry in itself and to the heroic poems of the South Slavs. (1933–35: 439)

At the very moment, then, that Parry's attention turned from the elaborate textual proof of Homer's *traditional* character to his necessary *orality*, he confronted the example of Murko's firsthand fieldwork in a living oral epic tradition.

The numerous aspects of Murko's influence may be summarized in a single point: more than any other reporter, even more than Radlov and Gesemann, he furnished an observed reality—encountered firsthand among the South Slavs—that corresponded to the hypothesis Parry had worked out for the Homeric poems. In place of an inevitably theoretical textual analysis, there now stood a measured, perceived proof that oral epic lived in a tradition of bards and verse-making. What is more, as much as Murko's accounts had to tell him, Parry also saw the opportunity to venture into the world Murko had reported and to conduct his own analyses. For the ethnographer had provided just enough information for Parry to identify the South Slavic epic tradition as an analogue for what he believed the Homeric tradition had to be, and yet had left enough questions unanswered or even unasked that the classical scholar must have felt the need for his own expedition, this time emphasizing collection and analysis over ethnographic description.[30]

Since Parry referred chiefly to the 1929 monograph in his writings,[31] we shall concentrate on a few major points in that document. It is well to note from the start that Murko was a native Slovenian and a professor of Slavic philology at Prague, who approached his nearly annual summer trips back to the Balkans from the perspective of both an experienced fieldworker and a professional linguist. His writings everywhere show him to be quite aware of the history of and latest developments in the study of *Volkspoesie*, and along these lines he suggests comparisons between the South Slavic epic and Ossian, Homer, the Russian *byliny*, and Romance and Germanic poetries. Likewise, he was impatient with the romantic excesses of *Lieder-theorie* and emphasized how the poetic tradition lived among individuals who served as its carriers.

In concert with his stated priority of providing an ethnographic description of the "folk poetry," Murko paid considerable attention to the territories in which it was still alive,[32] as well as to the particular kinds of songs that survived in each region. Murko also gave detailed (and sometimes anecdotal) pictures of the singers themselves, with notes on their religious affiliations and other sociocultural data. Included in such portraits were firsthand accounts of oral epic performances, complete with blow-by-blow descriptions of contests and other events, and a passage on semiprofessional singers of the day and itinerant court bards from an earlier time:

> In addition to the amateurs, one also encounters professional singers, especially among the Moslems, in northwest Bosnia and further to the south. Even those who in earlier times customarily sang in the Turkish cafés throughout the winter and during the month of Ramadan could and usually did have some occupation, but there formerly existed among them true professionals who journeyed from one to another of the courts of the Moslem nobility, remaining there weeks and months at a time to amuse the ruler and his guests. (1929: 11)

In addition to observations on the relative paucity of blind singers, the learning process for the prospective *guslar*, the length of songs in various regions, the question of a singer's repertoire, the pace of performance, and the problems of historical accuracy and the making of "new" songs,[33] Murko describes other features of the South Slavic tradition that were to be of primary interest to Parry and Lord. For one, his characterization of the

Moslem culture as generally the most conservative and traditional no doubt contributed to Parry's seeking the longer Moslem songs for comparison with the Homeric epics. The shaping function of the audience in attendance at an oral epic performance, an important dimension of traditional composition reported at length in Lord's *The Singer of Tales*, is noted briefly in Murko's monograph in his description of singers' adjustments of their songs to suit the audience and also in a memorable anecdote illustrating actual criticism of the performances:

> One time I reproached a singer for having given a favorite Moslem hero, Hrnjica Mujo, four brothers in place of the two who appear elsewhere; he retorted bitterly: "That's how it was told to me, I wasn't there when they were born." There is one critical process that does not lack originality: sometimes when the singer is absent during a rest-break, people grease the string [or strings] and bow of his instrument with tallow, so that it is impossible for him to continue. (22)

As mentioned above, Murko was well aware of the latest developments in the philological arena, so that he could observe with confidence that

> the singers retain such long songs thanks to the well-known epic repetitions, employed for example for messages, and also to various *clichés* devoted to celebrating feminine beauty, heroes, clothing [or war gear], horses, weapons, duels, etc. (18)

He also took care to mention and to illustrate the play of repetition and variation so typical of the formulaic structure of the oral epic language, obtaining examples of this multiformity by an experimental procedure very similar to that used by Parry and Lord some years later.[34] As one instance of this multiformity, he gives the opening lines of three versions of the same song by the same Moslem singer from Bosnia:[35]

> *Beg Osman beg* rano podranio
> [Osmanbeg arose early]
>
> *Beg Osman beg* na bedem izidje
> [Osmanbeg went out on the rampart]
>
> *Beg Osman beg* niz Posavlja gleda
> [Osmanbeg looked out over the Sava plain]

Although Murko himself was primarily interested in the demonstration these examples offered of whole-line substitution, we can sense their importance for Parry in what the German philologists called the *stehende Beiwort*, or "fixed epithet," of *Beg Osman beg*.[36]

As one who had spent many years in search of oral epic and its practitioners in his own and adjacent lands, Murko was understandably moved over its imminent passing away. He traced its demise to sociocultural and political factors, denominating "modern instruction" as its chief enemy, and closed his monograph, perhaps typically, by calling for further comparative scholarship on the South Slavic epic. Milman Parry was to hear that call.

As we move on to discuss the birth of the Oral Theory at the hands of Milman Parry and Albert Lord, it will be well to keep in mind the invaluable work of the investigators who preceded them, particularly those who truly influenced and did not simply anticipate aspects of the Theory. The Homeric Question had served as a touchstone for the best ideas of some of the leading classical scholars of the nineteenth and early twentieth centuries, scholars whose own thoughts had been shaped by those who came before them, from Josephus and Hédelin onward. The linguists had contributed a perspective on meter and language, together with a method of investigation, which Parry was to advance and use in a proof of traditional style that sixty years after its publication still stands as a model of philological acuity. And the anthropologists, as I have referred to the ethnographers Radlov, Gesemann, Murko, and others, served notice that there existed a living reality that corresponded to Parry's theoretical picture of Homer and his tradition; once his philological demonstration had been made in 1928, their work provided him with examples that urged the comparative method developed in cooperation with Lord. Thus it was that the Parry-Lord Oral Theory was to arise, as all theories of interpretation arise, in response to and in dialogue with the assumptions, methods, and findings of its age.

II.

MILMAN PARRY
FROM HOMERIC TEXT TO
HOMERIC ORAL TRADITION

With the work of Milman Parry we come upon the contribution of one of the two "founding fathers" of the Oral-Formulaic Theory, the other being his student and co-worker Albert Lord. As I attempted to show in the first chapter, Parry did not simply create the Theory ex nihilo; like all great thinkers, he carried on his research in the context, and with the benefit, of what had preceded him and what was happening in his own day. At various points the contemporary state of the Homeric Question, the findings of philology, and the reports offered by anthropology were all influential for the development of his thinking. Nonetheless, it is striking how much of his synthetic and comprehensive explanation of Homer and Homeric style may be found in even his earliest work, the master's thesis (1923), and further how easily and steadily his theories and demonstrations progressed from that point up to his final studies. Quite clearly, Parry's achievements are permanent contributions, in both their own reasoned analysis and their elegant presentation.

In this chapter we shall concentrate on the major writings, that is, the master's thesis, the two French doctoral theses (1928a, b), the two Harvard studies (1930, 1932), and the field notes from the Yugoslav expeditions (1933–35). Some attention will also be directed to Parry's comments on enjambement (1929), comparative formulaic diction (1933b), typical scenes (1936a), and the "winged words" phrase (1937). Our goal will be to understand the chief principles behind his revolutionary view of the Homeric poems and his establishment of a comparative method that has since been extended to more than one hundred language traditions.[1]

Analysis of the Homeric Texts

One can glimpse the depth of Parry's original vision in the master of arts thesis which he completed at the University of California at Berkeley in 1923, at the age of twenty-one. Here are the beginnings, however inchoate, of some of his most persuasive and far-reaching insights: the limitations of form on the expression of thought, the ornamental adjective, the persistence and conservatism of Homeric diction over time, metrical convenience, the "thrift" or "economy" of Homeric phraseology, the aesthetic excellence of an epitomized diction. In a sense this earliest of documents, although it does not pursue the various issues with the philological rigor that was to become Parry's trademark, does serve as a kind of map for most of his later explorations.

The opening paragraph of the thesis makes this point with its description of a poetic tradition:

> Just as the story of the Fall of Troy, the tale of the House of Labdakos, and the other Greek epic legends were not themselves the original fictions of certain authors, but creations of a whole people, passed through one generation to another and gladly given to anyone who wished to tell them, so the style in which they were to be told was not a matter of individual creation, but a popular tradition, evolved by centuries of poets and audiences, which the composer of heroic verse might follow without thought of plagiarism, indeed, without knowledge that such a thing existed. This does not mean that personal talent had no effect on style, nothing to do with the choice and use of the medium whereby an author undertook to express his ideas: Aristotle points out Homer's superiority to other writers of early epic verse in the organization of his material. It does mean, though, that there were certain established limits of form to which the play of genius must confine itself. (421)

Parry is speaking not about the collective consciousness of Lachmann's *Liedertheorie*, nor about the sequence of poets and redactors posited by the Analysts, nor about the original master bard imagined by many Unitarians; he is describing a *traditional* poet at the height of his powers,[2] one who is able to harness the artistic idiom fashioned by his many predecessors and to bring to his poems something more—an unprecedented ability to mold the traditional bequest into monumental epic poetry. It is also fair to note that at this period in the evolution of his thinking Parry is assuming, with almost all other classicists, a poet who writes his verse rather than an oral bard. It will be some years yet before a combination of factors—his own demonstration of the extent to which the Homeric texts are traditional, his mentor Antoine Meillet's encouragement, and the example of Matija

Murko and other ethnographers—will bring him to the conclusion that the only explanation for that traditional character is in fact an oral tradition.

But even at this juncture, Parry was enough aware of the implications of what he was formulating to anticipate the oversimplification that has dogged his ideas up to the present day, namely, the notion that his theories represented a dismissal of Homeric art in favor of a mechanistic model for the composition of poetry. His response to this reductionist view was an inspired analogy to Greek sculpture, in which traditional conventions played such a large part. In such a medium, as opposed to modern sculpture, the ideal was not simply the combination of ready-made parts, not only because that description of plastic composition is too wooden and simplistic, but also because it does not take into account the aesthetic heritage that inheres in convention. The patterns within which the sculptor works, far from being restrictive or even handicapping, are by their very nature filled with meaning, that meaning which they have achieved through the ages and which they encode in the present creation:

> Like the Greek painter the Greek sculptor worked in fixed schemes. He was dependent upon the manner in which his subject had been represented in earlier art. So, Furtwängler points out, Phidias, in his Lemnian Athene, followed the traditional design of the peaceful Athene—an Athene with uncovered head and closely bound hair circled by a festal fillet, who holds a spear in one hand and a helmet in the other, and wears the aegis in unwarlike fashion aslope her breasts. Moreover, the expression of the statue, a repose of body and face which by its very quietness indicates a divine strength and intellect, was an expression which, at the time, any carver of divinity must represent to the best of his ability. By following this tradition of design and expression Phidias has filled his work with the spirit of a whole race: he has not only followed its conception of the nature of a goddess, he has also represented her in the position and with the attributes which the race had chosen and approved as the most fitting to represent the beauty, the strength, the calmness of her nature. (424–25)

From the perception of traditional meaning in Greek sculpture it was then but a short step to its perception in Greek epic:

> We realize that the traditional, the formulaic quality of the diction was not a device for mere convenience, but the highest possible development of the hexameter medium to tell a race's heroic tales. (425)

In brief discussion and in modest-sized appendices to the thesis, Parry also began to illustrate by suggestion what his more thoroughgoing analyses (1928a, b) would later bear out in detail: that the traditional heritage behind Homer's genius could be tangibly demonstrated. The key to this insight was the use of the "ornamental adjective," already pointed out by Düntzer (whose work is not cited by Parry in the master's thesis), which denominates "some characteristic of an object without regard or reference to the special condition of that object in the narrative" (426). Here he argues firmly against the modern notion that epithets are summoned only or chiefly for their situation-specific applicability and in favor of the view that they serve in the role of a metrical convenience. What is often overlooked about this and later, more finely honed explanations of metrical convenience is the history that lay behind that compositional usage and the consequent referentiality of the phrase. Parry puts the matter succinctly when he contends that ornamental adjectives

> flow unceasingly through the changing moods of the poetry, inobtrusively blending with it, and yet, by their indifference to the story, giving a permanent, unchanging sense of strength and beauty. (426–27)

By way of conclusion he then turns to a comparative examination of Quintus of Smyrna, Apollonius of Rhodes, the earlier and later Homeric Hymns, and Hesiod with the *Iliad* and *Odyssey*, concentrating on the contribution of style to the compositional fabric and experience of each poem. In the works outside of the *Iliad* and *Odyssey* he finds in general a misconception of the "ornament" so natural (indeed crucial) to true Homeric style; the later poems affect an elegance that is not part of their making, while the earlier ones accomplish at best a decidedly lesser use of the traditional inheritance. The connection with orality, which we should distinguish from the later perception that Homer himself must have composed orally, is made during discussion of Quintus's attempts at artificial and individual adornment of his narrative with ornamental adjectives:

> For ornament could have no proper place in a diction that knew the traditional style and diction only by literary imitation; the traditional element was essentially a part of an oral poetry, a poetry that was learned by the ear, not by the eye. (429)

From that tantalizing point to the end of the thesis Parry says nothing further about the oral tradition that, at this point, he seems to have thought of as preceding Homer and serving as the crucible for the gradual creation of his phraseology.

From this juncture through the two doctoral theses (1928a, b), Parry turns his attention to development of the method he used to prove the traditional character of the Homeric texts. Armed with a full appreciation of the contributions made by Ellendt, Düntzer, and Witte, he adds to their insights a general theory of compositional method by a thorough analysis of one aspect of the diction.[3] The aspect he chooses for his testing procedure, the famous noun-epithet formulas for gods and heroes, is in fact the only one that would have provided the kind of proof he sought; as Parry himself later admits (1930: 306–7), only the noun-epithet phrases are tightly enough woven into a system of diction to present sufficient textual evidence for traditional character within the limited compass of the sample we have in the *Iliad* and *Odyssey*.[4]

The central credo behind Parry's demonstration in the first of his doctoral theses, "The Traditional Epithet in Homer" (1928a), was the perception that the action of meter upon phraseology produced formulaic diction, and that that process and its results could be unambiguously illustrated through analysis of the noun-epithet formulas:

> To create a diction adapted to the needs of versification, the bards found and kept expressions which could be used in a variety of sentences, either as they stood or with slight modifications, and which occupied fixed places in the hexameter line. (9)

Because the Homeric hexameter was a complex metrical mesh which admitted certain word- and phrase-shapes only at particular positions, the line served as a kind of selector mechanism, sorting elements of phraseology according to their metrical makeup. Once admitted to the appropriate metrical position, these noun-epithet formulas were useful to the composing poet and so, over time, became part of the special diction employed by each bard and handed down to his successors. By his concentration on the noun-epithet phrases, Parry was able to show with precision how these relatively large and unchanging elements were systematized by tradition and so made available to Homer and his fellows as part of a special traditional idiom.

From the start Parry emphasized two features of this compositional idiom: the simplicity and the length of the system. By the former term he meant to indicate the unique metrical values of the elements involved, and therefore their utility, while by the latter he designated the length of the smaller systems of phraseology within the diction as a whole. Both features are apparent in this selection from one of his examples, which documents the way in which Homer formulaically says "and X replied" (10):

τὸν ⎫
　　⎬　δ' ἠμείβετ' ἔπειτα ⎰ πολύτλας δῖος 'Οδυσσεύς (3)
τὴν ⎭　　　　　　　　　⎱ ποδάρκης δῖος 'Αχιλλεύς (2)
　　　　　　　　　　　　 βοῶπις πότνια ''Ηρη (4)
　　　　　　　　　　　　 Γερήνιος ἱππότα Νέστωρ (8)
　　　　　　　　　　　　 θεὰ γλαυκῶπις 'Αθήνη (7)
　　　　　　　　　　　　 βοὴν ἀγαθὸς Διομήδης (1)
　　　　　　　　　　　　 βοὴν ἀγαθὸς Μενέλαος (2)

What this system of phraseology provides is a unique and traditional way to relate the commonplace narrative occurrence of a god or hero making answer, whether that character be "much-suffering divine Odysseus," "swift-footed divine Achilleus," "ox-eyed queen Hera," "Gerenian horseman Nestor," "goddess gray-eyed Athena," "Diomedes of the great battle-cry," "Menelaos of the great battle-cry," or any of the many other gods and heroes whose noun-epithet formulas participate in this same useful pattern.

Or, since the poet can construct lines by joining any formulas that fit together in form[5] and essential idea, Parry illustrates the possible complements for a single noun-epithet formula (selections, 11):

$$
\left.\begin{array}{l}
\text{αὐτὰρ ὁ μερμήριξε (1)} \\
\text{αὐτὰρ ὁ βῆ διὰ δῶμα (1)} \\
\text{αὐτὰρ ἐπεὶ τὸ γ' ἄκουσε (1)} \\
\text{τὸν δ' αὖτε προσέειπε (8)} \\
\text{ἔνθα καθέζετ' ἔπειτα (1)}
\end{array}\right\} \quad \text{πολύτλας δῖος Ὀδυσσεύς}
$$

Thus, whether Homer wishes to say of Odysseus "But he pondered," "But he walked through the house," "But when he heard," "But on the other hand he addressed him," or "But then he sat down there," he has the means to do so formulaically, in a just measure of verse. The simplicity in both of these two systems consists of the unique metrical value of the constituent parts, and their extension is indicated by the mere fact that their full illustration in Parry 1928a includes twenty-seven members for the first and twenty-four for the second. As a rough approximation of the multiformity of traditional diction, we may note that each predicate action in the second system can be matched to any of the metrically equivalent noun-epithet formulas in the first, yielding a total of 648 different combinations for these two systems alone. When one adds that numerous other noun-epithet and predicate systems are available for the poet's use, it quickly becomes apparent how powerful an instrument Homeric phraseology is.[6]

On the basis of evidence such as this, Parry went on to define the *formula* as "an expression regularly used, under the same metrical conditions, to express an essential idea" (13), a definition developed in the first doctoral thesis for the noun-epithet phrases and later applied to other sorts of phraseological patterns as well. Phrases that filled the same part of the line and were equivalent in function (though usually unrelated in actual verbal makeup) he called the same *formula type*, denominating in this way the extension of the formulaic diction. Other important distinctions included the *particularized* epithet, which concerns the immediate action in a given narrative context, as opposed to the *ornamental* epithet, which has no specific relation to any of its given contexts.[7]

Within the same formula type one finds a wide selection of phrases for

different gods and heroes, but very few instances of more than a single
formula of the same metrical definition for a single character. This economy
of expression so typical of Homeric diction Parry termed *thrift*, later defining it as "the degree in which [a formula type or system] is free of phrases
which, having the same metrical value and expressing the same idea, could
replace one another" (1930: 276; cp. 1928a: 18, n. 1 and 100–101). He
reasoned, in other words, that a diction which in the great majority of cases
provided only a unique metrical solution to the problem of relating a given
action or idea was a consummately useful diction; by the practical virtue
of lacking alternatives, the traditional phraseology saved the poet from the
dilemma of choice by presenting the one epitomized expression appropriate to the task.

Most of the remainder of the first doctoral thesis is devoted to a thoroughgoing examination of the role of *principal-type* noun-epithet formulas
of gods and heroes, that is, of those phrases that exactly fill the metrical
space between line-beginning or -end and one of the regular caesuras or
diaereses.[8] This aspect of Parry's investigation—the exemplary care and
thoroughness of analysis—provided the philological basis upon which the
Oral Theory was erected. In these pages he broached the idea of *generic*
versus *distinctive* epithets, that is, words which could pertain to any god or
hero versus those which could be employed for only one particular god
or hero. He also offered an explanation of the dynamics or process of the
making of traditional diction to accompany his exhaustive investigation of
the evidence as we encounter it in the texts. Behind the data of the systems
Parry perceived the operation of a principle he named *analogy*:

> the bards, always trying to find for the expression of each idea in their poetry
> a formula at once noble and easy to handle, created new expressions—in so
> far as the result was compatible with their sense of heroic style—in the
> simplest way possible: they modified expressions already in existence. (68)

It was to this process of development that Parry ascribed the systematization
that he felt was proof of the traditional character of Homeric diction,[9] and
it was this explanation that he presented to counter the charges that his
description of Homeric poetics was mechanical or reductive of the poet's
art.[10]

Out of these analyses and deductions emerged a new way of confronting
the *fixed epithet*, the *stehend Beiwort* of Düntzer and others, that emphasized
four qualities:

1. Fixed epithets are used in accordance with their metrical value and not
   in accord with their signification;
2. they are traditional;

3. they are always ornamental [rather than particularized];
4. they are often generic [as well as distinctive]. (165)

Once one adds to this description the perception that "for [Homer] and his audience alike, the fixed epithet did not so much adorn a single line or even a single poem, as it did the entirety of heroic song" (137), one gains a sense of how far Parry advanced the findings of the linguists. Where they based their observations on a mélange of chosen examples, he conducted an exhaustive analysis of one type of example as the best test case for his purposes; where they sought to illustrate a principle, he sought to prove a system ordered by a principle operating over time; and where they were satisfied with pointing out one aspect of Homeric style, he searched for a comprehensive explanation that would shed light on all of Homeric compositional technique.

Just how powerful and generative the practice of analogy proved in the formation of traditional formulaic diction was the major thrust of Parry's supplementary doctoral thesis, "Homeric Formulae and Homeric Metre" (1928b). Instead of explaining metrical anomalies as always and everywhere the telltale mark of interpolation, and therefore as grist for the Analysts' mill, he showed how the combination of formulas could produce some phrases that exhibited short or long syllables in hiatus. While for a later, nontraditional poet, such infelicities would be considered violations of the rules of versification, and would thus demand correction, for Homer and the traditional epic bards they simply comprised those few cases where the juxtaposition of formulaic units failed to produce a perfect metrical fit.

More important than this demonstration, however, and more significant even than the preliminary observation that a large percentage of such metrical flaws occur at natural points of division in the hexameter (and therefore at formulaic seams in the verse), was the reasoning behind the explanation. Simply put, the traditional formulaic diction as a whole provided too important a compositional technique to abandon its entirety over the few anomalous cases in which it produced a metrical "error":

> Once the central fact has been understood that the genius of Homer manifested itself in the expression of traditional ideas by means of equally traditional words and groups of words, it will be seen that there is hardly any reason to suppose that to repair the hiatus of a short vowel, he would have abandoned the bardic style. (206)

Once again we see Parry's emphasis on a traditional technique rather than on a simple principle uncontextualized by an overall theory of composition.[11]

Before taking the second step in the evolution of the Oral Theory, Parry located another aspect of Homeric traditional structure in the distinctive quality of enjambement in the *Iliad* and *Odyssey* (1929). Here his basic concern was with the integrity of the single line as a compositional and expressive unit, and his measurements were intended to calculate the extent to which Homeric epic verses followed one of three possibilities: (a) no enjambement, with the thought complete at line-end and no optional continuation; (b) "unperiodic" enjambement, with the thought complete at line-end but optionally continued to the next verse; and (c) "necessary" enjambement, which entailed either incomplete syntax or division in the middle of a word-group, thus leading to an obligatory continuation in the following line (253). He found evidence that in Homer almost one-half of the verses show no enjambement whatever, with unperiodic enjambement twice as frequent as in Apollonius or Virgil and necessary enjambement twice as infrequent as in the literary writers of epic.[12] Parry reasoned that these findings constituted further evidence that Homer thought and composed formulaically and paratactically in natural linear units, that he made his epic in the style given him by tradition. We sense a hint of his developing vision of the oral bard in this commentary on the exigencies and opportunities associated with this method:

> Oral versemaking by its speed must be chiefly carried on in an adding style. The Singer has not time for the nice balances and contrasts of unhurried thought: he must order his words in such a way that they leave him much freedom to order the sentence or draw it out as the story and the needs of the verse demand. (262)

An Oral Tradition behind the Texts

Perhaps the chief reason for Parry's incipient notion of an oral tradition in the 1929 essay on enjambement was the influence of Antoine Meillet and Matija Murko. As shown in the last chapter, he was convinced that Meillet had hit upon the main weakness of his doctoral theses by pointing out that the traditional poet described therein must also have been an oral poet. In addition, his mentor had seen to it that Murko was present at the *soutenance*, and we recall that Parry himself vouchsafed that "it was the writings of Professor Murko more than those of any other which in the following years led me to the study of oral poetry in itself and to the heroic poems of the South Slavs" (1933–35: 439). At any rate, the two Harvard (or "Studies") essays, the first on "Homer and Homeric Style" (1930) and the second on "The Homeric Language as the Language of an Oral Poetry"

(1932), mark the crucial shift in Parry's thinking from a simply traditional to a necessarily *oral* traditional Homeric poetry.

In the first of these studies, Parry presented his new and more complete theory—which from this juncture onward may be termed the Oral Theory—in part as a response to two criticisms of the doctoral theses. These charges were (a) that formulas are to be found in virtually all poetry, and thus cannot be understood as a litmus test for traditional structure, and (b) that the noun-epithet formulas constitute a special case and thus should not serve as the model by means of which all of Homeric diction is to be characterized.[13] To both objections he answered that consideration of the *system* behind the use of fixed epithets and further probing of other aspects of the diction would provide more evidence for his position.[14]

A key element in the demonstration he proposed to undertake was, just as in the 1928 essays, the criterion of usefulness, that is, the degree to which "a group of words which is regularly employed under the same metrical conditions to express a given essential idea" (1930: 272) serves the versificational and tale-telling needs of the poet composing in oral performance. With the hypothesis of oral verse-making, then, comes an additional aspect of the utility described earlier as a traditional imperative; now Parry conceives of an oral bard, making his verse under the pressure of performance before an audience, who has at his command the formulaic "words" that allow him to tell the story fluently in the oral traditional idiom. A second modification should also be noticed, for in its simplicity it has far-reaching implications for both theory and analysis. This change has to do with the extension of the idea and definition of *formula* as applied strictly to the noun-epithet phrases so systematically deployed by Homer and ancient Greek tradition to, in effect, all phrases that make up the hexameter verses of the *Iliad* and *Odyssey*.[15] While he recognizes that the difference between formulas and mere repetitions, since it depends on systematization and utility, is of the greatest importance, he also realizes that it is difficult, and sometimes impossible, to indicate precisely how these two qualities pertain to every phrase in Homer.[16] He thus adopts the repetition of a phrase as a practical criterion of formulaic structure, noting that "the repeated use of a phrase means not only that the poet is following a fixed pattern of words, it means equally that he is denying himself all other ways of expressing the idea" (279).

But foremost among the modifications or extensions which Parry made in the 1930 study was the proposal of the *formulaic system*, which he defined as "a group of phrases which have the same metrical value and which are enough alike in thought and words to leave no doubt that the poet who used them knew them not only as single formulas, but also as formulas of a certain type" (257).[17] This construct, not a part of the theory in the 1928 essays because noun-epithet formulas are stable except for inflectional changes, allows consideration and analysis of the more fluid, more adaptable multiform phraseology outside of the formal designations for gods and heroes. Consider the following example, drawn from his own illustration of the concept (276):

$$
\text{αὐτὰρ ἐπεὶ}
\left\{
\begin{array}{l}
\text{δείπνησε (2)} \\
\text{κατέπαυσα (1)} \\
\text{τάρπησαν (3)} \\
\text{ῥ'} \left\{
\begin{array}{l}
\text{ἕσσαντο (3)} \\
\text{εὔξαντο (4)} \\
\text{ἵκοντο (3)} \\
\text{ἐνέηκε (1)}
\end{array}
\right.
\end{array}
\right.
$$

This diagram indicates telegraphically how the oral traditional diction outside the noun-epithet formulas is systematized: whether one wishes to include in the "But when" phrase the action of "had a meal," "rested from," "enjoyed," "took a seat," "prayed," "reached," or "let in," and further whether one is dealing with a verb that begins with a consonant or with a vowel,[18] the traditional phraseology offers a formulaic way to accomplish that goal, a method of portraying the desired action in a just measure of verse.[19] The inclusion of the formulaic system thus solves, at least theoretically and by example (see note 15), the thorny problem of explicating diction that does not as readily reveal the same kind of systematization that was shown to be the organizing principle underlying the use of noun-epithet formulas.

With this new concept in hand, Parry was prepared to conduct his famous analyses of the openings of the *Iliad* and *Odyssey*. It is important to note that he prescribed certain practical limits and conditions on the formulas he would investigate in these two passages, denominating by that term "only expressions made up of at least four words or five syllables, with the exception of noun-epithet phrases, which may be shorter" (275, n. 1) and "only those in which not only the metre and the parts of speech are the same, but in which also at least one important word or group of words is identical" (301). Even a glance through his marking of the two 25-line samples, in which he designates exactly repeated expressions with a solid and formulaic expressions with a broken underlining, shows how much Homer depended on the traditional phraseology. Parry argues that, far from serving any particular aesthetic purpose, these stylistic redundancies are signs of the poet's knowledge of, dependence on, and systematic deployment of traditional diction.

From this quantitative demonstration he proceeds to ask why Homer and his brethren kept so strictly to the formulaic style, and, with the support of sources mentioned in the first chapter, comes to the conclusion that only one explanation can be contemplated: "the necessity of making verses by the spoken word." He conceives of the process in this way:

> The answer [to this question] is not only the desire for an easy way of making verses, but the complete need of it. Whatever manner of composition we could suppose for Homer, it could be only one which barred him in every verse and in every phrase from the search for words that would be of his own finding. . . . Without writing, the poet can make his verses only if he has a formulaic diction which will give him his verses all made, and made in such a way that, at the slightest bidding of the poet, they will link themselves in an unbroken pattern that will fill his verses and make his sentences. (317)

This *proof by necessity* is, to be sure, solidly based in textual analysis, but it must by definition remain a hypothesis, however probable, that cannot be certified as fact without the firsthand observation that is of course beyond our grasp.[20] It was in order to gain a complementary *proof by analogy* that Parry was soon to adopt the next best available method—that of firsthand observation of the still extant oral epic tradition of the South Slavs.

The second of the two "Studies" essays (1932) carried the new hypothesis of oral tradition to the very language of the *Iliad* and *Odyssey*, an area that, like authorship and textual history, had long been a vexed question in Homeric scholarship. By applying the conclusions reached on the traditional formulaic style and on the long process of the evolution of that style under the conditions of oral performance, Parry was able to present an explanation for the often puzzling mix of dialectal and chronological forms that comprise the Homeric *Kunstsprache*. His basic principle for the formation and maintenance of the heterogeneous language was the natural operation of the diction over time:

> the Homeric poems were composed in a poetic language wherein old and foreign forms had been kept and new forms brought in by reason of the help they gave the epic poets in making their hexameters. (328)

Since words and inflections from various times and places proved metrically useful to the tradition, and further, since they became encoded (even fossilized) in the diction by virtue of their participation in formulaic phrases which then became the indivisible "words" in the traditional poet's lexicon, outmoded and foreign forms could survive as long as they served a compositional function. Likewise, new words and inflections could enter the Homeric language under the same conditions, and the process of analogy,

that estimable force to which Parry attributed the multiformity of phraseology, could encourage the formation of artificial elements, that is, forms
which never appeared in any version of the spoken language but which
were created by the exigencies of oral traditional style.

The Homeric scholar will want to consider the technicalities of Parry's
proposals carefully, weighing, for example, the eight principles associated
with his view of the language (340–42); these observations have implications
not only for the language, but also for the criticism of the texts and interpretations of the poems. For the comparatist, the idea of a multidialectal,
archaized, artificial language also has great importance. To take a convenient analogue, the South Slavic epic language is a similarly heterogeneous
idiom, with extremely old words and outdated inflections alongside recent
and even new elements, and with numerous inflections from dialects other
than the poet's own.[21] For Parry, this theory solved the nagging problem
of the "provenience" of the poems, that is, whether one was dealing with
an Ionic, Aeolic, or Arcado-Cyprian poet, allowing him to see the poems'
language as the gradual creation of the Aeolians and Arcado-Cyprians:

> the formulaic diction was learned by the Ionians from the Aeolians, and
> though under the stress of habit of their own speech they made it Ionic
> wherever that could be done without harm to the technique of its use, they
> otherwise kept it almost without change, since the way in which verse is
> orally made forced them to do so. (360)

The Analogy of South Slavic Oral Epic Tradition

Parry's reasons for turning to the analogy of the South Slavic tradition are
best summarized in his own fieldnotes, entitled "Ćor Huso" (1933–35) and
unpublished during his lifetime.[22] Having postulated an oral Homeric poetry on the basis of his textual analyses, Parry found himself

> in the position of speaking about the nature of oral style almost purely on
> the basis of a logical reasoning from the characteristics of Homeric style,
> whereas what information I had about oral style as it could be seen in actual
> practice was due to what I had been able to gather here and there from the
> remarks of different authors who, save in a few cases—that of Murko and
> Gesemann for the Southslavic poetries, and of Radloff for the Kirgiz-Tartar
> poetry—were apt to be haphazard and fragmentary—and I could well fear,
> misleading. Of the various oral poetries for which I could obtain enough
> information the Southslavic seemed to be the most suitable for a study which
> I had in mind, to give that knowledge of a still living oral poetry which I
> saw to be needed if I were to go on with any sureness in my study of Homer.
> (440)

By observing and collecting an oral epic poetry, and further by measuring with precision its defining features, Parry proposed to flesh out his theoretical findings with data that reflected a firsthand acquaintance with an extant analogous tradition.[23] He intended, in effect, to test theories developed from textual analyses of the Homeric poems in the living laboratory of South Slavic oral epic song.

The story of Parry's Yugoslav expeditions begins with a summer's reconnaissance work in 1933. It continues with the intensive collecting period from June 1934 to September 1935 when he was accompanied by his student and co-worker Albert Lord.[24] Over these sixteen months, they ranged from their base in Dubrovnik far and wide throughout various regions of the country, always seeking the best singers, the most gifted bearers of the oral epic tradition. Parry's electronic recording apparatus, powered initially by a generator and later by batteries, inscribed the oral performances onto aluminum discs, thus making possible the preservation of a live performance without translation into a written medium. He also took care to experiment with the usual recording by dictation, and reflected on the differences between the more conventional dictated texts and the acoustic recordings in his fieldnotes.[25]

Seeking especially songs from the Moslem epic tradition, songs which, being on the average considerably longer than their Christian counterparts, more closely approximated the Homeric poems in fullness of style and outright length,[26] Parry and Lord concentrated on seven centers: Macedonia, Novi Pazar, Bijelo Polje, Kolašin, Gacko, Stolac, and Bihać. From these areas they recorded nearly fifteen hundred epic texts from a wide variety of *guslari*,[27] including in that group not only numerous different songs from the same singers but also numerous versions or performances of the same song from the same and different singers. With this wealth of oral epic material in hand, Parry was certainly justified in saying, in a report quoted by Lord (*SCHS* I: 15), that "I believe I shall bring back to America a collection of manuscripts and discs which is unique in the world for the study of the functioning and life of an oral narrative poetry." This invaluable material, augmented by later trips by Lord and David Bynum,[28] forms the core of the Milman Parry Collection of Oral Literature at Harvard University, a fitting legacy to his philological acuity and imaginative comparative work.[29]

The first visible sign of Parry's engagement with the living analogue (and the only evidence published during his lifetime) is his article on whole formulaic verses in Homeric and South Slavic epic (1933b). Having spent the summer in Yugoslavia but still very much at the beginning of his fieldwork, he resorts to citing examples from the great nineteenth-century collection of Vuk Karadžić to counterpose to verses from the *Iliad* and *Odyssey*.

To illustrate his comparative technique, we may quote the following sets of lines meant to show how formulaic lines are employed to begin discourse (selections, 379):[30]

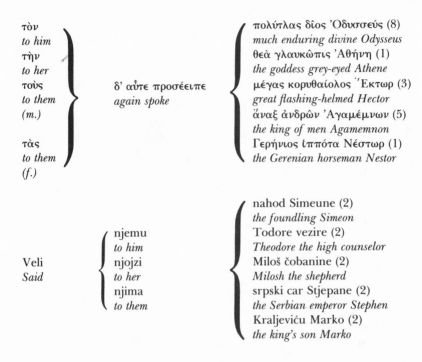

τὸν
to him
τὴν
to her
τοὺς
to them
(m.)

τὰς
to them
(f.)

δ' αὖτε προσέειπε
again spoke

πολύτλας δῖος 'Οδυσσεύς (8)
much enduring divine Odysseus
θεὰ γλαυκῶπις 'Αθήνη (1)
the goddess grey-eyed Athene
μέγας κορυθαίολος ῞Εκτωρ (3)
great flashing-helmed Hector
ἄναξ ἀνδρῶν 'Αγαμέμνων (5)
the king of men Agamemnon
Γερήνιος ἱππότα Νέστωρ (1)
the Gerenian horseman Nestor

Veli
Said

njemu
to him
njojzi
to her
njima
to them

nahod Simeune (2)
the foundling Simeon
Todore vezire (2)
Theodore the high counselor
Miloš čobanine (2)
Milosh the shepherd
srpski car Stjepane (2)
the Serbian emperor Stephen
Kraljeviću Marko (2)
the king's son Marko

Through these and many other illustrations, Parry shows how a verifiably oral traditional phraseology operates in much the same way as does Homeric phraseology, and then draws the indicated conclusion:

> The diction of Southslavic heroic poetry we know to be oral and traditional. The diction of Greek heroic poetry, which has those features which in the Southslavic poetry are due to that traditional and oral nature, such as the feature of whole formulaic verses which we have looked at in these pages, must therefore also be oral and traditional. (389)

The investigation is at root philological, in that it takes its cue from an analysis of the two traditional idioms, but the comparative dimension adds considerable weight to the argument,[31] and soon the anthropological aspect behind that comparison would figure importantly in the Oral Theory.

Parry was not to live to carry out the investigations he had imagined so clearly and planned so carefully. The closest thing we have to an account of his further thoughts on the comparative method is the collection of fieldnotes called "Ćor Huso." In this document we glimpse ideas that developed during the course of his earlier fieldwork, ideas that would have led to examinations of the narrative unit of "theme," to hypotheses about transmission of the texts, to observations on the greater rigor of Homeric as compared to South Slavic prosody, to an explanation of the advantages of dictated as opposed to recited or sung oral texts, and to treatments of numerous other topics, and all this in addition to his ethnographic notes on the Yugoslav tradition itself.

But even in articles on parallel subjects published after his death on December 3, 1935, the influence of the South Slavic analogy is apparent. The abstract which Parry submitted for the American Philological Association meetings of 1935 treated the issue of the singer's rests in Homeric and South Slavic song, bringing the experience of fieldwork to bear on the ancient Greek texts that have reached us.[32] Likewise, his review (1936a) of Walter Arend's study *Die typischen Scenen bei Homer* drew on his conception of a narrative unit that corresponded in its compositional utility to the phraseological formula, a unit that he called "theme" in his few brief references in "Ćor Huso." In responding to Arend's sound philology but lack of a realistic explanation for the structures he located, Parry observed that

> the fixed action-patterns and the fixed formulas, of course, depend on one another: an action which each time took a new form would call for new words, and in the same way the formulas are useful only inasmuch as the singer uses the schemes of composition in which they are meant to serve. (406)

His final published contribution to Oral Theory appeared in 1937, and, perhaps fittingly, struck at the core of the debate his work had engendered and continues to foster even up to the present day.[33] The immediate concern of this piece consists in rebutting the ideas of George Calhoun, whose article two years earlier had challenged Parry's proposal that formulaic phrases in Homeric diction are conventional and do not bear any special meaning uniquely appropriate to context. The phrase in question in this series of papers, *epea pteroenta* (or "winged words"), was viewed by Parry as a metrically suitable way to bring in a speech when "the character who is to speak has been the subject of the last verses, so that the use of his name in the line would be clumsy" (1933a: 372). After treating the particular points raised by Calhoun, Parry turns to the broader question:

> the issue at stake here is one which probably stands beyond such minute arguing. It seems to me to be the whole issue of whether we should read

Homer as we read written poetry, which is for us the natural form of poetry, or whether we should not rather try to gain for our reading the sense of style which is proper to oral song. (1937: 418)

Then, presaging the larger comparative view which his work was to make possible, he continued:

The reading of the *Iliad* and the *Odyssey* must be abetted by much reading of the other early European heroic poetries, and by the study of some of the many oral narrative poetries which still thrive in those places of the world where reading and writing have as yet gained no hold. (ibid.)

In the next chapter we shall consider how this program was realized and carried further by the achievements of Parry's co-worker and scholarly heir, Albert Lord.

III.

ALBERT LORD
COMPARATIVE ORAL TRADITIONS

Milman Parry had made a momentous beginning, both in his imaginative yet exacting conception of a Homeric oral tradition and in his plans for testing that conception in the laboratory of the South Slavic oral epic tradition. But after his accidental death in 1935 it was left to Albert Lord to continue their fieldwork in Yugoslavia, to shape the material they had already gathered into the Milman Parry Collection of Oral Literature, to ready important texts from this archive for publication in the series *Serbo-Croatian Heroic Songs (SCHS)*, and, most importantly, to realize the program of comparative studies Parry had in part outlined.

Besides the published and unpublished works mentioned in the preceding chapter, Parry's literary estate included seven pages of a projected book-length manuscript to be entitled "The Singer of Tales."[1] Of course, both the scholarly oeuvre and the field collaboration had to an extent prepared Lord for the task that now presented itself, but it is also fair to say that what he accomplished after 1935 went far beyond any blueprint Parry provided, either formally or informally. For Lord not only fulfilled plans for comparative study; through his version of *The Singer of Tales* (1960), submitted as a dissertation in 1949, he made Oral-Formulaic Theory a discipline of its own, a field that was eventually to touch on more than one hundred ancient, medieval, and modern traditions.[2] In the process the old Homeric Question became the Oral Traditional Question, as scholars sought to uncover the roots of some of our most cherished texts in an originative oral tradition. The promise and achievement of Milman Parry's first steps were fulfilled and augmented by the research and scholarship of Albert Lord.[3]

The South Slavic Analogy and Early Writings

The collecting trips of the thirties had resulted in a unique sample of Serbo-Croatian oral epic texts, the core of an archive to be supplemented by later expeditions carried out by Lord and David Bynum. Thus in 1936 Lord began a series of articles dealing with specific problems in the Homeric poems which could be addressed by analogy to the Yugoslav oral tradition. In the first of these papers,[4] he confronted the hypothesis that the book divisions in Homer were in some sense "chants" or chapters of heroic song. Did the singer choose an appropriate (or at least what we, acquainted with the literary "chapter," would see as appropriate) place to stop his performance, and was there in fact any evidence of a "performance unit" in the *Iliad* and *Odyssey*? Referring to Parry's then unpublished "The Falsity of the Notion of Chants in the Homeric Poems" (1933–35: 454–55), he demonstrated that the Yugoslav *guslar* may stop at almost any point, either for a rest from his considerable physical exertion or simply because of the audience situation.[5] Near the end of this essay Lord makes an important comment about comparative context, an observation that echoes Parry's concern for a proper criticism of Homer: "Nor does Homer suffer, as some would have us think, from this comparison with what is sometimes disparagingly called 'folk epic.' Rather, I believe, he emerges an even greater figure, because we are no longer seeking to compare him with the literary geniuses of another kind of tradition, but are trying to see him in his own time and place."[6]

In the second article (1938) in this same series, he considers the problem of narrative inconsistencies, the textual "blemishes" upon which the Analysts in part founded their theories of chronological strata. He explains such textual incongruities by describing how the *theme*, defined here as "a subject unit, a group of ideas, regularly employed by a singer, not merely in any given poem, but in the poetry as a whole" (410), has both a certain stability and a measure of self-sufficiency: "two of these units may be put together in the same poem because they are fitting, and yet they contain details which are incongruous. This, of course, does not upset the singer, intent as he is on the theme on which he is working at the moment" (411). A third aspect of Homeric style that Lord clarifies by comparative reference to Serbo-Croatian oral epic is that of enjambement (1948a). Showing how the South Slavic decasyllable contains the singer's unit of thought even more rigorously than does the Homeric hexameter, he explains that "the answer to the question of why necessary enjambement is more frequent in Homer than in the Southslavic poetry, therefore, is that Homeric style is richer in traditional devices for carrying the thought beyond the end of the line" (123). All three of these early "Homer and Huso" studies participate in establishing Lord's comparative methodology, a continuation of Parry's trademark procedure of combining copious and detailed evidence with imaginative, far-ranging analysis.

A few years later a comparative survey of traditional units appeared in

"Composition by Theme in Homer and Southslavic Epos" (1951a). In addition to differentiating between the units of formula and theme, Lord offered a second definition for the latter: "a recurrent element of narration or description in traditional oral poetry. It is not restricted, as is the formula, by metrical considerations" (73). He also sets forth in this article the outlines of a process he will later treat in detail—the singer's appropriation of the tradition.[7] He goes on to distinguish between "essential" and "ornamental" themes, giving examples from both ancient Greek and Serbo-Croatian texts, and concludes that Homer's skill in ornamenting these typical scenes figures prominently in his overall mastery of the traditional style.[8]

Serbo-Croatian Folk Songs (1951), co-edited with Béla Bartók, presented a sample of the so-called women's songs (*ženske pjesme*) in the South Slavic tradition, that is, the shorter lyric songs performed by women and young men without the accompaniment of the *gusle*.[9] Lord's section of the book contains the texts and translations of seventy-five of these women's songs, together with an introduction that describes the circumstances of their collection, especially in the Gacko region. Some of the lyrics are sung on particular occasions, such as at weddings and other ritual occasions, or as lullabies; the majority are love songs which could be performed at any time. Parry and Lord concentrated on recording epic, and Lord's analyses have treated primarily the heroic material, so this edition of and commentary on the folk or lyric poems is especially valuable in bringing another aspect of the tradition to light.

"Homer's Originality: Oral Dictated Texts" (1953a) furnished an answer to the opinion that Parry's work was an attack on Homer's genius. Lord's close study of actual sung performances as compared to poems taken down from dictation produced a number of new insights. First, he found that the formulaic repertory exhibits a higher degree of variation—of creation and re-creation—than Parry had originally thought. After noting how the theme and the story as a whole show a similar kind and amount of variation within limits, Lord concludes that the traditional medium provides for the exercise of creative imagination within the bounds of the conventions of narrative structure. Arguing by analogy from his experience in collecting both sung and dictated texts, Lord then makes the case for the Homeric poems as oral dictated texts, as songs written down from performance. He bases this claim primarily on the greater length and quality of such texts in South Slavic tradition:

> The chief advantage to the singer of this manner of composition is that it affords him time to think of his lines and of his song. His small audience is stable. This is an opportunity for the singer to show his best, not as a performer, but as a storyteller and poet. He can ornament his song as fully as

he wishes and is capable. . . . The very length of the Homeric poems is the
best proof that they are products of the moment of dictation rather than
that of singing. The leisureliness of their tempo, the fullness of their telling,
are also indications of this method." (132–33)[10]

In 1953 and 1954 the first two volumes of *Serbo-Croatian Heroic Songs*
(*Srpskohrvatske junačke pjesme*) appeared, containing material from the region
of Novi Pazar. Besides the poems themselves, these volumes offer an introduction to the fieldwork and an index to Parry Collection holdings,
conversations with the singers whose songs are published therein, and helpful summaries and notes. Lord's clearly stated criteria for selection of the
published material account for the composition of *SCHS* I and II: "In
investigating an oral epic tradition, it is necessary to begin with a study of
the songs of an individual singer and then to proceed to a consideration
of the other singers in the same district. One thus sees the singer both as
an individual and in relation to the community of singers to which he
belongs. For that reason our selected texts will be published by districts,
and within each district the songs of a single singer will be grouped together" (I: 16). The texts gathered together in this sampling of songs from
Novi Pazar present the scholar with a unified referent of known oral epic
much more extensive than that of the ancient Greek or any of the conti-
nental or insular medieval literatures. While no one would contend that
these songs are of the quality of the *Iliad* or *Beowulf* or the *Chanson de
Roland*, it should also be remembered that few poems of any period or
literature can be said to equal or surpass the very best that these other
traditions have to offer. These "first fruits" from the Parry Collection were
published in order to give Slavists and comparatists the opportunity to study
the metamorphosis of formula, theme, and story pattern from song to song
and from singer to singer within a defined geographical area, a local tradition. As for approaching the Homeric poems in terms of length and
aesthetic quality, this task was left to volumes III and IV and the *guslar*
Avdo Medjedović.[11]

Lord's article on Avdo (1956a) is a paean to all great traditional singers.
Included in the biography are some remarkable statistics. We learn, for
instance, that in 1935 the nonliterate Avdo had a repertoire of some fifty-
eight epics and that he dictated one song of 12,323 lines ("The Wedding
of Smailagić Meho," *SCHS* III–IV) and sang another of 13,331 lines ("Osmanbeg Delibegović and Pavičević Luka," *SCHS* VI)—each, in other words,
about the length of the *Odyssey*. After illustrating the singer's techniques of
ornamentation and flashback, Lord then recounts Parry's experiment of
having the great singer present when another *guslar* was performing a poem

that Avdo had not heard before: "When it was over, Parry turned to Avdo and asked him if he could now sing the same song, perhaps even sing it better than Mumin, who accepted the contest good-naturedly and sat by in his turn to listen. Avdo, indeed, addressed himself in his song to his 'colleague' (*kolega*) Muminaga. And the pupil's version of the tale reached to 6,313 lines, nearly three times the length of his 'original' on his first singing!"(327).[12] Lord recorded some epics from Avdo, including the "Smailagić Meho," during his 1951 trip; though ill, the master singer still managed more than 14,000 lines within approximately a week. This most Homeric of *guslari* was fittingly honored by Parry's and Lord's field assistant, Nikola Vujnović: " 'Onda kad ne bude Avda medju živima, neće se naći niko ko bi bio ovakav za pjevanje'—'When Avdo is no longer among the living, there will be no one like him in singing' " (329–30).

In the same year of 1956 Lord took up a fundamental aspect of oral tradition in "The Role of Sound Patterns in Serbo-Croatian Epic." He shows in this article that not only syntactic parallelism but also alliteration and assonance patterns help to guide the poet in his formula usage and deployment. These sound clusters, groupings marked by phonemic redundancy, seem to be organized by a "key word," which "is, as it were, the bridge between idea and sound" (302). A detailed explication of sound patterning in a passage from Salih Ugljanin's *The Song of Bagdad* (versions in *SCHS* I–II) illustrates how the acoustic patterns are linked to the essential ideas expressed by formulas. Far from working against the formulas, then, sound aids the singer employing the traditional method and adds another dimension to the compositional process. This rather short paper thus proves significant, both in the effect it has on later theory and in focusing attention on the oral/aural reality of traditional narrative song.[13]

Lord again treated sound patterns and their role in oral epic composition in an article that appeared three years later, "The Poetics of Oral Creation" (1959). In addition to comments on formula, theme, acoustic sequence, and syntactic balance, however, he also discussed the continuing force of myth in epic, using the example of the *guslar* Sulejman Fortić's versions of *The Song of Bagdad* (*SCHS* II: nos. 22 and 23) as illustration. He showed how "Djerdelez Alija has taken over a theme belonging to the god who dies and goes, or is lost or banished, to the other world and who is sought, when disaster threatens, to save his people by return. . . . *Fortić does not know this, of course*, but the force of the myth prevails" (6).[14] Through the singer's art the myths of times long past are maintained alive and vital, and the poetics of oral epic derive ultimately from their continuing influence. This observation typifies Lord's concept of oral epic tradition as fundamentally diachronic, as an evolutionary process that continues to develop while still preserving that which is important to the people who transmit it.

The Singer of Tales and the Comparative Method

The impact of *The Singer of Tales* (1960) has, as indicated above, been enormous.[15] Suffice it to say that the book has held its position as the bible of Oral Theory for more than twenty-five years; it will always be the single most important work in the field, because, simply put, it began the field as we now know it.

Lord's methodology is straightforward: he applies the personal experience of a living oral tradition in Yugoslavia to earlier literatures, illustrating by analogy the traditional oral form of those literatures. Following the introduction with a chapter on the performance and training of the *guslar*, he sketches in the usual milieu and social setting of epic singing and describes three stages in the poet's "apprenticeship." After a first period of simple listening and absorption of narrative and phraseological rhythms, the second stage starts with the boy's initial attempts at singing: "It begins with establishing the primary element of the form—the rhythm and melody, both of the song and of the gusle or the *tambura* (a two-stringed plucked instrument). This is to be the framework for the expression of his ideas"(21). The third period dates from the time a singer can perform more than one song all the way through and can add or subtract ornamentation to suit his performance to the audience and the situation.

Lord's remarks on the *formula* in the third chapter assume Parry's definition, "a group of words which is regularly employed under the same metrical conditions to express a given essential idea," which Lord supplements with phrases of his own, such as the formula being "the offspring of the marriage of thought and sung verse" (31), and with a large number of examples from South Slavic oral epic. In conceiving of the formulaic repertoire as a kind of oral poetic language and stressing the formative

function of rhythm and melody, he points the way toward a dynamic view of the formula, a view that emphasizes the active multiformity of the substitutable phrase. He then moves on to describe and exemplify the technique of formulaic analysis, finding, for instance, the lengthy formulaic system given above (48). This system is composed of some form of the verb *zasediti* ("to mount") and any one of these thirteen terms for "horse." His examination of songs by Ugljanin (*SCHS* I–II) proves that "in making his lines the singer is not bound by the formula. The formulaic technique was developed to serve him as a craftsman, not to enslave him" (54). Near the end of this chapter he briefly discusses allied features such as syntactic parallelism and word-boundary patterns, with all the evidence indicating that "the poetic grammar of oral epic is and must be based on the formula" (65).[16]

Complementary to this phraseological grammar is a narrative grammar consisting of units Lord (following Parry) has called *themes* and now defines as "the groups of ideas regularly used in telling a tale in the formulaic style of traditional song" (68). Chapter 4 of *The Singer of Tales* amounts to a clear and precise treatment of the dynamics of these large and plastic narrative units in Serbo-Croatian oral epic tradition, with an application of the findings to ancient Greek, Old English, Old French, and modern Greek texts later on. We may isolate three characteristics of themes that are among their paramount qualities: (1) they are groupings of ideas rather than of words; (2) their structure allows for variation in the form of compression, digression, or enrichment; and (3) they have both individual and contextual identities. The first characteristic, that of the core of the unit being comprised of associated ideas rather than of specific words,[17] leads to the second feature: versions of the same theme vary considerably, although the correspondence between essential ideas and formulaic expressions will keep that variance within limits.[18] In response to the audience and in line with his own talent and aims, a singer can make his rendering of the "arming of a warrior" or "assembly" long or short, studded with ornamental detail or spare and forthright. The third characteristic means that themes occur in divergent as well as similar contexts, that is, wherever their content proves useful to the poet; these units "have a semi-independent life of their own" (94) that supersedes any given individual usage. This quality makes themes extremely useful to the singer composing in performance. In fact, one might well conceive of the theme as a narrative formula.

In chapter 5, "Songs and the Song," we confront most clearly the differences between our "literary" view of the oral epic and the poem as it exists in tradition, as "a flexible plan of themes" (99). Our concept of an original text becomes oblique: "Each performance is the specific song, and at the same time it is the generic song. The song we are listening to is 'the song'; for each performance is more than a performance; it is a re-creation" (101). Making reference to examples from the Parry Collection, and especially the songs of Avdo Medjedović, Lord illustrates the fairly conservative structure of the oral epic song and its fluid parts; even from the same singer, stability from one performance to the next is likely to lie not at the word-for-word level of the text, but at the levels of theme and story pattern. Modes of variation include elaboration, simplification, change in order within a series, addition or omission of material, substitution of themes, and, frequently, different ways of ending the song. Our usual notion of "text" must therefore be modified considerably, for "in a variety of ways a song in tradition is separate, yet inseparable from other songs" (123).

The sixth chapter, "Writing and Oral Tradition," addresses the various kinds of interfaces between the worlds of print and song.[19] Lord's most important single point, however, is to debunk an assumption which we as members of a highly literate culture implicitly make: "When writing was introduced, epic singers, even the most brilliant among them, did not realize its 'possibilities' and did not rush to avail themselves of it. Perhaps they were wiser than we, because one cannot write song. One cannot lead Proteus captive; to bind him is to destroy him" (124). The very fluidity which is the life of traditional song can exist only when no fixed text interposes itself between singer and tradition; once *a* performance becomes "*the* song," the variorum nature of tradition ceases to play its role. Of course, as Lord mentions, such a fixed text could be elicited from a singer without disturbing his participation in the tradition, but the elicited text must be assessed for what it is—a single performance—and not as *the* poem. However, when literacy enters the process, the traditional ways of composing oral epic by formula, theme, and story pattern will eventually lose their raison d'être. Even the fixed text itself, if made available for memorization (as it was among younger *guslari* already in 1933–35), spells death for the tradition. In either case, composition soon comes to focus on a single model, usually a model committed to memory, and the multiforms that make up the tradition fall away.

The final four chapters of *The Singer of Tales* apply the principles derived from the Serbo-Croatian tradition to ancient Greek and medieval epic. They include formulaic and thematic analysis of the *Iliad* and *Odyssey*, *Beowulf*, the *Chanson de Roland*, and *Digenis Akritas*. Lord argues cogently for these poems as oral traditional poems, and discusses the hypothesis against the background of what is known about the history of their transmission. There are also in these pages, especially in those devoted to Homer, unique insights into the larger structure and meaning of these great works, insights made possible by the understanding of the true nature of the texts which have reached us in fixed form. Finally, Lord places a closing emphasis on the terms which define the new avatar of the old Homeric Question:

> Yet after all that has been said about *oral* composition as a technique of line and song construction, it seems that the term of greater significance is *traditional*. Oral tells us "how," but traditional tells us "what," and even more, "of what kind" and "of what force." When we know how a song is built, we know that its building blocks *must* be of great age. For it is of the *necessary* nature of tradition that it seek and maintain stability, that it preserve itself. And this tenacity springs neither from perverseness, nor from an abstract principle of absolute art, but from a desperately compelling conviction that what the tradition is preserving is the very means of attaining life and happiness. The traditional oral epic singer is not an artist; he is a seer. (220)

Later Writings (to 1979)

Two years after the first printing of *The Singer of Tales*, Lord commented on striking similarities of detail in the Serbo-Croatian "Return Song," a subgenre of epic, and the *Odyssey* in "Homeric Echoes in Bihać" (1962a).[20] Working with a song dictated by Franje Vuković, "The Captivity of Šarac Mehmedagha," he related an episode in the South Slavic epic to scenes in the Homeric poem, enumerating the points of contact between the two. The essay then turns to a brief look at another "deceptive tale," that which Odysseus tells to Athena just after he lands at Ithaca; the same scene also contains elements of the "Nausicaa theme," wherein the hero meets a woman or women near a well, and thus acts as a structural midpoint in the *Odyssey*. On the basis of these descriptions, Lord asks the question which they beg—whether there is a continuous tradition of Return Songs in the Balkans from at least Homeric times. Though proceeding with characteristic caution, he affirms the possibility: "Stories, or their narrative essences, cling tenaciously together and pass easily from language to language, providing only that there is a singing tradition. I like to think that in 'The Captivity of Šarac Mehmedagha' and in other similar songs in the Yugoslav tradition one is hearing the *Odyssey* or other similar songs, still alive on the lips of men, ever new, yet ever the same" (320).

"Homer and Other Epic Poetry" (1962b) offers a context for Homeric oral narrative by setting the *Iliad* and *Odyssey* against the backdrop of epic from all over the world and from as early as 2000 B.C. Lord recapitulates many of the analyses and descriptions carried out at length in *The Singer of Tales*, adding useful comparative observations on, for example, the relative complexity of the hexameter, the Serbo-Croatian epic decasyllable, and the verse-forms of relevant medieval poetries. He also illustrates in detail the multiformity of theme and song and places Homer in an oral tradition, a tradition which by its very nature would not consider the use of writing in the composition of epic: "Were one to discover epics written in Linear B having all the characteristics of oral narrative poetry, one would have uncovered another period of collecting. We now know that the answer to whether the Homeric poems are oral or not lies in the analysis of their style and not in the presence or absence of writing, or even in the presence or absence of a literary tradition" (197). In the final sections of this essay, Lord gives examples of sound patterns in Homer, suggests connections between epic song and ritual, and describes the functions of the epic as history, teaching, and entertainment.

One of Lord's most wide-ranging and important articles, "Homer as Oral Poet," appeared in 1968. His first point is the effect of literacy on oral tradition, made in answer to Adam Parry's "Have We Homer's *Iliad*?" (1966). On the basis of his fieldwork experience, Lord notes that a singer well established in the oral technique is unlikely to be attracted to reading and writing; likewise, even one who does appropriate the new medium may still continue to compose orally if he is thoroughly enough steeped in the prior oral tradition. On the other hand, "a singer who is not secure in the oral technique, no matter what his age, when the newer ideas come to him, will succumb quite easily to the concept of the fixed text, and he will rapidly lose whatever ability he had in oral composition" (5). Thus the influence of the *pjesmarica* ("songbook") makes itself felt, differentially and over time, to the eventual destruction of the oral tradition.[21] Of course, this topic leads naturally into the next: the value of the South Slavic analogy for studies of Homer. Here Lord shows that T. B. L. Webster's hypothesis that "literacy killed the Yugoslav poets because it brought them into touch with a higher culture" and that "there is no reason why it should have had the same effect on Greek oral poets" (1963: 157) is undocumented and critically uninformed. Likewise, he demonstrates the limits of Adam Parry's understanding of the situation in the latter's characterization of Serbo-Croatian oral epic as a "backwoods phenomenon" (1966: 212), affirming the integrity of the Moslem epic tradition from the rise of the Ottoman Empire.[22]

At the heart of the disagreement over whether quantitative formulaic analysis can prove Homer's orality, Lord believes, lies a fatal variation in definition and application. Taking studies by Joseph Russo (1966) and G. S. Kirk (1966b) as a point of departure, he shows that available data do indeed point toward a significant correlation between formula density and orality, but that more analysis and less speculation are needed.[23] He then describes the kinds of investigations undertaken for medieval texts and for both oral and imitation oral texts of the Serbo-Croatian epic narratives. Lord's own techniques and an additional method developed by David

Bynum successfully distinguish between the oral and the imitation poems. In comparing the formulaic density of samples taken from the *Batracho-myomachia* and the *Iliad*, Lord finds the Homeric poem much more formulaic and interprets this quality as proof of its orality.[24] What informs all of his analyses is a concern for a fair amount of material, a (presumed) single singer, and careful definitions of formula and formulaic.[25] The remainder of the article focuses on specific instances of what Lord feels is "subjective interpretation" of Homer, impressionistic explication which goes against the traditional nature of the poems. His arguments in response to the ideas of Kirk (1962, 1966b) and Anne Amory Parry (1966) are too detailed to treat in summary fashion, but we may say in general that he advocates meticulous research into the formulaic structure of the passages involved in order to shed a new and truer—because objective—light on their meaning:

> We must be willing to use the new tools for investigations of themes and patterns, and we must be willing to learn from the experience of other oral traditional poetries. Otherwise "oral" is only an empty label and "traditional" is devoid of sense. Together they form merely a façade behind which scholarship can continue to apply the poetics of written literature. (46)[26]

The next two articles in chronological sequence both concentrated mainly on the larger paradigm of oral story structure, what Lord has called the "story pattern." As he puts it in "The Theme of the Withdrawn Hero in Serbo-Croatian Oral Epic" (1969), his "basic assumption is that in oral tradition there exist narrative patterns that, no matter how much the stories built around them seem to vary, have great vitality and function as organizing elements in the composition and transmission of oral story texts" (18). In fact, he believes the Return Song story pattern treated in this essay, which involves the five-element sequence of Absence, Devastation, Return, Retribution, and Wedding, to be as old as the Indo-European oral tradition and to be preserved in, for example, the Homeric *Odyssey*.[27] Tracing the pattern in a number of South Slavic oral epics, significantly from both the Moslem and Christian singing traditions, he is able to illustrate the multiformity in narrative of this simple elemental sequence as well as the connection between the Yugoslav poems and Homeric epic tradition.

Although his primary interest in "Tradition and the Oral Poet: Homer, Huso, and Avdo Medjedović" (1970) turns to the relationship between history and the epic, Lord's methodology again touches on the story pattern in a comparative context. After a demonstration of how an oral story text cannot be reconstructed from "later" variants because of the fluidity of themes and sequences and the anachronism of tradition as a whole, he discusses duplication and agglomeration, two processes by means of which stories evolve within tradition. The emphasis here falls on the combination and recombination of story elements, and also on the "interpretation" of songs, that is, on the exchange of elements across boundaries between stories. He then applies these findings to the *Odyssey* and locates duplications of arrival and shipwreck. The final stress rests on the primacy of the story pattern, on the mythic paradigm which precedes and even gives shape to historical facts:

> Historical events cannot give to a pattern the intensity and force needed for it to survive all the changes of tradition. These changes are not the corruption of time, but the constant reinterpretation of succeeding generations and societies. Not corruption, but constant renewal and revivification. The patterns must be suprahistorical in order to have such force. Their matrix is myth and not history; for when history does have an influence on the stories it is, at first at least, history that is changed, not the stories. (27–28)

The relationship between myth and historical event remained the central concern in three of Lord's next four articles. In the first of them, "Homer, the Trojan War, and History" (1971b), he takes issue with interpretations by Denys Page and M. I. Finley of the Iliadic catalog of Greeks and Trojans, arguing that any theme, including a catalog, will exhibit variation over time and therefore cannot be expected to preserve "historical fact." A comparative look at Avdo Medjedović's catalogs in "The Wedding of Smailagić Meho" and "Osmanbeg Delibegović and Pavičević Luka" proves that the "accuracy" of the oral epic, as we understand the concept of accuracy, is not absolute: "Fact is present in the epic, but relative chronology in the catalogue is confused. Time is telescoped. The past of various times is all assembled into the present performance. . . . Oral epic presents a composite picture of the past" (90–91). The second of the papers studied "The Effect of the Turkish Conquest on Balkan Epic Tradition" (1972a). Along with a useful geographical and historical survey of Moslem oral epic from earliest times, Lord considers the Turkish elements now part of the Serbo-Croatian singing tradition. His comments range from particular lexical glosses to an appreciation of the elegant style of Balkan epic that derives from Turkish Moslem culture. In addition, he relates the Return Song story pattern to "the vegetation pattern of death and resurrection, the dying god who returns" (311). Finally, in "History and Tradition in Balkan Oral Epic and Ballad" (1972b), Lord again instances the work of Avdo Medjedović to suggest epic's roots in myth, arguing that "history *enters into* or is in its general characteristics reflected in oral epic and ballad tradition, rather than originating it" (60).

In 1974 the long-awaited text and translation of "The Wedding of Smailagić Meho," dictated by Avdo Medjedović in July 1935, was published by
Lord and David Bynum as the third and fourth volumes of *Serbo-Croatian
Heroic Songs (SCHS)*. This is the epic that Lord had previously described
in a number of articles, the most Homeric of Yugoslav oral epic songs both
in length and in traditional quality.[28] In the translation and especially in
the original language, Avdo's consummate skill—his ability to sing a great
song *within a tradition of singing* which also includes, inevitably, lesser songs—
shines through, affording a view of the master poet in perfect control of
his medium. His characteristic ornamentation gives a sense of fullness to
the poem, an effulgence and dynamism that derive directly from the Pro-
tean possibilities which form the context for its making and reveal the depth
of its roots in tradition. In coming to grips with Avdo's art, we can see most
clearly the poetic reality behind the theoretical message of *The Singer of
Tales* and understand the comparison of the Serbo-Croatian and ancient
Greek traditions in a new light. Lord and Bynum incorporate a helpful
and informative apparatus: the translation volume (III) includes essays on
Avdo and his originality, conversations with the singer, notes, and appendices covering related texts, while the original text volume (IV) adds
material on Avdo's background, his repertory, conversations (in Serbo-
Croatian), and notes. In short, these volumes and the poem they present
offer a unique view of a monumental epic which deserves careful scholarly
attention from Slavists and comparatists alike.

A collection of essays edited by Lord, *The Multinational Literature of Yugoslavia*, also appeared in 1974. His own contribution, "The Nineteenth-
Century Revival of National Literatures: Karadžić, Njegoš, the Illyrians,
and Prešeren," offers an overview of the complex group of traditions at
the root of more modern Yugoslav literature. Of interest are his comments
on the oral traditional context of important events and trends in the nineteenth century; for instance, he notes that "the literary language chosen
by Vuk and by the writers of the Illyrian movement in Zagreb was neither
the dialect of Zagreb nor that of Belgrade but that of oral literature in
Herzegovina" (103). Included as well are a brief listing of significant collections of oral literature from the period, an account of "purely literary"
original writings by individuals, and placement of those individuals in their
contemporary context. The primary value of this article lies in the sketch
it gives of the movement from oral to written in the nineteenth century;
much study remains to be done on this crucially important interface of
literatures.[29]

Lord's "Perspectives on Recent Work on Oral Literature" (1974c) surveys
contributions to Oral Theory in a number of traditions, among them Serbo-
Croatian, Russian, Albanian, modern Greek, central Asiatic, various Af-

rican linguistic communities, Ugaritic, Sumerian, early Chinese, Sanskrit, medieval Greek, Old Irish, ancient Greek, Old French, and Old English.[30] Much more than a bibliographical supplement, this essay treats many problems in depth, especially in the last three literatures just listed. Two points on Homeric tradition and the Yugoslav analogy and another on Old English are particularly noteworthy. In commenting on Bernard Fenik's study of the *Iliad* (1968), Lord reminds us of the contribution made by the comparison to the South Slavic tradition and goes on to note that "we have been able to see in the modern Balkans the *whole* of a tradition and that over a long period of time—not just two songs from one singer but many songs from many singers" (12). This wider view is especially valuable, he continues, because of the limited sample of Homeric epic poetry at our disposal. Likewise, Lord finds comparison of Serbo-Croatian epic and Anglo-Saxon poetry pointing toward the possibility that the Old English religious poems are "transitional" or "mixed" texts. One of the primary reasons for this position is his discovery of few genuine themes in these poems, few scenes that demonstrate a core of verbal correspondence among their occurrences. In his view idea-patterns without a regular verbal component cannot claim to be true compositional themes, and it is this distinction that then leads to an important and explicit new definition of this oral traditional unit as "a repeated narrative element together with its verbal expression, that portion of a poem, an aggregate of specific verses, that tells a certain repeated part of the narrative, measureable in terms of lines and even words and word combinations" (20). As we shall see in the next chapter, this two-part emphasis on idea-pattern and verbal component is in conflict with what specialists in some other traditions have found.

Comparative extension of theories and observations based on the Homeric texts took another direction in "The Heroic Tradition of Greek Epic and Ballad: Continuity and Change" (1976c).[31] In this essay he traces Greek oral song from its ancient beginnings through its medieval transformations to its modern forms, making the point that the tradition preserves as well as discards, continues as well as changes. Comparisons are drawn between the medieval hero Digenis Akritas and the classical Herakles, shifts in language and religion (and the resultant syncretism of pagan and Christian in medieval times) are described, and the various modern modulations in narrative pattern typical of the Akritic and klephtic songs are exemplified.

Lord's "The Traditional Song" (1976a) was presented to a colloquium on "Oral Literature and the Formula" in 1974. Once again he focuses on large narrative patterns, this time in "Bojičić Alija Rescues Alibey's Children" (*SCHS* I–II: no. 24), the *Odyssey*, "The Wedding of Smailagić Meho," the fourteenth-century Old Turkish romance of Sajjid Batthal, and the *Iliad*. A comparison is drawn between Bojičić Alija and Telemachus on the basis of their similar backgrounds and roles within the poems; Lord detects a single story pattern involving (1) a father absent or dead, (2) a challenge, (3) a helper-donor, (4) borrowed equipment, and (5) a journey cast in two different narrative situations. He then relates the stories of two more initiatory heroes—Meho and Dschaafar (Batthal)—to the same pattern. Lord also explains Achilles as a participant in this mythical structure, understanding the special armor as a traditional precursor to Achilles' fight against the river, a supernatural opponent. What we have in the *Iliad* is thus a composite structure: a tale of human vengeance that has at some point become linked with the dragon-slaying pattern. His closing remarks on Meho indicate the diachronic depth and multiform nature of the South Slavic epic as well.[32]

Some of the comparative points raised in the 1976 essays were again addressed in a paper that appeared the next year, "Parallel Culture Traits in Ancient and Modern Greece" (1977). Here Lord investigates the possible continuity of the ancient and modern Greek traditions through analysis of narrative pattern and formula. He also relates the Greek and Serbo-Croatian traditions through (a) "songs containing supernatural elements whose protagonists are historical figures of the past" (tales of Digenis Akritas and Marko Kraljević) and (b) historical and elegiac songs (72). The argument from formula, intended to indicate a relationship between the Homeric hexameter and the fifteen-syllable *politikos* line, proceeds from a study of metrical word-position; Homeric and *Digenis Akritas* formulas are placed side by side to illustrate their agreement in the constraints placed on the positioning of *teknon* and *akouô*.[33] His conclusions about continuity are in principle quite convincing, and they open up many new areas for research at levels of oral traditional structure from formula to story pattern.

Another essay, "The Gospels as Oral Traditional Literature" (1978a), is a long and experimental application of the methodology of Oral Theory to a new subject.[34] He begins by reiterating and developing earlier ideas about the primacy of mythic patterns and their shaping function in the determination of what we are accustomed to call "history." A number of biographical events in the Gospels are shown to proceed from generic life patterns common to other oral texts such as the *Theogony*, the Babylonian *Enuma Elish*, and many others. By weighing common and divergent themes, he seeks to establish the transitional character of each Gospel and at the same time to indicate their lack of dependence on a single archetype. The remainder of the study is devoted to a comparative analysis of traditional motifs and verbal correspondence in Matthew, Mark, and Luke. Carefully taking note of the necessarily tentative nature of conclusions based on this bold first step in an almost unexplored direction, Lord then summarizes:

As I see it at the moment, the events in Jesus' life, his works and teachings, evoked ties with "sacred" oral traditional narratives and narrative elements that were current in the Near East and in the eastern Mediterranean in the first century A.D. These were stories whose deepest meanings were concerned with: (a) establishing order in the world by invoking divine models and divine intervention, and (b) assuring, as part of this order, a continuation of life for a humanity that was puzzled by and anxious about its own mortality. (91)

Most Recent Writings (1980 and After)

This period in Lord's scholarship has seen a number of fresh departures as well as continuation of previous work, as he sought to bring Oral Theory to new areas and to new topics within areas already treated, as well as to restate and amplify observations made and theories propounded in earlier writings. In the process he has offered valuable insights on the question of memorization versus re-creation, on the matter of genre, on the interface of oral tradition and the written word, and on the problem of meaning in oral tradition.

Thus the period begins with an analysis of two Ukrainian *dumy* (1979–80; see also 1981b), the ballad genre composed orally in strophes rather than in the stichic lines of oral epic. After cautionary words on the necessary difference between narrative and non-narrative genres, and also about the special considerations due ballad structure, Lord examines five variants of each of the two *dumy*; even though the texts are as many as two hundred years apart, he shows the traditional "sameness" of the variants—not in terms of memorized, repeated verses but in terms of the multiformity typical of oral traditional composition. Just like the South Slavic epic and other traditions studied earlier, the *duma* texts are variants "not of any given text of the song, nor even of any particular version of it, but of the song as narrative, as a story" (576). Although he can describe the opening scene of the two *dumy* in terms of familiar, recurrent ideas, no performance is ever entirely predictable, just as no past performance could ever be reconstructed, regardless of the number of variants one had collected: "Not memory, but the natural process of language itself—dynamic, creative, ever in movement—is the basis of traditional composition and recomposition" (583).[35]

Some of the same concerns are examined in "Memory, Fixity, and Genre in Oral Traditional Poetries" (1981a). Once again Lord illustrates how the traditional oral poet, here the South Slavic *guslar* Salih Ugljanin, does not memorize his lines or scenes, no more than he improvises them. He remembers the essential ideas rather than the exact verbal expression, and, having learned to compose in the traditional idiom, then renders the ideas of the song in the special language of the tradition. The result is that versions of the same idea have a distinct verbal correspondence that identifies them as "the same," even if a line or scene does not repeat verbatim. This, then, is the kind of fixity one would be led to expect in poetry composed in the traditional style.

But there are important qualifications to be made as well. For instance, Lord notes that while a certain fixity may characterize the work of a single singer, that particular fixity will not be transmitted to another singer; each *guslar* is an individual. The realities of local tradition versus national tradition will also enter the picture. In a similar vein, he observes that the role of memory varies from one genre to the next:

> Obviously, shorter lyric songs tend to greater fixity of stanza than long epics. If one were to generalize about fixity from the observation of it in lyric poetry and apply the result to epic, the conclusions drawn would not be accurate. The reverse, of course, is true. In general the smaller the unit the greater the degree of fixity, whether one speaks of lyric, or praise song, or whatever. Often non-narrative poetry consists of a series of short units which may be more or less fixed, but their order is customary, rather than fixed, and metathesis is frequent. (459–60)

After acknowledging the existence of another possibility, that of shorter poems composed in the mind and then spoken orally without the aid of writing (a type of poem he views as oral "only in the most literal sense of the word," 460), he summarizes by observing that true oral epic composition can owe nothing to memorization, since the process of memorizing proves much too rigid and fixed to serve the singer as he turns essential ideas into actual verbal expression.[36]

About the same time Lord enlarged upon earlier studies of mythic pattern in a study of the structure of *Beowulf* (1980a).[37] Here he described (a) the Withdrawal-Devastation-Return (WDR) pattern and (b) the pattern involving encounters with a male monster and female monster leading to a journey of enlightenment, both of which occur in other Indo-European traditions and can therefore be ascribed, hypothetically of course, to an original Indo-European tradition. The first of these patterns he sees as informing the sequence of Hrothgar's powerlessness against Grendel (absence of a hero), the devastation wrought during Grendel's and his mother's perverse rule, and the advent of Beowulf as the conquering hero. The deaths of Hondscio and Æschere then figure forth the second pattern, as they image the "Death of the Substitute" and lead toward the hero's meeting first Grendel, the male monster, and then his mother, the female monster.

Lord then explains the modifications in *Beowulf* as Germanic specifications of the common mythic structures, offering comparisons to *Gilgamesh* and the *Odyssey* and illustrating how the traditional inheritance operates in the Old English context.

In "Memory, Meaning, and Myth in Homer and Other Oral Epic Traditions" (1980c), Lord explores a number of issues that had arisen over the more than twenty years since the appearance of *The Singer of Tales*. Among the most interesting points is his distinction among various types of repeated lines and phrases; in addition to the classic formula and system, he locates the repeated gnomic line or couplet, the repetition of part of a preceding line (often called "terracing" or pleonasm), the Homeric run-on line, and the rhetorical series. He also distinguishes the type-scene, as studied by Walter Arend (1933), from the theme by stipulating that "the type scene does not involve any degree of verbal correspondence, whereas the theme requires a major degree of verbal correspondence" (44).[38] All of these observations are supported by detailed analyses of examples, as is his illustration of the mythic meaning behind the story-patterns that underlie an epic narrative. Associative meaning is inscribed in these structures by the poetic tradition and emerges in the narration of the tale, as the momentary telling recalls important values fostered by the tradition: "Through the images, patterns, and stories of these oral literary traditions and their combinings and recombinings to assure their effectiveness the singers of epic brought promise of renewal of life, of continuity and succession" (63).

Aspects of both similarity and divergence from one tradition to the next form the subject of "Comparative Slavic Epic" (1981b), in which Lord considers the formulaic and thematic structures typical of oral poetry in Russian (the *bylina*), Ukrainian (the *duma*), Serbo-Croatian (the epic), and Bulgarian (again the epic). His opening focus is on the variant metrical systems, the syllabic line of the South Slavic material and the tonic, nonsyllabic line of the East Slavic; in the process he proposes a possible relationship between this distinction and that involving the bowed or plucked instruments used to accompany performance in each genre and tradition. He emphasizes the importance of meter, which provides "the molds, or matrices, into which thought is poured" (416), and of the characteristics of the individual language in assessing variant types of formulas over the four traditions. Although each tradition has developed its own way of expressing essential ideas, so that there certainly exist tradition-dependent formulas, he also notes that each includes phrases and systems that are common to all of the poetries. On the thematic level as well, Lord finds that "as on the level of the formulaic language, we come to realize that we are dealing with 'dialects,' i.e., local narrative variations within a common stock of narrative possibilities, the sum total of which we might call 'the language of narrative' " (428). Given these correspondences and the fact of ongoing variation (really re-creation), he warns against searching for Common Slavic archetypes of traditional structures or story patterns.

Two more recent articles open up directions in scholarship heretofore unexplored by Lord. "The Battle of Kosovo in Albanian and Serbocroatian Oral Epic Songs" (1984) takes issue with the view of the relationship between these two epic traditions of Kosovo as described by Alois Schmaus, presenting evidence that the "classical" South Slavic and the Albanian traditions "emerged more or less independent of one another" (82) and were later joined in the Sandžak tradition as represented by Salih Ugljanin, one of the Parry-Lord *guslari* whose works help to comprise *SCHS* I–II. Also of significance is Lord's account of collecting Albanian songs from 1937 onward, a valuable supplement to earlier reports on the field expeditions (see note 11). In the second paper (1985), he treats the problem of "text-stanzas" in Yugoslav folk songs, specifically the collection edited by himself and Béla Bartók (1951). In addition to finding and describing such units in the folk songs, Lord notes the tectonic difference between this genre and that of the South Slavic epic: "in folk songs the text stanzas are syntactic and semantic units as well as units of length, but . . . this is not so in epic. In this way, it would seem that we can note a formal differentiation between the two genres in an aspect that at first it appeared they shared" (403).[39]

Lord's contribution to *Oral Tradition in Literature: Interpretation in Context* (1986a) confronts two difficult problems that have been concerns of the Oral Theory since its beginnings in the work of Milman Parry. The first of these amounts to the question of exactly what has been the historical impact of the world of literacy on the world of orality, and therefore whether "transitional" stages exist and, if so, what their characteristics might be. Using the South Slavic oral tradition as his point of reference for the investigation, Lord shows that the merging of the two worlds produced different results in each of the regions he examines—Serbia, Dalmatia, and Montenegro. Early Dalmatian written literature, he finds, was exclusively the creation of a lettered and learned élite, while the oral tradition was the medium of the peasant class; thus no merger of any sort could take place until the eighteenth century, when sophisticated literary people undertook to write imitation oral poems. In Montenegro, on the other hand, Petar II Petrović Njegoš presents quite another case: this greatest of Montenegrin poets learned the traditional style from actual singers (including his father) as a boy and was later taught to read and write in the monastery at Cetinje. His own compositions show a variety of form; some are versions of "folk epics" done in the oral traditional style, while others are much more literary. The example of Njegoš leads Lord to observe that "there *are* transitional texts in South Slavic epic, probably several kinds" (34).

Further examples of the differential effects of the merging of the worlds of orality and literacy in the South Slavic tradition are added, in particular a careful analysis of the case of Parry's and Lord's field assistant Nikola Vujnović, himself both a singer and a literate man. The recurring message of these examples is that one cannot generalize freely about "the transition," that it must be recognized that the nature and results of the merger depend on the life history of the individual and the role of literacy in his culture. Lord closes this wide-ranging and important essay with a consideration of ring-composition, the structural device so common in the Homeric epics,[40] as it is found in South Slavic oral epic. His particular aim in this part of the study is to treat the matter of "structure versus meaning," that is, the question of whether ring-composition serves as a mnemonic device or as an aesthetic feature. Making reference to "The Wedding of Smailagić Meho," he shows that Avdo Medjedović both used the traditional inheritance, with all of its mythic attachment of meaning, and deployed the symmetrical features in a fashion we would identify as "conscious artistry" (63–64).

The next item in Lord's bibliography is "Perspectives on Recent Work on the Oral Traditional Formula" (1986b), an essay that combines a continuation of his former survey of scholarship (1974c) with a close analysis of certain trends and methods in the field of Oral Theory. After some preliminary remarks on performance and context, issues that have become more prominent in the last few years, he discusses advances in the study of Central Asiatic epic, the Pabuji epic of western India and South Indian poetry, Celtic oral literature (both Old Irish and contemporary storytellers), Xhosa praise poetry, various African traditions, Arabic oral poetry, and the Latvian *dainas*. Lord notes that these traditions hold out the promise of much new knowledge and especially of fruitful comparison, but adds the caveat that "like should be compared with like" (472).[41] He also surveys work on the more well-trodden areas of ancient Greek, Old and Middle English, Old French, medieval Spanish, Scandinavian, and the Gospels.

The remainder of the article is devoted to a commentary on formulaic analysis since Parry's writings and on ancillary modes of investigation. Lord recounts the history of the formulaic test, in which density was understood to be a litmus test for determining the orality of a manuscript or other printed text whose provenance was uncertain, and notes that he now credits the possibility of a "transitional text": "There seem to be texts that can be called either transitional or belonging to the first stage of written literature" (479–80). Nonetheless, he points out that quantitative assessment of formulaic character can still provide valuable information about a work, such as its degree of dependence on traditional or nontraditional style. Further, he suggests that in Anglo-Saxon poetry, formulaic density "should also be reckoned in terms of larger syntactic and semantic units, such as the whole sentence, and within boundaries, therefore, that go beyond the single line" (481). After a discussion of John Miletich's method (e.g., 1974, 1978) for determining probable orality on the basis of other stylistic features, Lord closes with cogent remarks about the differences between the traditional formula and mere repetition and on the importance of emphasizing the role of tradition in the oral literatures that come under scrutiny.

Some of these same points are again taken up in "The Nature of Oral Poetry" (1986c), in which the major agenda consists of (a) the memorizing oral poet, (b) composition in performance, and (c) the transitional text. In the first section Lord examines claims for the Xhosa *imbongi*, the black South African singer of praise poetry as described by Jeff Opland (e.g., 1975), and the Somali *gabay*, the composer of occasional poetry on a recent event, as oral poets. On the basis of textual analysis and field reports, he classes the *gabay* and the older *imbongi* as memorizers who are "oral poets" only in the most literal sense, since they do not appear to rely on the oral traditional method of composition. The second part of the essay engages Ruth Finnegan's interpretation of African evidence (e.g., 1977) in coming to terms with the difference between improvisation and the kind of composition in performance practiced by the South Slavic *guslari*. Lord calls for thematic analysis, for precision in phraseological comparisons, and most crucially for recognition of the invaluable function of the poetic tradition, the diachronic inheritance, for the composing oral poet. In the last section of the article, he offers further comments on the transitional text, citing passages from songbooks in the Parry Collection and making reference to Old English poems such as *Andreas* and *Elene*. He warns that we need more studies of bona fide oral texts in order to be able to point out with confidence and exactness the nontraditional aspects of transitional texts.[42]

Thus Albert Lord has fulfilled the plans drawn up by Milman Parry for the comparative study of oral epic, and he has accomplished much more. With *The Singer of Tales* the Oral Theory became not merely a methodology but a discipline, so that today we can identify scores of traditions that have felt its influence. With the series *Serbo-Croatian Heroic Songs,* collected with Parry and edited with David Bynum, Lord has presented Slavist and comparatist alike with unambiguously oral epic material for close study. And, perhaps most impressive of all, his articles have more than kept pace with the work of other scholars in the field, reacting to the myriad new ideas from any number of areas and proposing new theories and interpretations of his own for more than fifty years.[43] In the next chapter we shall be in a better position to appreciate the real magnitude of his and Parry's work by looking at some of the most significant research and scholarship that it has stimulated.

IV.

THE MAKING OF
A DISCIPLINE

With some idea of the seminal work of Parry and Lord behind us, we shall now consider the enormous expansion of their pioneering efforts from ancient Greek, Serbo-Croatian, and, to a lesser degree, other traditions to more than one hundred separate language traditions. Since a full treatment of this growth, which amounts to the making of a new discipline, would pass far beyond the limits of this chapter,[1] I shall focus on scholarship in three principal areas: (1) ancient Greek, (2) Old English, and (3) selected other traditions. Parts one and two will survey the most important contributions to research in the respective fields, and part three will look more selectively at a variety of traditions.[2] At the appropriate points throughout all three sections, the major counterarguments and suggestions for revision or modification of the Oral-Formulaic Theory will be mentioned.

Ancient Greek

1928–1949

As we discovered in the opening chapter, Milman Parry's theories were not without partial anticipation nor, for that matter, without true precedent. Nonetheless, scholarship immediately following Parry's first studies was not quick to absorb the importance of his synthetic and iconoclastic thinking. A few items in the thirties and forties do, however, take serious notice of, and sometimes serious issue with, certain of his positions. Pierre Chantraine's 1932 article on formulas in Book I of the *Iliad*[3] was the first to acknowledge Parry's work and to put it into practice, but it was George M. Calhoun who, in papers published in 1933 and 1935, offered the earliest commentary in depth on the initial statements of the Oral Theory. In the former study, "Homeric Repetitions," Calhoun sought to establish a Homer who composed as easily in whole lines and even groups of lines as modern poets do in words. Two years later he came squarely at odds with Parry over the criterion of metrical usefulness in Homeric formulas. In what has become a *locus classicus* in the history of oral theory, Calhoun argued that the *epea* ("words") in Homer are not simply conventionally and formulaically *pteroenta* ("winged"); that is, he understood the poet's use of the formula *epea pteroenta* or "winged words" as one which is employed with a conscious aesthetic design and a sensitivity to context rather than as a metrical convenience.

Since the Theory has long run the gamut of utility versus context-sensitivity—in other words, of convention versus originality—we may be justified in quoting from Parry's response to this first plea for the poet's aesthetic choice. In "About Winged Words," he counters: "The various *epea pteroenta* verses, I believe, are used to bring in speech when 'the character who is to speak has been the subject of the last verses, so that the use of his name in the line would be clumsy' " (1937: 414). Calhoun argues for the aesthetic association of winged words with impassioned speech-making, while his adversary speaks of a metrical exigency and stylistic convenience. The issue is clearly much larger than the meaning of the epithet *pteroenta*; at stake, as Parry himself foresaw, was to be "the whole issue of whether we should read Homer as we read written poetry, which is for us the natural form of poetry, or whether we should not rather try to gain for our reading the sense of style which is proper to oral song" (418). Just as the argument over the meaning of "winged words" has found no easy solution in the more than fifty years that have followed,[4] so the more comprehensive question of utility and aesthetics remains unanswered—though, in view of the debate aroused, one might say *productively* unanswered—to this day.

Apart from the rather unconvincing objections of J. T. Sheppard (1935 and 1936), who relied more on rhetoric than on philological precision,[5] the only other dissenting voice to be heard and appreciated in this period was that of Samuel E. Bassett, chiefly in his influential study *The Poetry of Homer* (1938).[6] Like Calhoun and Sheppard, Bassett was concerned, as he saw it, to liberate Homer from Parry's too mechanical conception and to restore what amounted to a literary originality to the epics.

James Notopoulos, on the other hand, began at about the same time a long and distinguished series of articles on oral literature sympathetic to Parry's theories with an application of Oral Theory to the figure of Mnemosyne in ancient Greek literature (1938).[7] In explaining Mnemosyne as the personification of the creative force behind oral memory, he says: "As the foundation of the technique of oral poetry, Mnemosyne was rightly invoked as 'mother of the Muses' " (473).

At the very end of our first chronological period, Notopoulos published another study, "Parataxis in Homer" (1949), this time differentiating Homer's oral and "paratactic" style from later written and "hypotactic" styles.

That is, he showed how Homeric poetry is ordered by a unity much different from the organic relations of parts familiar to literary critics, that such poetry is imbued deeply with a principle of thought and structure that juxtaposes rather than subordinates: "the *Iliad* and the *Odyssey* have a unity; but unlike that of the drama it is inorganic and, moreover, the digressions, far from being, like Homer's similes, for purposes of relief, are actually the substance of the narrative, strung paratactically like beads on a string" (5–6). This principle of parataxis, as it informs both the relationship between the parts of a work and the relationship between one work and another within a tradition, was to influence not a few entries in the later bibliography of the Oral Theory.[8]

A number of more general works from this period touched upon oral theory in one way or another. As we saw in chapter 2, Walter Arend's *Die typischen Scenen bei Homer* (1933) established the proliferation of typical scenes in Homer and led to Parry's comments (1936a) on the traditional nature of these units. The same year saw the appearance of Martin Nilsson's *Homer and Mycenae*, which warmly commended Parry's studies and enlisted his theories in the aid of proving the antiquity to be uncovered in the Homeric poems. Although Nilsson's main interest was the discovery of knowledge about Mycenaean times, and Parry's apparent proof of the age of Homeric diction seemed to serve his thesis well, he did bring a version of the Oral Theory to a wider audience at a very early stage. Another scholar greatly in sympathy with Parry's ideas, especially as they furthered his own cause, was Rhys Carpenter. In his *Folk Tale, Fiction, and Saga in the Homeric Epics* (1946), Carpenter invoked the ancient witness of the poems' diction in a search for points of comparison with European folktale patterns, but not before he offered the opinion that Parry had given the scholarly world an "unanswerable and unassailable proof that [the] Iliad and Odyssey belong to the class of oral literatures—composed in the mind and not on paper, retained in the memory and not in books, recited to audiences, heard and not read" (6).

1949–1959

The second period of activity in ancient Greek is demarcated at one extremity by the date of submission of Lord's dissertation, later to become *The Singer of Tales*, and at the other by the year before the actual publication of that groundbreaking study in 1960. Thus in 1952 appeared C. M. Bowra's encyclopedic *Heroic Poetry*,[9] still a useful reference on a large number of poetries and their probable milieux and methods of composition. About the same time, directly influenced by Parry but concerned above all with the master poet Homer, Richmond Lattimore wrote in the introduction to his stately translation of the *Iliad*:

> Formulae are words, and they come down in the tradition, though many may be the work of a single man, and in the incredible skill of their manipulation in the Iliad we may be justified in seeing a single, original poet. But not original in the sense that he would throw away a ready-made phrase for the sake of making a new one, his own. In this respect later Greek poets, such as Pindar and Aeschylus, are as remote from Homer as are Donne, Crashaw, and Browning. (1951: 40)

Also during this middle period, Notopoulos contributed a significant number of innovative articles to the development of the field. In 1950 he sought to relate the generic types of Homer's characters to formulaic composition and the next year to show how the oral poet has at his disposal devices of ring structure, foreshadowing, and the like to unify his poem inorganically (that is, paratactically). Later on he would employ Parry's ideas to posit an oral Hesiod, the foremost representative of a second major branch of the ancient Greek tradition (1960a, 1962).[10] Notopoulos added an article (1952) which effectively made the argument for the comparative applicability of the modern Cretan heroic poetry which he himself recorded and later bequeathed to the Parry Collection.[11] Finally, in 1957 he explored the relationship between the structure of Homeric epic and the paratactic designs typical of Greek pottery of the Geometric period.[12]

The most convincing and thoroughgoing demonstration of this same analogy between literature and art is one of the major themes of Cedric Whitman's *Homer and the Heroic Tradition* (1958), a study that also touched on the Oral Theory. Among the many aspects of Homer addressed in a stimulating and careful manner, Whitman includes challenging accounts of the unity of the poems, the Geometric structure of the *Iliad*, and the interrelationship of image, symbol, and formula. But whatever the topic, his informing aesthetic for Homer is based on the research and scholarship of Parry and Lord. "In seeking Homer's original genius," he remarks, "we must not seek the newly turned phrase, the nonformulaic line, or even the character who, we might somehow persuade ourselves, did not exist in previous tradition. It is not outside tradition that Homer has triumphed, but within it" (6). About the same time Denys Page's *History and the Homeric Iliad* (1959) appeared, in which its author posited, on the example of Parry's investigations, the existence of fifteenth-century B.C. phraseology imbedded in the Homeric texts which have survived to us. In thus agreeing with Nilsson's general argument (1933) and summoning linguistic and archaeological evidence in support of this assertion, Page derives several sensible hypotheses about the history and prehistory of the *Iliad* (that is, of the epic and not simply of our text of the epic) and presages the later revival of interest in a diachronic, evolutionary perspective on the textual analysis of Homer.[13]

1960 and Afterward

After the publication of *The Singer of Tales* in 1960, research in ancient Greek gained particular momentum. G. S. Kirk, who was to contribute many significant works on Homer and the question of orality, followed an early article (1960) disputing Lord's "oral dictated text" theory with a now often-cited book, *The Songs of Homer* (1962). After chapters on the historical background, Kirk turns in part II of the longer study to "The Oral Poet and His Methods," a discussion of Homeric formula and theme which parts company with Lord's work on the questions of originality and the application of the Yugoslav analogy. The three differences which Kirk finds between the *guslar* and Homer are important enough to quote in his own words: "First of all, . . . neither the Yugoslav poetry nor any other oral poetry of which we know has anything like the strict formular system, with its high degree of economy and scope, that is exemplified throughout the Iliad and Odyssey" (88). This divergence points to a second and related one, "the difference in metrical strictness" which allows the South Slavic singer "greater freedom" (89). And finally, he suggests, "the third great difference between the *aoidoi* and present-day *guslari* is, to put it crudely, that the former were primarily creative oral poets while the latter are primarily if not exclusively non-creative and reproductive" (91). These points of perceived incongruity lead Kirk to advise caution in considering the Yugoslav analogy; together with his pronouncement on the Homeric poems' superior quality, a judgment founded (it must be observed) on weighing the translations of the Novi Pazar songs (*SCHS* I) against the original language texts of the *Iliad* and *Odyssey*,[14] they form the basis for an opinion which was to attract a modest constituency.[15]

On the basis of these and other judgments, Kirk then posits a four-stage life cycle for an oral tradition: originative, creative, reproductive, and degenerate (96). Within the second stage he finds a creative and original Homer able to make radical and individual changes in the tradition he inherits, a monumental poet-composer able to mold the tradition in an extraordinary way. This singer is to be distinguished from the "*reproductive* one exemplified by the Novi Pazar singers" (96–97); in this third phase of the cycle, repertoires are not extended by individual invention and older patterns prevail for a time before the advent of the rhapsode, or performer from a fixed text, who characterizes the final stage. A great deal of the rest of the book, including chapters on the possibility of Mycenaean epic, the conditions for poetic tradition in the subsequent Dark Age, cultural and linguistic backgrounds, structural anomalies, and so on are built upon this hypothesis of the step-by-step evolution of oral tradition. Much that Kirk has to say agrees at least in part with Parry-Lord theory, and his departures from their views on oral epic can almost all be traced to this central theorem on originality. His position on Homer and his tradition is well stated in the coda to the final chapter:

> Yet ultimately [the *Iliad* and *Odyssey*] owe their qualities to a rare and almost unique coalescence of virtuosity and, precisely, tradition: to the directness and inevitability of a language evolved over many generations of singers, to the formalized and severe repetition of descriptions and themes, but also to a deeper vision in which infatuation and mortality, the stresses of heroic personality and the tensions and rewards of existence in peace and war, are subjected to an oblique but penetrating scrutiny. (384)[16]

Soon after Kirk's book was published, Eric A. Havelock's *Preface to Plato* (1963) appeared. Havelock's contribution was nothing less than an entire revamping of the way in which scholars had thought about Homer and the epics; he argues, persuasively and with considerable evidence, that the poems served as the educational "encyclopedias" of their time, storing information that an oral culture could not commit to the convenience of the manuscript or printed book but had nonetheless to have ready at hand:

> Poetry is central in the educational theory. It occupied this position so it seems in contemporary society, and it was a position held apparently not on the grounds that we would offer, namely poetry's inspirational and imaginative effects, but on the ground that it provided a massive repository of useful knowledge, a sort of encyclopedia of ethics, politics, history and technology which the effective citizen was required to learn as the core of his educational equipment. (27)

The oral state of mind, he goes on, is Plato's real enemy in his well-known attack on the poets in the *Republic*, for the barrier between Homer and Plato is not simply one of genre or history, but more fundamentally a difference in phenomenologies—between oral and written phenomenologies taken each in its fullest, most far-reaching sense.[17] Both the incantatory medium and the generically formed but individually applicable message were uniquely suited to the oral culture, and so Plato's ideal state, imposing regulation from without, came into primal conflict with deeply ingrained habits of thought and action which functioned from within. The Homeric society as Havelock construes it acted out the encoded patterns of the *Iliad* and *Odyssey* mimetically, just as the bard himself transmitted the tradition mimetically. This philosophical view of ancient Greek oral poetry adds a new dimension to the Oral Theory, and much has followed in its wake.[18]

Other new directions were being described almost concurrently by A. Hoekstra, whose *Homeric Modifications of Formulaic Prototypes: Studies in the Development of Greek Epic Diction* (1964)[19] probed beneath the surface of Homer's diction in an attempt to establish elements of its prehistory, and by scholars engaged in the debate over the so-called structural formula. While Hoekstra's studies sought to understand the Homeric poetic language diachronically, the controversy over structural or syntactic patterns was prompted by primarily synchronic views of the *Kunstsprache*. As a response to what they saw as a too mechanical or restrictive model of Homeric language, some scholars, chiefly Joseph Russo, argued for a kind of formula that was basically metrical and syntactic in shape and consistency rather than verbal. This idea, introduced by Russo in 1963, was critiqued by William Minton, who, in "The Fallacy of the Structural Formula" (1965), contended that such a non- or extraverbal concept of the formula precluded its use as a test to differentiate between oral and written texts.

J. B. Hainsworth joined in objecting to the structural model (1964), and was answered by Russo (1966) in a volume of *Yale Classical Studies* that has since become collectively noteworthy as a source of information and disputation on Homer and Oral Theory.[20] The debate was to continue, fueled by Hainsworth's *The Flexibility of the Homeric Formula* in 1968,[21] as some tried to win for "their Homer" a measure of aesthetic control over his medium and others concentrated more on demonstrating the usefulness and dynamics of the Homeric idiom. In reality, this struggle had at its heart the much older issue of originality versus convention, and within the same decade the newer metaphor would show more obvious signs of that fundamental and irksome issue.

It was this same spirit of searching within apparent formulaic rigidity for an informing aesthetic control that characterized the writings of Adam Parry and Anne Amory Parry. In an earlier paper on the idiosyncratic language of Achilles (1956),[22] a contribution in 1966 on the *Iliad* and the Oral Theory, and a later article on characterization in Homer (1972), Adam Parry described a poet who is able to invest the commonplace with rich and carefully developed meaning. Anne Amory Parry's focus was similar; "The Gates of Horn and Ivory" (1966; cp. 1963) and especially the posthumous *Blameless Aegisthus* (1973; cp. 1971) set out to prove that the Homeric poems are both formulaic and consciously crafted and that the Oral Theory as contemporarily constituted may stand in the way of understanding their artistry. Along with articles by Dimock (1963), Rosenmeyer (1965), Russo, and others,[23] these studies by the Parrys strived to offer an alternative view of Homer that de-emphasized what Milman Parry and Albert Lord had claimed were the necessary consequences of orality and that concentrated instead on discovering a poetic craftsmanship in full and conscious control of a formulaic idiom.[24]

In the middle and latter part of the 1960s, many other studies of various aspects of Homeric oral epic appeared. I shall single out a few of the more important for comment. Notopoulos's "Studies in Early Greek Oral Poetry" (1964) considered the possible rate of composition/performance of ancient Greek oral verse in the modern field context of the Cretan oral poetry which he had himself collected, and discussed, as he had done for Hesiod (1960a) and the Homeric Hymns (1962), the place of the cyclic epics in oral tradition. But the most important section of this paper for later criticism is Notopoulos's call for a new and more suitable aesthetics for oral literature; and indeed, in the following years the questions of whether such a poetics was needed and how it might be attempted continued to figure prominently in the history of the Oral Theory.[25] Two years afterward the first in a series of significant studies by Mark Edwards, "Some Features of Homeric Craftsmanship" (1966), presented further evidence of an artisan-poet able to confer poetic meaning more effectively than Edwards believed the original Parry-Lord model could indicate.[26] In this respect his point of view closely resembles that of Adam and Anne Parry, Kirk, Russo, and others, but his emphasis on the multiformity of patterning at various levels and on the value of tradition to the composing poet set his scholarship apart.

In addition, two interesting but very differently focused books were published during this same period. In 1968 Bernard Fenik's authoritative *Typical Battle Scenes in the Iliad*[27] blended the close analysis and documentation most often associated with the German Neoanalysts with the insights of Oral Theory in order to achieve a thorough discussion of longer traditional narrative units in Homer. And soon afterward William Whallon published his comparative study, *Formula, Character, and Context* (1969a),[28] which treated epithets, kennings, and word groups and their relationship to poetic context and characterization in Homeric, Old English, and Old Testament verse. Although it would be unfair to generalize too much about this book, we may say that Whallon concentrates—unusually, given other instances of comparative oral literature research—on actively differentiating among various oral poetries, that is, on reaching beyond obvious similarities to points of contrast and distinction.[29]

As we move into the 1970s and early 1980s, quite a number of relevant works on ancient Greek literature loom large enough in the overall evolution of the field to merit separate treatment as "new directions" in chapter 5, so our task at this particular spot is correspondingly reduced in scope. Nevertheless, there remains a substantial group of books and articles which may be very briefly summarized here, in addition to those already mentioned in relation to earlier works. Comparative studies on the Oral Theory were aided in 1970 and 1971 by David M. Gunn's "Narrative Inconsistency and the Oral Dictated Text in the Homeric Epic" and "Thematic Composition and Homeric Authorship," both of which brought the author's observations on oral structure in the original-language texts from Novi Pazar (*SCHS* I–II) to bear on problems in the Homeric epics.[30] About the same time Tilman Krischer's book on typical scenes (1971), William Hansen's monograph on more extensive agglomerations (1972), and William Scott's *The Oral Nature of the Homeric Simile* (1974)[31] all provided copious and carefully presented data on the traditional character of the poems. In addition, Harald Patzer (1972) undertook, as had Adam Parry, Anne Amory Parry, and others in the 1966 *Yale Classical Studies* and elsewhere, to reconcile the method and idiom of the oral poet with the literary subtlety many have found in the epics, and Richard Shannon described, in what amounts to a study in oral poetics (1975), the structural relationship between the arms of Achilles and major patterns, themes, and characters in the *Iliad*.

Other publications later on in the decade included Norman Austin's *Archery at the Dark of the Moon* (1975), which offered a revision of Milman Parry's formulaic analyses, claiming as had others that a diction so construed cannot account for Homeric artistry, and also considered larger structures in the *Odyssey*, reacting in this latter case against Bruno Snell's *The Discovery of Mind*. Formulaic structure and the Homeric hexameter comprised the main concerns of Wayne Ingalls's forthright and convincing series of articles during this period,[32] and Leonard Muellner attempted a poetics true to the traditional character of the poetry in *The Meaning of Homeric* eukhomai *through Its Formulas* (1976). Working in part from the analytical program described by Hainsworth (1968), N. Postlethwaite contributed a pair of articles (1979, 1981) that argued for the possibility of a "personal tradition," as exemplified in the Homeric Hymns, within the general formulaic style and in favor of the so-called Continuation of the *Odyssey* (23.297–end) as the oral creation of a poet other than Homer.[33]

Old English

Beginnings to 1949

Aside from ancient Greek, the field that has seen the most sustained research on the Oral Theory has been Old English poetry.[34] As early as the mid–nineteenth century, German Higher Criticism was practicing a kind of formulaic analysis in its attempts to establish the text and authorship of the more significant Anglo-Saxon poems. The very first sign of activity on the formula, however, and more thoroughgoing than Vilmar 1862, was in the related Old Germanic language of Old Saxon, namely in Eduard Sievers's "Formelverzeichnis" appended to his edition of the *Heliand* (1878).[35] Like many other scholars of this period, Sievers conceived of the *Formel* not as Parry's later "group of words which is regularly employed under the same metrical conditions to express a given essential idea," but rather as a consistency of *idea only* which might take a number of different, verbally unrelated forms. A year later Franz Charitius (1879) proposed that investigators concentrate on the phrase rather than the single word or synonym, and in 1889 Richard Meyer published a comparative study of Old Germanic poetry that proposed a whole range of figures of repetition with careful definitions for each. At the same time, Johannes Kail (1889), reacting primarily against the authorship studies of Gregor Sarrazin (1886, 1888), took a large step forward by arguing that the repetitive *Parallel-stellen* were not the trace of a conscious, individualized author but rather a general indication of epic style and thus comprised, to use his term, a *Phrasenvorrat* ("store or reservoir of phrases").[36] With E. C. Buttenwieser's admission of aesthetics to the study of repeated phraseology in a work that appeared in the last year of the century, we come to the end of theoretical development of the "formula" concept in the Higher Criticism. While over-all this group of scholars sought, as did the Homeric Analysts, to dissect the poems they examined—trying to show that this or that poet, redactor, or *Bearbeiter* had his influence on the text that has reached us, their methodology evolved away from a simple fingerprinting device toward a consideration of diction as style, a central tenet of what was to become the Oral Theory.

A few slightly later developments in American criticism of medieval English literature also contributed to the history behind the advent of the Oral Theory in this area. In 1923 John S. P. Tatlock published two articles on formulas in Middle English[37] and other literatures. In the more important of the two, "Epic Formulas, Especially in Layamon" (1923a), he argues for the poet's conscious and aesthetically sensitive deployment of the repetitive phrase, contending that "formulas are magnifying and imposing, no mere convenience, but often a means of embellishment" (513). With reference to Anglo-Saxon poetry, he goes against preceding critics by positing a "conscious Ars Poetica" (516). Tatlock's impressive data, concern for exactness in concept and definition, and comparative perspective (he treats Old and Middle English, other Old Germanic literatures, medieval French and Spanish, and ancient Greek) lend authority to his work, even if some of his deductions have proved untenable. Six years later, writing in the *Klaeber Miscellany* of 1929, Francis P. Magoun, Jr., was to take quite an opposite tack: in analyzing the verbal changes rung on compounds in *Beowulf* and the *Elder Edda*, he comes very near positing a tradition of verse-making in suggesting that "the tendency to make recurrent use of the same first compounding elements no doubt arose in seeking alliterative words" (77; cp. Bryan 1929) and that a study of substitutable positions in the line "might ultimately lead to an understanding of the actual technique of composition" (ibid.). This early note illustrates how close Magoun was to conceiving of an oral tradition of Old English poetry fully twenty-four years before his seminal article of 1953.[38]

1949–1960

Old English studies in this eleven-year period included some of the most innovative studies on Oral Theory to date. Spurred on by Lord's recently completed dissertation,[39] Magoun presented in 1953 the first application of the Parry-Lord approach to Old English verse, "The Oral-Formulaic Character of Anglo-Saxon Narrative Poetry." Using Parry's definitions of *formula* and also of the substitutable frame which he called the *formulaic system*,[40] Magoun carried out a formulaic analysis of lines 1–25 of *Beowulf*. His findings, namely that 70 percent of his sample was repeated elsewhere in the approximately 30,000 lines of the poetic corpus, proved, so he claimed, that *Beowulf* was an oral epic. In retrospect, this demonstration, followed soon by an explanation of Bede's story of the miracle of Cædmon as a "case history" of an oral singer's appropriation of the tradition (1955a),[41] seems to have been too doctrinaire; today few specialists would agree with Magoun's particular view on the necessary and exclusive connection between formulaic structure and orality in the case of Anglo-Saxon verse. But his early writings fired the imagination of a whole generation of scholars and, even before the publication of *The Singer of Tales*, transferred the vital methodology of the Oral Theory to a new literary arena.

The first voices of dissent against the Magoun hypothesis were raised in the years immediately following, with Claes Schaar (1956) pointing out that "the proposition 'all formulaic poetry is oral' does not follow, either logically or psychologically, from the proposition 'all oral poetry is formulaic' " (303), and with Kemp Malone (1960; see also 1961) peremptorily dismissing the possibility that *Beowulf* was an improvised poem on the model of the *guslar* composing in performance, as assumed by Magoun. In opposition to these objections, two of Magoun's students were at the same time developing new applications of the Oral-Formulaic Theory. Robert P. Creed, after completing in 1955 a dissertation that included a formulaic analysis of all of *Beowulf*, published an article on the formulaic system for "answering" in Anglo-Saxon verse (1957), as well as two manuscript readings based on oral theory (1956, 1958). And in what has become a *locus classicus* for later criticism, Creed presented in 1959 a recomposition of lines 356–59 of *Beowulf*, a formulaic remaking in which he illustrated the flexibility of oral poetic diction. To the subsequent objections of Robert Stevick (1962), having to do mainly with what the latter felt was the greater role of memory in the compositional process, Creed granted the importance of past performances but stressed the need to understand the active participation of the poet in his tradition. And to R. F. Lawrence's contention that "if [Creed] can effectively use the oral techniques in the privacy of his study, then how much more effectively might the Anglo-Saxon monk have done likewise?" (1966: 177–78, n. 27), he replied: "I should like to point out that the 'monk' who was as much concerned as I was about possible substitutions of the sort I have suggested above either performed the same elaborate and painstaking operations I performed with the aid of [the concordance] Grein-Köhler-Holthausen's *Sprachschatz* or was a singer-poet thoroughly trained in the tradition" (Creed 1959 [Fry rpt.]: 152).

Another of Magoun's students, Robert E. Diamond, took a quite different position on the basis of his formulaic analysis of the works usually ascribed to the poet Cynewulf. In an article published in 1959, "The Diction of the Signed Poems of Cynewulf," which reported a relatively high formulaic density in these works, he echoes Schaar's reservations while employing Magoun's methodology, contending that "on the basis of internal evidence alone (there is no external evidence), it is impossible to determine whether the Cynewulf poems were composed orally and written down by a scribe, were composed pen in hand in the ordinary modern way, or were composed by a learned poet who was making use of the traditional poetic formulas handed down to him from an age when all poems were oral" (229). The essence of his formulation was thus a direct contradiction of Magoun's central theorem concerning the necessary interrelationship of oral and formulaic; this article and Diamond's other contributions along the same line (1958, 1963, 1975) established an opinion since adopted by not a few Anglo-Saxon scholars, an opinion that maintained its position alongside the arguments of those who subscribed to the original exposition of the Oral Theory.

Research on the narrative *theme* as an oral compositional unit in Old English was also vigorous in this middle period, and, if we pass over the observations Lord made in his dissertation and which appeared later in *The Singer of Tales*,[42] we shall again find Magoun, this time in the company of Stanley B. Greenfield, at the point of origination. Two years after his groundbreaking study of formulaic structure, Magoun's "The Theme of the Beasts of Battle" (1955b; cp. Renoir 1962a) treated what is certainly one of the most common and recognizable of Old English typical scenes.

As he isolated it, this narrative commonplace had a definite pattern—"the mention of the wolf, eagle, and/or raven as beasts attendant on a scene of carnage" (83)—and a certain formulaic content, although this latter aspect was not clearly defined. Greenfield's article on the theme of "Exile" (1955)[43] analyzed an even more pervasive idea-complex, the stereotypical description of a figure ostracized by society because he has lost his lord and therefore his entire social context and identity, and showed how this idea-complex was consistently made up of certain integral parts: status, deprivation, state of mind, and movement in or into exile. Departure from the original Parry-Lord concept of "theme," which includes a measure of verbal correspondence between and among occurrences, was complete in 1960 with David Crowne's extremely influential exposition of what he called the "Hero on the Beach" theme.[44] All mention of repetition in terms of formulas or words vanishes with Crowne's description of the recurrent motif as "(1) a hero on the beach (2) with his retainers (3) in the presence of a flashing light (4) as a journey is completed (or begun)" (368). As time went on, this notion of the theme as a pattern of ideas without the requisite feature of verbal correspondence more and more became the prevailing concept in Old English studies.

1960 and Afterward

By the mid-1960s a movement had begun in Anglo-Saxon formulaic studies, just as a similar movement had started about the same time in the study of ancient Greek, to make the concept and definition of the formula more flexible, so that the poet might be more easily understood as the master rather than the slave of his diction. One way in which this tendency manifested itself was in the works of a group of scholars who, like Russo in Homeric studies, posited a structural, syntactic formula. Assimilating data from Wayne O'Neil (1960a)[45] and Godfrey Gattiker (1962), Frederic Cassidy described a limited number of syntactic frames at the basis of the compositional process and pictured the poet as much freer in actual word choice than the Parry-Lord-Magoun idea of formulaic structure had permitted.[46] A few years later Donald C. Green (1971) added more evidence of the formative role of syntax with a report on his computer studies of the relationship among verbal formulas, metrical types, and syntactic frames. Greenfield (1963; see also 1967b) came at the issues involved in formulas and syntax from the point of view of artistic design, as did Randolph Quirk (1963) in an article stressing the fulfillment or frustration of traditional poetic expectations. Greenfield was soon to declare his outright opposition to the writings of many of the oral-formulaic theorists, and especially the new school of syntactic pattern recognition, in "The Canons of Old English Criticism" (1967a), a significant work in the history of oral studies in medieval English.

An article which has proven even more pivotal to the application of the Oral Theory to Old English poetry, and to the interdisciplinary field in general, is Larry D. Benson's 1966 paper, "The Literary Character of Anglo-Saxon Formulaic Poetry." Analyzing four of the metrical texts most probably the work of writers rather than oral composers, Benson demonstrates that they have about the same formula density as do *Beowulf* and the Cynewulf poems. This congruity, which of course would not be predicted by the Parry-Lord theory as applied by Magoun, leads Benson to suggest an Old English poetic canon which is not oral-formulaic but written-formulaic: "we can see that not only can literate poets write formulaic verse, they can do it pen in hand in the same way any writer observes a literary tradition" (337). Furthermore, this hypothesis must, he feels, affect the way in which we view the poems: "Because Old English poetry is formulaic, our study of it must begin with the exciting and useful techniques developed by students of oral verse, but because this poetry is also literature, our study need not end there" (340). Three years later Ann Watts joined in questioning Magoun's direct translation of Oral Theory—as evolved originally for ancient Greek and South Slavic epic—to Anglo-Saxon verse. In *The Lyre and the Harp* (1969),[47] which treats ancient Greek and Old English comparatively, she criticized the flaws in application of the theory and the practice of analogy in general: "Rules for one will not fit the other. Any comparative investigation, whether of epithets or of other verbal arrangements, finally ends not only in a recognition of the distinct characters of the two traditions of poetry but in uncertainty about the oral nature of Old English poetry" (124).

Nearly concurrently, Donald K. Fry, Jr., began a series of articles on traditional phraseology with "Old English Formulas and Systems" (1967b),[48] which was to enjoy a wide currency in the field. Instead of taking what became known in ancient Greek scholarship as the "hard Parryist" position (Rosenmeyer 1965: 297ff.) of charting and counting repetitions according to the original definitions, Fry adopted a generative model of flexible systems from which, in performance, the poet produced individual formulas. These formulaic systems were built along the prosodic plan of the Old English half-line, with verbal, metrical, and syntactic dimensions, and were, he claimed, learned not as a list of phrases but as an idiom of systems. His new definitions thus reflect these theoretical modifications; the *system* is "a group of half-lines, usually loosely related in form by the identical relative placement of two elements, one a variable word or element of a compound, with approximately the same distribution of non-stressed elements" (203), and a *formula* is "a group of words, one half-line in length,

which shows evidence of being the direct product of a formulaic system"
(204).

Fry went on a few years afterward (1974; see also 1981) to use these
concepts and definitions to explain, as Magoun had attempted to do before
him, the miracle of Cædmon's spontaneous composition of Christian song
and its implications. After a formulaic analysis of *Cædmon's Hymn* against
the background of the rest of Old English verse, he remarked:

> I find it more likely that the half-lines in the corpus originated in systems
> Cædmon used than that Cædmon originated the systems himself. That
> would be a miracle. Cædmon did begin Old English vernacular poetry, the
> value of which Abbess Hild and her scholars immediately recognized. . . . I
> suspect that Hild grasped the potential of converting the secular poetry of
> the Germans to Christian uses, in the spirit of Pope Gregory's admonition
> to Abbot Melitus to convert pagan temples into churches, because the English
> "will be able to banish error from their hearts and be more ready to come
> to the places they are familiar with, but now recognizing and worshipping
> the true god." Cædmon did just that. (60–61)

More revisionist studies of the formula appeared in the next few years,
among them articles by Thomas Gardner (1973), James P. Holoka (1976),
and John S. Miletich (1976). Gardner argues for a literate *Beowulf*-poet,
one who is able to manipulate the tradition he inherits to aesthetic advan-
tage. Not dissimilar is Holoka's thesis of a literate sensibility behind the
poetics of "The Wife's Lament" and "The Husband's Message." In an important distinction not usually made by scholars working in oral literature,
Holoka also maintains that the nature of the genre—in this instance the
shorter, lyric elegy as opposed to the longer narrative genre of epic in Old
English—must come into play: unlike the epic, "short, elegiac poems could
conceivably attain a fixity indistinguishable from that of a written text"
(572).[49] Besides offering a multidisciplinary bibliography, Miletich's article
calls for a consistent application of Parry-Lord Oral Theory (which, he
feels, denies the orality of *Beowulf*) and more comparative statistical analyses
to help differentiate categories of oral, imitation oral, and written texts.[50]

Of the more recent studies of the Old English formula, I shall mention
only a few, and those very briefly, reserving as in the case of ancient Greek
some space in the next chapter for additional commentary on new directions. My computer study of metrical patterns in *Beowulf* (Foley 1978c)
reported the distribution and density of various metrical figures in the poem
and mentioned another aspect of the analysis—the discovery and documentation of a purely metrical level of formula.[51] At about the same time,
Geoffrey R. Russom's "Artful Avoidance of the Useful Phrase in *Beowulf*,
The Battle of Maldon, and *Fates of the Apostles*" (1978) found the Oral Theory

unable to explain the formulaic artistry in those poems. Their poets, he reasoned, had more control of their verbal designs than the conventional theory would predict: "Their diction stands out as superior because they knew more of the tradition than singing demanded, and controlled it with greater felicity" (390).

Other perspectives on the formula included Creed's explanation of the role of sound patterning in *Beowulf* (1981a), an investigation based in part on Berkley Peabody's study (1975) of traditional structure in Hesiod. My contribution to the Lord Festschrift (Foley 1981c) treated the tradition-dependence of formulaic units, with emphasis on the differences among phraseological structures typical of ancient Greek, South Slavic, and Old English. Likewise, John D. Niles (1981a) described the incongruencies between Homeric and Anglo-Saxon formulas as part of his suggested revision of Fry's work on systems, and added a study of compounding (1981b) that further explicated his model of composition through flexible systems and denied Benson's 1966 proposal of literate formulaic composition. The most recent study of the Anglo-Saxon formula, by Anita Riedinger (1985), fashions new definitions and examines "the meanings of traditional thematic formulas in context" (294).[52]

Scholarship on the Old English theme in the period following the publication of *The Singer of Tales* has been nearly as copious as that on the formula. In 1961 Creed suggested, in his "On the Possibility of Criticizing Old English Poetry," that "it is on the level of the theme that we can legitimately expect to find differences in the work of mature singers which has survived to us" (99); this observation led him to prescribe thematic articulation against the traditional backdrop of other occurrences as the locus of the singer's art. On the subject of the poetic portraits of the singer in the *Odyssey* and *Beowulf*, Creed (1962) and, some years later, Jeff Opland (1976; see further 1980a) reached complementary conclusions, examining what the poems tell us of poetic practice and performance in the context of all other related information. At approximately the same time, Diamond described other themes—of war, sea voyages, the comitatus, and cold weather—in his "Theme as Ornament in Anglo-Saxon Poetry" (1961), and Renoir turned the emphasis from structure to aesthetics in his masterful account of the cinematographic, visual effect of oral narrative in "Point of View and Design for Terror in *Beowulf*" (1962b). Later, Renoir published a comparative examination of the traditional motif of the boast before battle (1963), George Clark (1965b; cp. 1965a) documented "the traveler recognizes his goal" as a theme in Crowne's sense of the term as an idea-pattern, and Lord (1965a) pointed to thematic similarities in the *Odyssey* and *Beowulf* having to do with the passages just preceding the Euryalus story and the Unferth episode, respectively.

In 1966 Fry began his series of articles on the Old English theme with "The Hero on the Beach in *Finnsburh*," which took its subject from Crowne's earlier work and supported the contention of diachronic continuity put forward by Renoir in "Oral-Formulaic Theme Survival: A Possible Instance in the *Nibelungenlied*" (1964; cp. 1976a). But Fry's most important study of the narrative multiform, one from which many other scholars would draw their definitions for units, was his "Old English Formulaic Themes and Type-Scenes" (1968). Here he described not just one but two traditional units: the *type-scene* as "a recurring stereotyped presentation of conventional details used to describe a certain narrative event, requiring neither verbatim repetition nor a specific formula content," and the *theme* as "a recurring concatenation of details and ideas, not restricted to a specific event, verbatim repetition, or certain formulas, which forms an underlying structure for an action or description" (53). In other words, he conceived of the former as an action-pattern and the latter as a static association of images and details. Neither of these two units closely matched what Lord had meant by *theme* in *The Singer of Tales* and elsewhere, since the criterion of verbal correspondence between or among occurrences was now dispensed with altogether.

Lord's "Perspectives on Recent Work on Oral Literature" includes an extensive section on the Old English theme (1974c: 19–24). Because his definition of the narrative pattern demands a repeated verbal element as well as a grouping of ideas, he finds the Christian poems of the Anglo-Saxon canon lacking in real evidence of orality: "If the religious poems were truly oral traditional songs, I would expect to find a higher degree of verbal correspondence among the various instances of a theme within a given poem, after making due allowance for adjustment to the specific position in the poem which it occupies" (23). Renoir's "Oral Theme and Written Texts" (1976a), on the other hand, worked with the narrative multiform as idea alone, locating the same theme in two different traditions in Catullus's *Poem IV*, *The Dream of the Rood*, and *The Husband's Message*: "an elongated, man-made, wooden object of any size . . . with a pragmatic effect upon the speaker of the poem or a protagonist thereof . . . speaks up to tell how it once had a previous existence under the form of one or more live trees" (340–41). Comparing similar narrative clusters in Homer and Virgil, Renoir suggests that the oral-formulaic theme—whether or not the work in which it appears is itself oral—offers a critical context free of the sometimes insoluble problems posed by conventional literary history. Also in 1976, I argued in "Formula and Theme in Old English Poetry" that the Anglo-Saxon multiform should be assessed as a tradition-dependent unit, a narrative commonplace whose verbal correspondence will, because of prosodic differences, not consist of the line or caesura-bound partial line of Homeric Greek or South Slavic epic, but rather of a series of single root morphemes, "principally the roots of alliterating words, although non-alliterating words may at times be included" (Foley 1976: 221, italics deleted).[53]

Two years later I explored this idea of tradition-dependence comparatively in "The Oral Singer in Context: Halil Bajgorić, *Guslar*" (1978b). Using example passages from the *Odyssey*, two versions of Bajgorić's *Marko and Mina od Koštura* (Parry Collection texts hitherto unpublished), and *Beowulf*, I demonstrated that each poetic tradition has its own kind of theme and is comparable with the units of other traditions only to a certain extent. In the comparison between the "heroic oath" in Old English and Serbo-Croatian, for example, I found that both themes exhibited relatively little verbal correspondence, either formulaic or morphemic, among occurrences, whereas the Odyssean "feast scene" shows heavy formulaic correspondence among its occurrences. This situation turns out to be typical of some Serbo-Croatian themes and atypical of others.[54] All themes, in short, cannot be reduced to a single, limited set of qualities, any more than all languages and, more to the point, all poetic languages can.[55]

In 1981 Jean Ritzke-Rutherford published two companion articles which, though focusing most immediately on the Middle English *Alliterative Morte Arthure*, have direct reference to and bearing on Old English poetry as well. She posits a six-level taxonomy of traditional structure—formula, formulaic system, motif, type-scene, theme, and cluster—and shows how Old and Middle English poets were able to manipulate associations inherent in these structures. Studies of particular themes include articles by Harry E. Kavros (1981) and Joanne De Lavan (1981) on the feasting and sleeping complex in *Beowulf*. One of the most significant developments in thematic analysis in the past few years has been the continuation of Renoir's series of papers on the aesthetic interpretation of narrative structures. Working with materials as heterogeneous as *Beowulf*, Riddle 89, the *Odyssey*, the *Hildebrandslied*, *Sir Gawain and the Green Knight*, and even Dickens's *Great Expectations* and Gauguin's *Ia Orana Maria*, Renoir has provided an avenue for the recovery of long-lost associations that revivify the traditional work of art.[56]

Selected Other Traditions

Although it will not be possible to cover other traditions in the same detail as ancient Greek and Old English, even an overview of the more important scholarship in these other fields will help to illustrate the spread and applicability of the Oral Theory. In each case I shall treat primarily studies which derive directly from the Parry-Lord impetus, but reference will also be made to less obviously related scholarship on oral literature that nonetheless has bearing on the problems to be discussed.[57]

Serbo-Croatian

Much has already been said in earlier chapters about the field of Serbo-Croatian oral tradition, from its influence on Parry through the work of Murko and Gesemann, to the great collecting trips of the 1930s and afterward that resulted in the Parry archive at Harvard, and on to Lord's comparative studies. In the 1960s we may add Maximilian Braun's *Das serbokroatische Heldenlied* (1961),[58] a historically oriented volume, and important papers by David Bynum (1964, 1968). In the latter piece, Bynum's comparative analysis leads him to this insight on the Odyssean Telemacheia: "Because they so closely resemble each other, the modern Yugoslav experience described in this paper suggests that Telemachus, like Mehmed Smailagić or Omer Hrnjica, would have been *expected* to fail in his initiatory quest to bring about restoration of his father's authority, and that the failure itself is a significant part of the story that confirms the place of Telemachus in the *Odyssey*" (1300). In later years he would add a series of articles on such subjects as genre in oral narrative (1969), character transformation through thematic structure (1970), the "principle of redundancy" in formulaic phraseology (1981), and a reconstruction of the earliest known oral narrative text (1986).[59]

Benjamin A. Stolz has also contributed a series of papers on South Slavic epic, among them a study of the two prominent meters for oral narrative (1969), a comparative thematic analysis of Christian and Moslem variants of the tale of Nikac and Hamza (1970), and an interesting paper on the historicity of a song by the Parry-Lord *guslar* Salih Ugljanin (1967). Mary P. Coote, like Bynum and Stolz a former student of Lord, has enlarged the generic perspective on this traditional oral literature with her "Women's Songs in Serbo-Croatian" (1977), an account of lyric songs from the Parry Collection and elsewhere.[60] She has also added helpful bibliographical articles (1974, 1978), a study of the morphology of the "Return" subgenre of epic (1981), and a comprehensive thematic analysis of the repertoire of Ćamil Kulenović, a Parry-Lord singer (1980).

Although Yugoslav scholarship on oral literature has, quite naturally, not evolved hand in hand with the primarily American school of Oral Theory, both the importance of the native research per se and its many parallel concerns urge that a few key works should be mentioned in this section. Among the most significant and forward-looking of the relevant books and articles we may cite *Usmena književnost* (Oral Literature), edited by Maja

Bošković-Stulli (1971), an especially useful, wide-ranging anthology of re-printed papers and selections from longer works; Svetozar Koljević's *The Epic in the Making* (1980), a thorough and exacting history of oral epic in the Christian tradition from the fifteenth through the nineteenth centuries; a collection of articles in English on various oral genres in Serbo-Croatian tradition (Kolar 1976); and two papers by Z. Dukat on the validity of the Yugoslav analogy for Homeric studies (1976, 1978). John Miletich's survey of scholarship on Hispanic and South Slavic traditional narrative (1981a) also provides further bibliographical aid in this regard.[61]

In many ways the most important event of the 1970s and 1980s for the development of the Oral Theory in the Serbo-Croatian area was the ap-pearance of the translation and edition of Avdo Medjedović's *The Wedding of Smailagić Meho* (Bynum 1974b, Lord and Bynum 1974).[62] In addition to this major accomplishment and analytical essays by Lord, work continued on materials from the Parry Collection and the Serbian Academy of Sciences with my articles on story-pattern in Ibro Bašić's "Alagić Alija and Velagić Selim' " (1978a), comparative thematic structure in the songs of Halil Bajgo-rić, *Beowulf*, and the *Odyssey* (1978b), the applicability of the Oral Theory across traditions (1980), and the role of genre in comparative investigations (1983). In 1975 another field project in Yugoslavia, carried out by Robert Creed, Barbara Kerewsky-Halpern, Joel Halpern, and myself, concentrated on the non-epic genres of oral poetry in a Serbian village. Subsequent reports on this activity include general overviews (Foley 1977b, 1982) and analyses of oral charms or *bajanje* (Kerewsky-Halpern and Foley 1978a, b and Foley 1979), graveside laments or *tužbalice* (Kerewsky-Halpern 1981a), metrical genealogies (Kerewsky-Halpern 1981b), and other types of pat-terned speech.

Hispanic

The Hispanic area has seen a great deal of activity on the Oral Theory, much of it running parallel to the long-standing debate between the so-called Individualists, who would interpret the *Poema de Mío Cid* as the crea-tion of a single gifted poet, and the Traditionalists, who view the poem as the culmination of a rich tradition of verse-making.[63] The point of origin of work in this field may be found in Ruth Webber's groundbreaking mono-graph of 1951, *Formulistic Diction in the Spanish Ballad*, which looked at various kinds of formulaic structure in the *Primavera* collection of Spanish ballads. Understanding composition and performance as a process "of com-bining remembered terms rather than reciting from memory" (253), in accordance with the Parry-Lord model, Webber described the traditional forms taken by the essential ideas of the tradition and considered the impact of formulaic analysis on the problems of origin, dating, transmission, and the like. Webber was to go on to contribute a long line of distinguished studies in this and similar veins, among them analyses of diction in various narrative works (e.g., 1966) and of theme (1973), not to mention magisterial survey essays treating scholarship on the Oral Theory relating to the *Cid* (1986b) and to the Hispanic area in general (1986a).

As in other fields, the publication of *The Singer of Tales* encouraged much response and led to a series of studies of various texts. One of the earliest to engage the Yugoslav analogy was Alan Deyermond, who in 1965 published "The Singer of Tales and Mediaeval Spanish Epic," which attempted to adapt the findings of Parry and Lord to the complex situation of the Middle Ages.[64] Here and in later work (e.g., 1968, 1973) he seeks a middle path between those who claim actual orality for medieval Spanish narrative and those who deny any immediate connection with the unwritten word. Although he finds sufficient evidence of oral traditional structures such as formula and theme, Deyermond also feels that the poetry is stylistically too sophisticated to be orally composed. A year later the great Hispanist Ramón Menéndez Pidal took up the issue of the Yugoslav analogy (1965–66), arguing that the model presented by Parry and Lord was a special case and thus had limited applicability for the understanding of medieval poetry. His opinion was both based on and influenced by his own work on oral poetry, which had laid the groundwork for the advent of 'Neotraditionalism,' an effort to restore art and complexity to poems considered traditional.[65]

Edmund de Chasca's early view of oral tradition (1955) stemmed originally from that of Menéndez Pidal, firmly rooted in the Neotraditionalist school that saw no contradiction between tradition and artistic design. Later on, however, he tended more toward the criteria prescribed by Oral Theory, namely toward formulaic density, enjambement, paratactic style, and thematic structure as the hallmarks of verifiably oral material. His "Composición escrita y oral en el *Poema del Cid*" (1966–67) presented the first figures on formulaic analysis for that poem, a listing completed in his *Registro* of 1968. De Chasca also contributed a redefinition of the formula that attempted to take into account the possibility of aesthetic manipulation as well as both phraseological and narrative modes and the irregularity of the meter of the *Cid*;[66] his final statement on these matters (1976) reemphasizes the artistic design behind the deployment of traditional structures and, particularly in its adherence to the criterion of formulaic density, places him squarely in the Parry-Lord camp.

Other important figures in the development of Oral Theory in the Hispanic area, which as indicated above is often difficult to distinguish from Neotraditionalism, include Diego Catalán, the grandson of Menéndez Pidal, who heads the Cátedra Seminario Menéndez Pidal. This institute has taken on the burden of publishing all available ballad texts, as well as encouraging the collection of ballads and compiling catalogs and bibliographies.[67] Catalán's own scholarly analyses have also proven apposite, from the historically oriented *Siete siglos de romancero* (1969) to more theoretical works, such as "Memoria e invención en el Romancero de tradición oral" (1970–71). Likewise, Samuel G. Armistead has contributed enormously both to the collection and editing of the ballads and to scholarly exchange on all aspects of Hispanic oral tradition. Together with Joseph Silverman, he has compiled a fine series of volumes on the Judeo-Spanish ballad tradition (1971, 1986). Among his research publications are treatments of the *Mocedades de Rodrigo* and Neoindividualist theory (1978) and of the epic and ballad as a "single system of oral, traditional poetry, extending from the epic's remote and unknown origins, in an uninterrupted continuum, down to the twentieth-century tradition of the *Romancero*" (1981: 384). A significant dimension of all of Armistead's oeuvre has been its critically informed comparison with other European literatures.

In 1973 Franklin M. Waltman began a series of articles based on his statistical studies of the *Cid*; all of these investigations treated the problem of unity of authorship, each of them coming to the conclusion that there was a single author behind the composition of the poem. His complete formulaic analysis and commentary (1973) assumed a literate poet working with materials inherited from a prior oral tradition, and his article on the possibility of a divided heroic vision (1976–78) summoned the Yugoslav analogy to explain differing thematic emphases. A few years later Orest R. Ochrymowycz set out to prove that the Carolingian *romances juglarescos* are oral poems composed by "polished and mature" artists (1975: 10) by considering formulaic diction, twinning devices, enjambement, and irregular lines. Perhaps the most important point for scholars interested in the Oral Theory is his contention that the poet who has mastered the traditional formulaic language has the same freedom as the writing poet. Another quantitative measure was supplied by John S. Geary (1980), who, after establishing the formulaic density of the *Poema de Fernán González* and the *Mocedades de Rodrigo*, finds these two poems written but in many ways traditional.[68]

The comparative work of John S. Miletich has suggested another method of determining the oral or written provenance of texts about whose actual history we know little or nothing.[69] In lieu of the formulaic density test, Miletich prescribes a distinction between "elaborate" and "essential" repetition. The former, designated as typical of true oral texts, is anaphoric, parallel, nonessential, and retarding, while the latter, typical of other kinds of texts, is rapid and necessary to the narrative. From this distinction Miletich creates a variety of categories and a taxonomy of texts, including an intermediate kind of creation which he views as what Yugoslav scholars call *pučka književnost*, literally "popular literature." The *pučka* material is imitation oral; that is, it was composed by literate poets who were following the traditional style. As such, this material shows a lower density of the kinds of repetition Miletich associates with true oral traditional texts, and it is into this category that he places many medieval works.[70]

Old French

Just as was the case in the Hispanic area, the origin of writings on the Oral Theory in Old French can be traced back before the publication of *The Singer of Tales*, to Jean Rychner's seminal monograph, *La Chanson de geste: Essai sur l'art épique des jongleurs* (1955). Using a methodology derived from the work of Murko, Jousse, Parry, and Lord, Rychner claimed that the *chanson de geste* was an oral traditional genre, with the notable exception of the great *Chanson de Roland*, which he viewed as too finished to be anything but a literary work. In an article published a year earlier but not nearly as central to subsequent developments in this field, Rita Lejeune had discussed certain formulas in the *chanson de geste*, speaking of the poet's "mémoire auditive" as well as the metrical values of the "clichés" and their consequent usefulness to the poet and connotation for the audience. In a memorable reponse to those who would decry such patterned diction as monotonous or unimaginative, Lejeune noted that "les chansons de geste aux formes immuables sont 'monotones' comme sont 'monotones' les sculptures romanes—et même gothiques—de nos cathédrales, avec leurs thèmes identiques: 'Jugement dernier' ou 'Annonciation' à leur portail . . ." (1954: 331).

Response to Rychner's radical proposals was not long in coming. In 1959 Maurice Delbouille rejected the orality thesis on the basis of too little evidence of a *chanson de geste* tradition prior to the twelfth century and of disagreement with Rychner and Parry over the issues of improvisation, unity, laisse and strophe subdivisions, the technique of refrain and formula, and the significance of manuscript variations.[71] On the other hand, Stephen G. Nichols affirmed Rychner's findings in part though his 1961 analysis of formulaic structure, enjambement, and theme in the *Chanson de Roland*. Nichols assumes the text to have been composed by a literate singer trained in the tradition, a transitional figure who could have used his inherited materials creatively and occasionally have gone beyond the conventional limits of the *chanson de geste* genre.

In 1966 Joseph J. Duggan began an important series of studies on these problems, studies that were to feature a rigorously quantitative dimension that derived directly from the work of Parry and Lord. With respect first to the *Couronnement de Louis* (1966) and then to the *Chanson de Roland* (1973) and the *Poema de Mio Cid* (1974b), Duggan established the formulaic density of each text against the comparative background of the *chanson de geste* tradition. On the basis of thirteen Old French songs, he proposed a threshold of 20 percent straight formula (exact repetition, allowing for substitution according to assonance patterns) as the minimum measure of the orality of a poem. The *Roland*, standing 15 percent over this threshold figure, is thus judged an oral work. Taking into account the irregular meter of the Cid, he finds it 31.7 percent semantic formulas and comes to the same conclusion about the Spanish poem's provenience. Many of the issues raised by these analyses, as well as other problems in application of the Oral Theory, were taken up in the four-part debate between Duggan and William Calin (Duggan 1981a, b and Calin 1981 a, b); these scholarly duels bring into the foreground some of the most troublesome points of the Theory, with both sides of each question well represented.[72]

Other studies on Old French include Rudy S. Spraycar's comparative analysis (1976) of the *chansons de geste* and Andrija Kačić-Miošić's *Razgovor*, a literate composition in Serbo-Croatian done in imitation of the oral style. Finding the *Razgovor* more formulaic than the Old French material, Spraycar concludes that formula density is not a true measure of orality and that the oral/written dichotomy posited by the Oral Theory amounts to an oversimplification. Generative models for the Old French formula were suggested by Genette Ashby (1979) and MarjorieWindelberg and D. Gary Miller (1980). Ashby's paper is quite similar to the work of Nagler and Windelberg and Miller's is more in the vein of Hainsworth; in both cases, the emphasis is placed not on the formulas themselves but on the process of phrase generation that leads to specific surface structures in the moment of performance.

Finally, although it lies in large part outside the mainstream of the Oral Theory, I should mention the challenging work of Paul Zumthor, who has brought a much-needed concern for aesthetics and literary theory to the study of oral poetry. Zumthor understands the *chansons de geste* that have reached us as literary texts that derived from a primary oral traditon not unlike that observed by Parry and Lord in the Balkans (1973). But he considers conventional Oral Theory an insufficient approach to oral poetry because it concentrates too exclusively on a single feature of the *discours*, that is, on the formula. Noting that phraseology and all other traditional characteristics vary from one poetry to another, he stresses the function of the formula as an element of meaning: "à la fois signe et symbole, paradigme et syntagme, la formule neutralise l'opposition entre la continuité de la langue et la discontinuité des discours" (1982: 390). Zumthor's latest contribution, *Introduction à la poésie orale* (1983), moves outside the Old French canon to provide an international overview of oral traditional forms, concentrating on the presence of "voice" in oral re-creations.[73]

Medieval German

The first activity to stem directly from the Parry-Lord initiative in medieval German was that of Werner Schwarz (1965) and Robert Kellogg (1965).[74] Schwarz concentrated on the application of the Oral Theory to the epic *Dukus Horant* and other Middle High German texts by tracing the morphology of a single phrase and illustrating its shifts in meaning. Based on the evidence of common formulaic phraseology in the Old Saxon *Heliand*, the Old English poetic corpus, and Old High German verse, Kellogg posited a South Germanic oral tradition, "a more or less unified and indisputably oral tradition stretching back in time to the early centuries of the Christian era, and perhaps much further" (72).[75] In 1967 Michael Curschmann published a commentary on, and critique of, Parry-Lord scholarship on various medieval literatures. His later writings were to treat the *Spielmannsepik*, with emphasis on the role of tradition and the nature of poetic art (1968);[76] the formula as an impediment to the understanding of medieval poetry (1977);[77] and the relationship of the *Nibelungenlied* to the *Nibelungenklage* (1979).

Within a few years of the entry of Oral Theory into the Germanic area, Franz H. Bäuml began an insightful series of articles that attempted to shape Parry-Lord theory to the specific area of Middle High German and to study the social aspects of literacy and illiteracy in medieval society at large. As early as 1968, many of Bäuml's concerns were evident: the nature of the transition from oral to written composition, the different audiences for the different kinds of texts, and the blend of oral-formulaic diction with written style. Among his other essays, we may single out for special mention "Varieties and Consequences of Medieval Literacy and Illiteracy" (1980) and "Medieval Texts and the Two Theories of Oral-Formulaic Composition: A Proposal for a Third Theory" (1984). The first of these enlists Receptionalist theory in the service of an inquiry into the relationship between different kinds of texts and their audiences, observing that "with the evolution of vernacular literacy, textual as well as pictorial narrative changes its communicative function from commenting on 'reality' to constituting a 'reality' " (265). The latter article attempts to use such distinctions in a codified manner to come to terms with the transitional texts that are so common during the medieval period.

Edward R. Haymes has also contributed a number of important studies in the Germanic field, chief among them *Mündliches Epos in mittelhoch-*

deutscher Zeit (1970), which looks at oral traditional characteristics in a number of Middle High German works, and the more generally oriented *Das mündliche Epos: Eine Einführung in die "Oral Poetry" Forschung* (1977), which tracks the early progress of the Theory in certain European literatures.[78] Other works of note include Dieter Lutz's 1974 exposition of the tradition-dependent features of Middle High German epic, in which he disputes the necessary connection between formulaic density and orality, and Ruth H. Firestone's largely Proppian study of traditional structure in the Dietrich Cycle (1975). Finally, Renoir's comparative essays on oral traditional context and medieval narrative have often made mention of the Old High German *Hildebrandslied* (esp. 1979a, b), explicating the connotative power of the ubiquitous "Hero on the Beach" theme and its role in providing a traditional kind of unity for the fragment of the work that has survived.

Byzantine and Modern Greek

Scholarship on Byzantine and modern Greek has occupied pride of place in the expansion of the Oral Theory since Lord first considered the *Digenis Akritas* epic in *The Singer of Tales*.[79] In fact, Gareth Morgan's study of Cretan poetry (1960), which treated episodic structure, narrative inconsistencies, and the analogy with the Yugoslav *guslar*, appeared concurrently with Lord's classic book. A few years later C. A. Trypanis made a connection between the Parry-Lord theory and Byzantine oral poetry (1963), citing the multiformity of language and textual variants typical of oral poems in other traditions and commenting on the complexity of the manuscript tradition that was in part the result of oral transmission.[80] Soon afterward András Mohay (1974–75), discussing *Schriftlichkeit und Mündlichkeit* in Byzantine literature, denied the necessary link between formulaic structure and orality and contended that, since the chief function of what he interpreted as written formulas was to facilitate versification, literate poets could also employ the traditional diction.

Most of the later pertinent scholarship in the Byzantine area has been the contribution of Elizabeth and Michael Jeffreys, whose essays have been collected in *Popular Literature in Late Byzantium* (1983). Among these articles, Michael Jeffreys's analysis of formulas in the *Chronicle of the Morea* (1973) stands out as a judicious extension of the Oral Theory. Comparing this text against the certainly written and learned *Alexander* from about the same period, he is able to reinstate the *Chronicle* as a work of Greek literature rather than a translation, to confirm its oral sources, to describe its diction as a traditional *Kunstsprache,* and to comment on necessary procedures in textual criticism. Likewise, in a joint article that takes as its point of departure the difficulties of editing Byzantine verse romances (1971), the

Jeffreys propose a formulaic and memorial tradition of translation rather than the composition-in-performance model that is the cornerstone of the Oral Theory. Another joint essay on the traditional style of early demotic verse (1979) probes the poorly understood area of the transitional text, arguing that, given its combination of traditional formulas and idiosyncratic phrases in the service of a literate translator, the demotic Greek *War of Troy* amounts to a work "between oral and literary composition" (138). In these and other articles, the Jeffreys have helped to develop the explicative potential of the Oral Theory by adapting its concepts and models to the particular tradition under consideration.

In the modern Greek area, the most significant recent work has been done by Roderick Beaton, whose 1980 book, *Folk Poetry of Modern Greece*, considers the structure and history of the demotic tradition, with special attention to the formula, oral transmission, myth, the emergence of professional singers, and the state of the tradition in the twentieth century. His conclusions on the question of whether *Digenis Akritas* was an oral poem (1981) echo those reached by the Jeffreys on much of the Byzantine material: although the texts reveal oral traditional characteristics and can thus be shown to have oral roots, "no version . . . shows convincing signs that it is the product of composition in performance" (16). Beaton goes on to derive the poem from the convergence of the learned and literate Byzantine tradition with the oral heroic tradition of the eastern frontier, suggesting that our concept of "oral poetry" must be refined to take account of texts that have oral roots but which were not composed in performance.

Margaret Alexiou's perspective on the Greek lament allows her to review the history of this genre from Homer to the present (1974). In part III of this study, she examines the interaction of poetic originality with a "common tradition" of poetic conventions and structures, themes, formulas, images, and symbols. Similarly, her treatment of the "Lament of the Virgin" folksong pattern (1975) finds a common oral source for the Byzantine and modern examples. Anna Caraveli advocates a synthetic approach to modern Greek folk song (1982), combining attention to the traditional associations of structural elements with consideration of the living, present social context. In the process she argues, as does Renoir in his studies of Germanic poetry, that apparently fragmentary texts are filled out by traditional implications and context outside of the immediate song-text.[81]

Irish

Contributions to scholarship in the Irish field cover many stages in the evolution of oral tradition, from the earliest Old Irish narratives to modern Gaelic tales. Furthermore, with the momentum engendered by a scholarly enterprise as vigorous as the Irish Folklore Commission (founded in 1935), studies of oral tradition have taken many forms, relatively few of them to be directly derived from the Oral Theory.[82] Of those which do to some extent owe their methods to the Parry-Lord research, we may mention James Ross's exploration of the formulaic and thematic qualities of Gaelic oral poetry collected in recent times in the western isles of Scotland (1959), a study which proposes adaptation of the original model to the tradition at hand and suggests connections with prose tales. Challenging and insightful comparative studies of Irish material and Homeric epic have been published by Kevin O'Nolan, who in 1968 applied the Parry-Lord approach to a folktale entitled "Tóraíocht an Ghiolla Dheacair" and discovered noun-epithet formulas and other features typical of traditional phraseology. His investigations continued in 1969 with further exposition of formulaic structure in Homer and Old Irish narrative, concentrating as well on examples of context adjustment and the elaboration of set themes in both traditions. A third article (1975) treated the formulaic runs typical of modern Irish prose tales and found the formula to be basically independent of meter.[83]

In addition to Seán Ó Coileáin's useful overview of Irish saga literature (1978),[84] Daniel F. Melia and Joseph F. Nagy have contributed importantly to the relevant scholarship on Old Irish and later texts. Melia (1974) analyzes versions of "The Boyhood Deeds of Cuchulainn" within the *Cattle Raid of Cooley* to show that the narrative structure of the Ulster tales as a whole descends from oral tradition.[85] Nagy's 1985 book, *The Wisdom of the Outlaw: The Boyhood Deeds of Finn in Gaelic Narrative Tradition*, engages the tremendous complexity of the Fenian cycle of myths, stretching from as early as the twelfth century up to the present day in a formidable array of manuscripts and dictated texts, and illustrates the continuing traditional strands of narrative that even in their manifest variation preserve essential heroic and societal values from Indo-European culture onward. His remarks concern not only the multiform activities of the great hero Finn himself, but also the mythology attendant on poets and poetry, on rites of passage, and on the relationship of this world to the otherworld.[86]

Biblical Studies

Like Irish, the field of Biblical studies has had a long history of concern with the relationship of extant texts to oral tradition that predates and continues alongside work that stems specifically from the Oral Theory.[87] Although Charles H. Lohr's "Oral Techniques in the Gospel of Matthew" (1961) constituted the first instance of the Parry-Lord approach, it was Robert C. Culley's 1963 critique that opened the way for the contribution of Oral Theory. Culley maintained that while scholars had often remarked on the importance of orality for the Bible, their concept of oral tradition was inexact and the results of their research were therefore disappointing. He recommended taking account of scholarship on analogous traditions, particularly the work of the Chadwicks (1932–40) and Lord (1960). Culley's *Oral Formulaic Language in the Biblical Psalms* (1967) answered this call for application of the Parry-Lord methods, revealing a high density of formulas that he interpreted as evidence for the presence of a formulaic language if not for actual formulaic composition. His collection on *Oral Tradition and Old Testament Studies* (1976a), some of whose contents are separately reviewed herein, and his analytic monograph, *Studies in the Structure of Hebrew Narrative* (1976b), which concentrates on the episodic patterning that may be evidence of an ultimate source in oral tradition, continue this work.

In 1972 William J. Urbrock explored the units of formula and theme in the song-cycle of Job, explaining the differences between the Masoretic and Old Greek texts of the Book of Job as the result of an oral tradition underlying the manuscripts. He also interpreted the traditional word-pairs so much a feature of these texts as a formulaic device that operated in concert with the more customary units described by Oral Theory.[88] This latter observation was independently made a year earlier by Perry B. Yoder, who claimed that the word-pairs were equivalent to Parry's formulas, with the formal requirement of parallelism taking the place of the metrical constraint. Yoder summoned the analogues of Ob-Ugric and Toda poetry as comparative evidence for this assertion.[89] At the level of theme, David M. Gunn, who had written on oral traditional style in Homer (1970, 1971), turned his attention to narrative patterns in the Bible, specifically Judges and Samuel (1974a), the "battle report" commonplace (1974b), and the "succession narrative" (1976a). These articles also contain useful and interesting observations on prose formulas and other characteristics of oral style; Gunn thus endeavors to indicate the importance of oral tradition for the texts involved without insisting on actual oral provenience.

One scholar who disputed the findings of Culley, Gunn, and others is John Van Seters, who prefers to explain common patterns as symptomatic of common authorship or literary borrowing rather than of an active oral tradition. In 1972 he made this case for the two primary accounts of Israel's conquest of Sihon and Og, and in 1976 he responded specifically to Gunn's analysis of the "battle report" pattern. William R. Watters' *Formula Criticism and the Poetry of the Old Testament* (1976) likewise finds conventional Oral Theory lacking in some respects, but he acknowledges and exemplifies its usefulness if adapted to the Biblical texts. He also enters the discussion on the nature of word-pairs, pointing out that they occur in both oral and written material, and applies the Theory to problems of dating, authenticating, relating, and repairing individual texts. In the same year Robert B. Coote considered the judicious application of the Parry-Lord approach to Biblical literature, concluding among other things that one should take into account the idiosyncratic aspects of the Hebrew material and preferring the repeated phrase over the word-pair as the core formulaic unit of composition.[90]

Coote was one member of a small school of Biblical scholars trained by Frank M. Cross, whose *Canaanite Myth and Hebrew Epic* (1973) provided an early glimpse of the oral traditional background of Biblical and related materials. Cross noted, for example, that the mythic cycle of Ba'l and 'Anat "is marked by oral formulae, by characteristic repetitions, and by fixed pairs of synonyms (a type of formula) in traditional thought rhyme (*parallelismus membrorum*) which marks Semitic oral literature as well as much of the oral literature throughout the world" (112). Others of his students have produced works that bear on oral tradition in the Biblical and Near Eastern texts, including Susan Niditch (1985) and Richard E. Whitaker (1972).[91]

Into this scholarly arena Werner Kelber brought a new emphasis on the differing phenomenologies of oral and written in the history of the Gospels. Although his major work will be reviewed in the next chapter, I note here that his 1980 article, "Mark and Oral Tradition," charted the territory he was later to explore. Instead of seeing the shift from an oral to a textual tradition as a natural and gradual evolution, Kelber persuasively characterizes textuality as "a critical alternative to the powers of orality" (46), a shift from collectivity to individual authorship and a "crisis" of oral transmission brought on by the retreat of Jesus' oral presence into a necessarily textual history. He also notes the oral traditional features of Mark's Gospel (formulaic and thematic patterning, variants with respect to the other Gospels, modulation in the order of events) and the fact that Mark's chirographic enterprise went on in a milieu that included a contemporary synoptic oral tradition.

Arabic

The field of Arabic has also felt the influence of the Oral Theory, especially in relation to medieval texts.[92] The earliest example of such activity is an examination by Andras Hamori (1969) of convention in the poetry of Abū Nuwās, whose figures of speech, stock motifs, and other structures Hamori interprets as functional elements rather than mere commonplaces. He also distinguishes explicitly between the Parry-Lord formula and the phraseological patterns he finds by comparing the latter exclusively to the unchanging longer Homeric repetition that does not advance the narra-tive.[93] From a different perspective, James T. Monroe argues in "Oral Composition in Pre-Islamic Poetry" (1972) that the long debate over the authenticity of this body of material might well be resolved by recognizing its tradition as oral in the Parry-Lord sense. His explanation is supported by a careful treatment of formulaic density and distinctions among pure formula, formulaic system, structural formula, and conventionalized lan-guage.[94] In a similar vein, Bridget Connelly (1973) has proposed clearing up scholarly confusion over the *al-sira* tales in Middle Arabic by recognizing their orality.

This kind of application reached a new level of maturity with the research of Michael J. Zwettler. After a brief prolegomenon (1976) describing the need for acknowledging the orality of classical Arabic poetry and the re-sponsibility to adapt the Oral Theory to the specific case of this tradition, Zwettler proceeded to a full-length study, *The Oral Tradition of Classical Arabic Poetry: Its Character and Implications* (1978), that made the requisite adjustments in the Parry-Lord approach and presented a formulaic analysis of a sample *qaṣīda*.[95] He also demonstrates Arabic grammarians' disapproval of necessary enjambement, a feature Parry established as atypical of Ho-meric oral traditional poetry, and interprets the thematic structure of the poems under consideration as another sign of oral composition. The last two chapters of the book describe the poetic *koine*, analogous to the Homeric *Kunstsprache*, that serves as the traditional poetic medium and discuss the nature of variation and attribution within the classical Arabic tradition.[96] In the modern sphere, Semha Alwaya's "Formulas and Themes in Con-temporary Bedouin Poetry" (1977) treats the theme of hospitality in five versions of a poem and identifies associated systems of formulas.

Two additional works, both of them concerned with still-extant oral tra-ditions in Arabic lands, also deserve mention. Saad Abdullah Sowayan's *Nabaṭi Poetry* (1985) describes this genre's pre-Islamic counterpart and goes on to treat aspects of composition, performance, and transmission. Of spe-cial interest is his discussion of the applicability of the Parry-Lord theory, particularly his observation that

> Formulaic expressions are artistic conventions and stylistic devices that serve to alert the audience to the thematic movement of the poem and establish the necessary rapport and feeling of familiarity that attract the audience to the poem without jeopardizing its individual quality. It is therefore necessary to reevaluate such terms as *orality* and *formulaic* in order to understand their true importance and function in the Arabic poetic tradition as a whole. . . . (208)

Bridget Connelly's *Arab Folk Epic and Identity* (1986) explores another genre, the Banī Hilāl epic, again through firsthand study, this time in Egypt and Tunisia. Connelly probes the social significance of the epic, describing its genealogical and historical importance to those who preserve it through many Arabic territories. Although references to the oral theory abound throughout the study, her remarks on "Musical Improvisation and the Oral-Formulaic Mode" (69–87) are especially innovative in their attention to an often neglected but fundamental aspect of oral poetic phraseology.

African

As we turn to the last major area to be considered, that of African, it is well to emphasize that only a relatively small percentage of the enormous amount of research and scholarship on that continent's oral traditions falls under the shadow cast by Oral Theory.[97] Nonetheless, we may mention a few representative works, some more directly influenced than others by the Parry-Lord approach. Certainly the contributions of Jeff Opland must be placed in this category, since the major thrust of much of his writing has been to provide another living analogue for comparison with medieval and other manuscript traditions. Although his comparative articles on Bantu and Old English poetry begin as early as 1970 and 1971, the first thoroughgoing account of the Xhosa poet and oral tradition appeared in *"Imbongi Nezibongo"* (1975). Here Opland distinguished between (1) general improvising, (2) memorizing, (3) the refined improvising of the tribal poet, and (4) literate composition. In this and other essays[98] he seeks to qualify the Parry-Lord orthodoxy by showing how oral composition of short, non-narrative poetry and a literate poet are not mutually exclusive.

A wider, more synthetic perspective is offered by the scholarship of Ruth Finnegan. Although her initial publication, *Limba Stories and Story-Telling* (1967), reported the oral prose tradition in a single African tribe among whom she had carried on fieldwork, Finnegan's subsequent contributions were more comparative in nature. In 1970 her encyclopedic compendium, *Oral Literature in Africa*, appeared, with its documentation of oral performance, audience, assortment of genres, history of scholarship, and social, linguistic, and literary background for a great many African traditions. Through a series of articles (esp. 1976) and a longer study, *Oral Poetry: Its Nature, Significance, and Social Context* (1977), she went on to attack the Oral Theory for its overdependence on the South Slavic model of composition and tradition, denying that (1) there is a single, definable phenomenon we can call "oral literature," (2) a clear boundary can always and everywhere be drawn between oral and written forms of verbal art, and (3) oral composition is a single, universal process. Finnegan's observations, which are made from the viewpoint of an anthropologist and thus sometimes do not square with the linguist's or literary scholar's opinions, have been valuable in opening up Oral Theory to a necessary differentiation among various traditions and forms of oral material.

Another anthropologist who has contributed significantly to our understanding of oral tradition in Africa is Daniel Biebuyck. Among his many relevant publications, most of which treat the heroic epic (e.g., 1972, 1976), I would single out *Hero and Chief: Epic Literature from the Banyanga Zaire Republic* (1978) and his co-edition and -translation of *The Mwindo Epic* (1969) for special mention. The latter is a presentation in both the original Bantu and modern English of the text of the Nyanga oral epic taken down in writing from oral performance. The former volume has chapters on "The Bards" and "Formulas and Style Features," in which he describes noun-epithet combinations, phrases for time and space, introductions, and other typical phraseological elements.[99] Other studies of African oral traditional material, some of them more directly related to the Oral Theory than others, include Marion Kilson's report on the *kpele* song texts she collected in Ghana during the 1960s (1971); David Henige's analysis of Fante oral history (1974), with an account of the impact of literacy on oral tradition;[100] Harold Scheub's numerous explorations of Xhosa and other oral art in terms of his own system of description and analysis (e.g., 1975); and Deirdre La Pin's explanation of how oral narrative serves a pedagogical and homeostatic function in Yoruba society (1981).

Much of the pertinent scholarship in this area has revolved around the question of whether epic really exists in Africa and, if so, how it compares to the European concept of the genre. In addition to the testimony of Biebuyck and Opland on this score, the contributions of Isidore Okpewho and John W. Johnson should be noted. Okpewho's 1977 article found the oral epic in both the *Kambili*, from the western African Mande, and the *Mwindo Epic*, from the Banyanga of Zaire; he also pointed out the presence of formulas, themes, ornamental structures, and ring-composition in the two works. A few years later his *Epic in Africa: Toward a Poetics of the Oral Performance* (1979) continued this research, with comparative reference to Homer, the South Slavic *guslari*, and *Gilgamesh*. In the same year Johnson published an edition of the epic of Sun-Jata as told by Magan Sisòkò, a version recorded on tape by the editor in western Mali; it includes data on the bard, the language and transcription, and the circumstances of performance, as well as selections from an interview with Sisòkò. Thus it was that in 1980 Johnson answered the nagging question of genre in his article "Yes, Virginia, There Is an Epic in Africa"; among the features and criteria he ascribes to the genre is the Parry-Lord idea of theme.[101]

Others

The remainder of this section of the chapter will review pertinent scholarship on a selection of oral traditions that for one reason or another have not yet seen extensive application of the Oral Theory. The notations will thus be brief, sometimes treating only a single article or book.

The ancient world outside of Greece has been the subject of a modest amount of investigation from the point of view of Oral Theory. Bendt Alster's monograph, *Dumuzi's Dream: Aspects of Oral Poetry in a Sumerian Myth* (1972), amounts to a reconstruction of the poem from fragments, with particular attention to formulaic structure and thematic patterns. I. McNeill (1963) studies formulaic structure in the Hittite *Song of Ullikummi* in comparison to ancient Greek, and Frank M. Cross argues that certain Ugaritic texts were composed "in poetic formulae and patterns which reveal original oral composition" (1974: 1).[102]

The Indian region is represented in part by Murray B. Emeneau's fieldwork and writings on the Todas, which approach their subject from an ethnographic as well as oral-formulaic angle. After an original overview (1958), Emeneau studied various kinds of traditional phraseology (1966) and provided an edition (1971) and linguistic analysis (1974) of this material. Likewise, K. Kailasapathy's *Tamil Heroic Poetry* (1968) considers formulaic and thematic structure in Tamil verse, as well as provides portraits of the bards and a taxonomy of different kinds of singers in that tradition. John D. Smith (1977) describes a West Indian epic tradition that seems not to obey the tenets of the Oral Theory, in that it is formulaic but not improvisatory.[103] In the Turkish area, Ilhan Başgöz has published numerous articles having to do with his field research among tellers of *hikaye;* these papers touch on the nature of the genre, which is similar but not identical to the epic (1970), the relationship between singer and audience (1975), and formula in prose narrative (1978a).[104]

In other areas, Ching-Hsien Wang (1974) has applied the Oral Theory to the ancient lyrics of the Chinese *Shih Ching*, finding formulaic and thematic structures to be pervasive features and arguing that the texts that have survived were composed during a transitional period in which oral-formulaic devices were employed by lettered poets.[105] Vaira Vikis-Freibergs and Imants Freibergs used computer-assisted techniques to probe the formulaic structure of the Latvian *dainas* or "sun-songs" (1978), and Hèdi Sioud has carried the Parry-Lord theory to the realm of Tunisian oral poetry (1976, 1978), performing formulaic and other analyses on material he collected during fieldwork.

Somewhat more focused attention has been accorded the Old Norse and

Russian traditions. For the former, Joseph Harris has contributed surveys which include remarks on Oral Theory, with respect to both the poetic Eddas (1983) and the prose sagas (1986), as well as an analytical discussion of the *senna*, the stylized battle of words in Old Norse saga (1979).[106] His remarks touch on tradition-dependent features and on the possible role of memorization as well as on units of composition and provenience. Some years earlier Paul B. Taylor (1963) had identified formulaic and thematic structures in *Völundarkviða*, arguing that irony, foreshadowing, and subtle kinds of correspondences are accomplished through oral traditional techniques. Lars Lönnroth's essays have considered the Eddic poems as oral and formulaic creations, though he does not accept the standard Parry-Lord model (1971), and thematic patterns in the sagas (1979) and a formula that shows signs of originating in Common Germanic tradition (1981). In the Russian area, the primary work has been done by Patricia Arant, whose article on formulaic structure in the *bylina* (1967) was one of the first to suggest the need for adaptation of the Parry-Lord idea of the phrase to fit individual traditions. She has also written on thematic structure (1968, 1981a) as well as on the tradition of funeral lament in Russian (e.g., 1981b).[107] Elizabeth Warner (1974) offers an interesting glimpse of the reverse process of literary material entering the oral tradition in her discussion of Pushkin and Russian folk drama.

The Oral Theory has also affected scholarship on various kinds of music. Leo Treitler (1974, 1975) has used the approach to investigate the transmission of plainchant before the advent of musical transcription, explaining how oral formulas and formulaic systems played a role in the invention, maintenance, and passing on of melodies.[108] Other studies that show a direct connection to Parry-Lord methodology include Jeff T. Titon's *Early Downhome Blues: A Musical and Cultural Analysis* (1977a), which features a chapter on formulaic structure, specifically on the "generating systems" underlying the variety of tunes. Titon has also examined "thematic pattern," which he defines as "the thought sequence that controls attitudes toward human experience and selects a narrative pattern (that is, an event sequence) to illustrate those attitudes" (1977b: 316).[109] Similarly, John Barnie (1978) feels it is correct to say that country blues singers are working within a tradition not unlike that described by Parry and Lord, but he notes that further scholarship should take more careful account of meter, line and stanza structure, and thematics in the blues genre. In the area of jazz improvisation, Lawrence Gushee (1981) discusses the insights gained by applying Oral Theory to the work of saxophonist Lester Young, treating the collective structure of the performance as well as formulaic structure and pointing out that composition proceeds along several tracks at once.

The field of the folk ballad is of course tremendously complex, and much the greater part of its secondary literature bears in some way on the oral provenience or roots of the ballads. Nonetheless, relatively few studies can be said to be extensions of the Oral Theory, since methods developed prior to and alongside the Parry-Lord approach have occupied the attention of scholars almost exclusively. As the merest sampling of relevant activity, I might mention the exchange between James H. Jones (1961) and Albert B. Friedman (1961), in which the former sought to use Parry-Lord theory to release the English and Scottish popular ballads from the bonds of memorization, while the latter insisted on the dissimilarity of the ballads and the South Slavic epic songs and maintained that "memorization, not improvisation by means of commonplaces, is the basic vehicle of oral tradition" (114). W. Edson Richmond (1963), in his analysis of a Norwegian ballad, seemed to prefer an intermediate position whereby oral-formulaic composition could be understood to play a role in the transmission of ballads, with the additional condition that memorization and its lapses also had a part in the process.

David Buchan's *The Ballad and the Folk* (1972) uses the Brown corpus of ballads to study the ballad as oral poetry in the sense of the Theory; later on (1977), he explores the interaction of oral and written and finds two stages that follow true oral re-creation: a transitional period and rote memorization. In a 1973 article that attempts to encourage a necessary complexity in the study of ballad tradition, Eleanor R. Long contends that oral-formulaic composition is typical only of some and not all activities associated with transmission. The situation among the Faroese is explored by Patricia Conroy (1980), who examines the repertoire of a singer for formulas and themes against the sociocultural background.[110] In "A Tension of Essences in Murdered-Sweetheart Ballads" (1983), D. K. Wilgus uses Lord's concept of implicit narrative context to gloss the otherwise puzzling plot sequence of a particular ballad genre. A part of the same collection, Friedman's "The Oral-Formulaic Theory of Balladry—A Re-rebuttal" contests the proposals of Jones and Buchan and offers a full bibliography of controversy on the subject.

Finally, the fieldwork and scholarship accomplished by Bruce A. Rosenberg has brought to light an oral tradition that still exists in the United States, the black folk-preaching tradition of the rural South and Southwest.[111] In *The Art of the American Folk Preacher* (1970a), he analyzes the style and performance of the chanted folk sermon, with emphasis on the preacher's dependence on formulaic phrases and on the participation of the congregation or audience. Others of Rosenberg's studies touch on the grammar of formulas and themes and the mnemonic function of melody (1970b) as well as the psycholinguistic features of the sermon performance (1974). When one adds the application of Oral Theory to authors as much a part of the Anglo-American literary tradition as Edmund Spenser (J. Webster 1976), William Shakespeare (Trousdale 1981), James Fenimore Cooper (Walker 1981), and Nathaniel Hawthorne (Bayer 1980), the explanatory potential of the Theory begins to come clear.

Through the sections on ancient Greek and Old English and, more briefly, in the comments on selected other traditions, I have attempted to illustrate by example the enormous growth of the field of Oral Theory, especially since the publication of Albert Lord's *The Singer of Tales*. The evolution from 1960 to the present cannot be described as even or measured, since there have been numerous suggestions for modification and revision of the Theory, but the majority of the controversies have generated further understanding. As we move on to the closing chapter, which will examine new directions in the development of the field, it is well to remember that some of the most productive controversies—utility versus aesthetics, improvisation versus memorization, a universal Oral Theory versus a Theory tailored to each tradition or genre—will remain a part of the picture and in fact will help to move scholarship forward.

V.

RECENT AND FUTURE DIRECTIONS

In this final chapter I shall describe in somewhat more detail than was possible earlier in the volume a few of the most influential or promising contributions to the evolution of the Oral Theory over the past twenty years, concentrating on those books or articles that have in one way or another broken new ground in the field and thereby helped to define it further as an area of study in its own right.[1] Toward the end of the chapter, I shall make brief note of some general directions in which Oral Theory seems to be evolving at the end of the 1980s and suggest a few problems in research and scholarship which might profitably be addressed in future years.

The first book to be mentioned, *The Presence of the Word: Some Prolegomena for Cultural and Religious History* by Walter J. Ong, S.J., was originally published in 1967. In its eclectic and yet rationalizing fashion, this study treats the phenomenology of the oral as distinguished from the written word, taking as its subjects for demonstration and explication such topics as the differences among oral/aural, manuscript, and typographic media and their sociocultural implications; the psychosexual phases correlative to various stages in the development of the word; and a wealth of examples of media-culture interactions from a wide variety of times and places. In Ong's first stage of oral culture, as opposed to the second stage of alphabetic culture, the learning necessary for the society as a whole is encoded in oral epic; thus far he agrees with Eric Havelock, especially in the latter's *Preface to Plato* (1963; cp. 1982). But Ong also connects later rhetorical structuring with what he views as its origin in oral thought: "The formulary character of oral performance is responsible for the development of the doctrine of the commonplaces or *loci communes* which dominated skilled verbal performance from oral-aural times until the maturing of the romantic age. The *loci communes* were essentially formulaic modes of expression derivative from oral practice and perpetuating oral psychological structures" (1967: 31). In fact, this extension of oral phenomenology from its *prima facie* form

in verifiably oral material to later, alphabetic cultures and media which
nonetheless contained an "oral residue" (1965) has been one of Ong's major
contributions to the field and to humanistic studies in general.

More recently, his *Interfaces of the Word: Studies in the Evolution of Consciousness and Culture* (1977) has brought Ong's theories on the progressive
exteriorization of the word to a host of modern problems of perception,
from the "disambiguation" of African drum language to the position of
the authorial personae imagined by readers of literature. Although some
of these applications may seem far removed from the center of our concerns
in the present volume, they actually comprise a coherent and brilliant extension of Oral Theory from the text back to the perceiver, from object
back to subject. This retrograde movement of self-discovery is of course
part of the philosophical and critical tenor of our times, and Ong has been
able to marshal it in the service of oral studies. One result of such a dynamic
method has been the concomitant illumination of the other side of the
dialectic—the phenomenology of writer and reader, who converse in silence
with words quite distinct from those employed by their oral counterparts.
As Ong shows in "The Writer's Audience Is Always a Fiction" (53–81; orig.
version 1975), written communication is also a medium sui generis, with
its own ground rules: "No matter what pitch of frankness, directness, or
authenticity he may strive for, the writer's mask and the reader's are less
removable than those of the oral communicator and his hearer. For writing
is itself an indirection" (80).

Published in 1982, *Orality and Literacy: The Technologizing of the Word* serves
as an expert introduction to certain aspects of research on oral tradition,
a summary of Ong's own thinking to date, and a comparative evaluation
of Oral Theory in the context of other literary and philosophical approaches. In addition to tracing some of the origins of the Theory in the
Homeric Question and Parry's writings, Ong describes the psychodynamics
of orality, illustrating how writing restructures human consciousness. The
discrete events of script, print, and word-processing, he argues, determine
shifts in man's method of storing, retrieving, and making available the
knowledge he needs to get on in the world and, still more crucially, alter
his very modes of perception and expression.

Just such an alteration is the subject of Havelock's "The Linguistic Task
of the Presocratics" (1983), which follows on earlier work on ancient Greek
discussed in the last chapter. Havelock views these philosophers as "poised
between literacy and nonliteracy. Their style of composition is a form of
mediation between ear and eye. They expect an audience of listeners, yet
look forward to a reception at the hands of readers" (9). In painstaking
detail, he illustrates how the Presocratics reinterpret the narrative reality
of the Homeric oral world into an analytical representation replete with
newly invented abstractions. These abstractions had to be wrested from the

traditional Homeric language, decontextualized, as it were, from the event-centered medium that had served as the language of the transmission of knowledge. With the emergence of this focus on logos at the expense of mythos comes the birth of a new world view and a new discipline: "Philosophy proper arose as a commentary upon and correction of the cosmic imagery of Homer and the cosmic architecture of Hesiod's *Theogony*" (80). In two later essays (1986, 1987), Havelock offers further insights on this competition between mythos and logos, documenting the episodic structure of preliterate thought versus the fact-centered, analytical structure that characterizes the alphabetic mind.

On another front Joseph J. Duggan's *The Song of Roland: Formulaic Style and Poetic Craft* (1973) follows out the Parry-Lord methodology in a uniquely thoroughgoing manner by employing computer techniques to study the formulaic nature of this greatest of Old French *chansons de geste*. What is more, Duggan has had the good fortune to work in the only medieval European poetic tradition which offers a large sample of texts in a single genre (over one hundred possible comparanda exist for the *Roland*, though the best are many fewer in number) and the critical imagination to employ his quantified results to elucidate long-disputed textual cruces. After a review of earlier work on Old French epic and a scrutiny of the testing methodology applied by other investigators in various traditions, he places the *Roland* against the background of twelve other poems and comes to this judgment about formulaic density and orality: "in general, if an Old French narrative poem is less than 20 percent straight repetition, it probably derives from literary, or written, creation. When the formula density exceeds 20 percent, it is strong evidence of oral composition, and the probability rises as the figure increases over 20 percent" (29). The *Roland* itself is well over this threshold with a figure of 35.2 percent, and so qualifies easily as an oral poem by the stated criterion.

But Duggan's book is more than a summary of statistics, more even than an exacting philological description of diction and style. Later on, for example, Duggan considers the vexed question of the Episode of Baligant, the formal equivalent of the Iliadic Doloneia or Odyssean Telemacheia, which has long been singled out as the major problem in the unity of the *Roland*. His close examination of structure from the point of view of Oral Theory indicates a rather late date for the entry of the episode into the traditional story: "It must certainly have been integrated into the *Roland* tradition, or generated within it, no earlier than the eleventh century" (102). And although his analysis of formulaic language admits this assessment, he finds the inclusion of the episode, as preserved in the authoritative Oxford manuscript of the poem, "mythically authentic" even if, as he believes, it joined the main frame of the poem's tradition rather late: "Oxford is the most esthetically pleasing and archaic version we have, and we have it with 'Baligant'; it possesses mythical grandeur with 'Baligant,' despite the inconsistencies, and there is no alternate version which equals it in this respect. Whether 'Baligant' improved the poem or not is a matter of taste and conjecture: we have no choice but to accept the episode as an example of the ordinary process of mythical expansion carried out by the oral tradition upon Roland's poetic legend" (103–4).[2] In this manner he turns the insights made possible by Oral Theory into innovative aesthetic criticism.

In 1974 the long-awaited edition and translation of Avdo Medjedović's *The Wedding of Smailagić Meho (Ženidba Smailagina sina)* appeared as volumes III (English translation, Lord and Bynum 1974) and IV (original-language text, Bynum 1974b) of *Serbo-Croatian Heroic Songs*. For Slavists and comparatists alike, here was a remarkable event: an unquestionably oral poem of 12,311 lines, or about the length of the Homeric *Odyssey*, rich in finely woven detail, studded with similes, steeped in uniquely memorable descriptions and actions, and sung along a clear and relatively common story-pattern in South Slavic epic—that of the "Wedding Song." Moreover, as Lord points out in his discussion of "Avdo's Originality" (*SCHS* III: esp. 22–23), this song is an initiatory tale of a young man's coming of age that reveals many formal parallels to the story of Telemachus in the *Odyssey*. And, he goes on, in this most Homeric of Serbo-Croatian epics one can view at first hand the coalescence of history and mythic reality, and of tradition and originality, on a large scale. The manner of Avdo's appropriation and molding of the tale, which was read aloud to him from a songbook, illustrates this last nexus:

> While Avdo had not heard, so far as he remembered, at least, the song of "Smailagić Meho" before it came to him from the songbook some four or five years earlier, in 1927, 1928, or 1929, he had heard, and sometimes he sang, a multiform of part of it. In addition to adapting, probably quite unconsciously, one multiform to another—the usual mode of transmission and re-creation within a tradition—Avdo also added some original elements, one of which, to the best of my present knowledge, was the return of the exiled father of the bride. The reading of the songbook to Avdo was pretty much the same as his hearing it from another singer. If one remembers that in an oral tradition one is dealing constantly with multiforms and with parts of multiforms rather than with rigidly distinct songs, then the "Smailagić Meho" of Avdo is an excellent illustration of the processes of tradition in the hands of an extraordinarily gifted singer. (*SCHS* III: 27)

This, then, was the song dictated to Parry's assistant Nikola Vujnović from July 5 to 12, 1935, an epic with historical roots in the golden age of the Ottoman Empire and with mythic roots which probably reach back to a pan-Balkan or even Indo-European tradition. It is well to emphasize the fact that the song was both an embodiment of tradition and Avdo's own, and was therefore dependent for its shape in performance both upon the poetic inheritance which the singer had spent his life recasting and upon his own talents and perspectives. Lord's apparatus to the translation makes apparent this double identity of *The Wedding of Smailagić Meho*, especially in providing a description of Avdo's customary "ornamentation" of a song he had heard and in adding a summary of his 1950 performance of the same song. Read in its many contexts, but most importantly against the background of other Wedding Songs in the South Slavic tradition, the 1935 poem emerges as a masterfully crafted glimpse of the continuous tradition in the necessarily ephemeral form of a single performance: Avdo's young hero, seeking to validate his succession and cross the threshold to manhood, brings life to old patterns, revivifies the constant and permanent with the energy of the moment. The characters—one recalls most vividly the redoubtable companion Osman, the doting and stubbornly paternal Smail, Meho's more realistic uncle Cifrić Hasanaga, the desperate Lady Zajim, the treacherous vizier, the ubiquitous and magically unconventional Tale, not to mention the proud and increasingly poised Meho himself—are traditional and yet imbued with Avdo's own realism; they act more than are acted upon, moving in unique and individual tangents along the figures inscribed by tradition. The *Smailagić Meho* may not stand quite shoulder to shoulder with the Homeric epics, but it can be said to emulate their artistry. As Lord and Bynum show by presenting the poem in this editorial format, providing, along with text and translation, conversations with the singer, an essay on originality and comparative context, accounts of close textual relatives, and a biography and repertoire of Avdo, *The Wedding of Smailagić Meho* is both a memorable work of oral art and the most convincing argument yet made for the oral composition of the *Iliad* and *Odyssey*.[3]

Another book published in 1974, Gregory Nagy's *Comparative Studies in Greek and Indic Meter*, signaled the advent of a new and promising approach.[4] For many years the Oral Theory had explained formula, theme, and other traditional features chiefly through recourse to structuralist metaphors; that is, the level of explication had been in the great majority of cases *synchronic*. Now Nagy used the methods of comparative Indo-European reconstruction to probe the evolutionary, or *diachronic*, depths underlying the surface structures in the Homeric epics. Working from a single phrase, Homeric Greek *kléos áphthiton* and its Sanskrit cognate *śráva(s) ákṣitam* (translated in both cases as "imperishable fame"), he contends first that the Greek and Sanskrit metrical contexts of these phrases are also identical and that, diachronically, formula produced meter and not vice versa: "At first, the reasoning goes, traditional phraseology simply contains built-in rhythms. Later, the factor of tradition leads to the preference of phrases with some rhythms over phrases with other rhythms. Still later, the preferred rhythms have their own dynamics and become regulators of any incoming non-traditional phraseology. By becoming a viable structure in its own right, meter may evolve independently of traditional phraseology. Recent metrical developments may even obliterate aspects of the selfsame traditional phraseology that had engendered them, if these aspects no longer match the meter" (145). Thus, he argued, the true relationship between formula and meter is not that of an unyielding matrix and its tailored-to-fit diction, but rather of a gradual shift or modulation of priorities through which the phraseological material eventually generates its own matrix.

In other sections of the monograph, Nagy offers an "etymology" for the Homeric hexameter from a lyric meter known as the pherecratic and reverses the usual chronology assigned to ancient Greek epic and lyric by viewing the latter as historically precedent to Homer. This is not the place to rehearse the intricacies of his persuasive argument on metrical development, but we may mention an additional feature of his work which concerns the meaning of the Greek, Sanskrit, and ultimately Indo-European phrase for "imperishable fame." The adjective in this formula has, as he shows, "a least common denominator in context: *an unfailing stream* of water, fire, light, milk, semen, urine, vegetal extract (soma-sap)" (240). Further, he demonstrates, "**klewos* was the word once used to designate the hieratic art of song which ensured unfailing streams of water, light, vegetal sap, and so on. Since these streams were unfailing, the art of song itself could be idealized and self-servingly glorified by the Singer as 'unfailing.' Hence *śráva(s) ákṣitam* and *kléos áphthiton*" (254). These insights adumbrate the deep traditional meaning of an element of Homeric oral epic language, a meaning preserved far beyond its time of origin and initial context by the power of tradition, even as its most ancient religious intent came metaphorically to describe the art of epic song.

In an exhaustive study of Hesiod's *Works and Days* as an exemplar text, Berkley Peabody (1975) also probes the diachronic recesses of form and meaning in oral literature. His massive book, *The Winged Word*, begins as does Nagy's with a metrical genealogy of the Homeric line from Indo-European evidence and then proceeds systematically through a discussion of structure and function at five levels: phoneme, formula, enjambement, theme, and song. In each case, he believes, an orally composed work should reveal a consistency of pattern, and he describes at considerable length both the evolution which must have led to this consistency and its implications for the *Works and Days*. Clearly, Peabody's discoveries must be generalized to Homeric as well as Hesiodic epos, from the level of sound patterning through that of narrative structure, for they promise new and uniquely faithful ways of dealing with problems in the *Iliad* and *Odyssey* which the Oral Theory in its earlier forms had not completely solved. By enlarging the set of linguistic and narrative features typical of oral composition, and by explaining those already known in a manner mindful of their origin and evolution, he makes it possible to credit Homeric epos with the complexity we observe at every turn and yet to understand the poems as oral literature. In fact, it is not the least of Peabody's accomplishments that he demonstrates not simply a possible but a *necessary* connection between the complexity of ancient Greek epos and its orality.

A few observations may be noted to illustrate his method and its productivity. To begin, his theory of the evolution of the hexameter is markedly different from that of Nagy, but it shares the virtue of being grounded in a comparative view of cognate meters, in Peabody's case ancient Indic and Iranian verse forms. Whatever the preferable derivation may be, the section that follows on "The Form of Words" convincingly portrays the "word" in oral epos as being coextensive with the colon, the basic metrical shape and line-part first thoroughly discussed by Hermann Fränkel.[5] After a treatment of enjambement in which he distinguishes between syntactically and semantically closed periods, Peabody moves on to a discussion of *theme*, which he understands most immediately as a pattern of "phonic cores" or a redundancy in sound that may be overlain by a semantic unity of the sort that other investigators have led us to expect. In other words, his concept of the theme is only secondarily one of actual narrative pattern; at the core of the unit is a fundamental consistency in the texture of audible sound. At the upper level of Peabody's system of structures in ancient Greek epos is the *song*, which may be explained in the most general terms as a singer's memory of past performances, or "the conscious, phenomenalized aspect of the oral compositional process" (216). In the final chapter, "The Flight of Song," Peabody turns his system of structures to an explication of the *Works and Days*, concluding that it is a Contest Song, "the actual song of a challenged bard" (270). It is an original coda to an original book, and both the particular hypothesis and the study as a whole well deserve the attention of those interested in Oral Theory and its application to a variety of literatures.

Michael Nagler's *Spontaneity and Tradition: A Study in the Oral Art of Homer* (1974) takes a much different approach from the diachronic analysis exemplified in Nagy's and Peabody's books, but it shares with them a sense of the necessary connection between Homeric art and orality. Nagler had first broached his theory of ancient Greek oral composition in a 1967 article,

"Towards a Generative View of the Homeric Formula," and now expanded it in his opening two chapters on "The Traditional Phrase." The main thrust of his approach is to loosen the rigorous, text-centered definition of the formula by widening the contextual field of reference for a given phrase from the closed "formulaic system" to the open-ended "family" of "allomorphs." Thus Nagler would require as evidence for a poetic relationship between traditional phrases not the usual links of verbal repetition or Russo's syntactic pattern or finally even metrical criteria, but rather redundancies of pure sound free from prosodic or other formal constraints; needless to say, this relaxation of definition admits a much larger referent for any given phrase and is not subject to quantification. Nonetheless, the new concept does open up heretofore unacknowledged (or unheard) associations of sound and sense, as Nagler's excellent illustrations show, particularly in the example of the *krêdemnon* and its poetic signification of chastity (45–60). He locates both the source and the dynamics of this traditional poetics not in the fully formed surface structures usually called "formulas," but in what he terms a "preverbal Gestalt," an ideational nexus of traditional meaning which can take a variety of verbal forms. In the Chomskyan metaphor, *Gestalt* and *allomorph* would translate roughly as "deep" and "surface" structures, respectively. By directing attention away from obviously similar elements in the diction toward a more resonant context of structure and poetic meaning made evident by this linguistic model, he aims to dissolve the protests of mechanistic composition, claiming that "all is traditional on the generative level, all original on the level of performance" (26).

Nagler's discussion of narrative units also derives from his central theorem that "the oral poet is one who, at the moment of performance, makes spontaneous, and therefore original realizations of inherited, traditional impulses" (xxi). In the case of what he calls the *motif*, this impulse is a highly generic association of thought and words which may be specified in myriad ways; a motif is not so definitively a unit as the type-scene, but underlies and poetically connects a much wider range of narrative situations, just as the Gestalt underlies and poetically connects a large family of allomorphs whose membership could not be documented in terms of the conventionally defined formula. This idea of narrative structure invites comparison with the theme as defined by Lord or Peabody. In a later chapter, "The 'Eternal Return' in the Plot Structure of the *Iliad*," Nagler extends Lord's story-pattern of Withdrawal-Devastation-Return to a poetic Gestalt, tracing its various avatars throughout the *Iliad*. His analysis of these WDR cycles is too complex to summarize here, but we may quote from his conclusions regarding the problems of Achilles as an example of the fruit of his method:

Positively put—that is, as it happens, in the mythic perspective, Achilles "withdraws" to enter a realm of prior causes (destiny), where he comes closer than ordinary mortals can come to wellsprings of the actions carried out below, on the Trojan plain. All the apparent "devastations" are in reality the agonizing adjustments that human beings must undergo to bring their lives into harmony with that divine ordination, as is clearest in Achilles' belated submission to Zeus at the climax of the river fight. Negatively, from what may be called a literary perspective, his withdrawal cuts him off from living companionship and the network of social values in which he belongs. This withdrawal *is* devastation because it is a withdrawal from reality into egotism—that is, spiritual ignorance. (163)

In 1976 the proceedings of a 1974 interdisciplinary conference arranged by Gerald Else at the University of Michigan on "Oral Literature and the Formula" appeared under the editorship of Benjamin Stolz and Richard Shannon. The essays included in that volume treat ancient Greek (G. Nagy, Russo), Old English (Foley), African (Finnegan), Finnish, Sanskrit, and linguistics (Paul Kiparsky), Fulani (Paulène Aspel), and comparative epic (Lord). Along with a summary by Henry Hoenigswald, the editors also furnish transcripts of the prepared individual responses made to each paper and of the spontaneous general discussion which each paper stimulated. In addition to those contributions treated earlier, we may single out Kiparsky's essay for its influence on subsequent scholarship. By developing a linguistic model for the formula that views traditional expression as different types of bound phrases, he is able to come to a grammatical definition that allows explanation of the various kinds of patterning that typify Homeric Greek diction. Further, by bringing Finnish and Vedic Sanskrit analogues into the discussion, both of which show less flexibility among different versions than do the Yugoslav songs, he suggests a process of gradual text fixation for the *Iliad* and *Odyssey* within a family or guild of singers.

Another of the main participants at that conference, Ruth Finnegan, was soon to publish *Oral Poetry: Its Nature, Significance, and Social Context* (1977), a worldwide survey of poetries associated in one way or another with orality. Especially because her earlier works had proved so helpful (chiefly *Oral Literature in Africa* [1970] and *Limba Stories and Story-Telling* [1967]), much was reasonably expected of this book. For the anthropologist or sociologist, Finnegan's survey proves very useful in its emphasis on the context of oral performance in a spectrum of traditions. And although the literary specialist may find fault with the lack of philological underpinning, everyone engaged in research that touches on the Oral Theory should be grateful for Finnegan's insistence on a pluralistic model of oral literature. Indeed, if we are to evolve an Oral Theory that faithfully treats the complex mass of materials that have heretofore too easily been forced into the simplistic oral-versus-written dichotomy, we must heed the warnings of Finnegan and others on the *differences* among oral traditions.

One of the most original books to appear in the field over the past ten years is David E. Bynum's *The Daemon in the Wood: A Study of Oral Narrative Patterns* (1978). What validates his recourse to such an eclectic group of materials—numerous African folktales, Biblical stories, *Beowulf*, British fable, Serbo-Croatian epic, and so on comprise the literary itinerary—is his patient unraveling of their surface identities to discover a single narrative pattern, that of the "Two Trees." He explicates this apparently universal motif as a structure in which green wood and hewn wood act as narrative signs for separation and unity, respectively, marking also the arena of a protagonist's defeat of a threatening preternatural. Other details attach themselves in what he calls a *cluster,* and permutations of the commonplace, especially permutations in the sequence of motif constituents and events, yield a ubiquitous story multiform. The ogre or preternatural is initially associated with green wood and the hero's triumph with its hewn result. The Grendel monster's defeat in *Beowulf* provides an example:

> Even in death Beowulf's ogre retains its association with the wood, except that now both are in a hewn state. But although the pole with the dread head on it is fashioned from wood and fitted with the product of Beowulf's hewing in the wilderness, it is still only a transitional motif . . . and not the primary wooden artifact that represents human unity in *Beowulf.* That motif, the Anglo-Saxon equivalent of the Lamba flutes and the Hebrew Tree of Life, is Heorot itself, Hrothgar's magnificent wooden banquet-hall, assembly-place, and seat of government, the very home of man's desire to eat, be merry, and enjoy companionship. (96)

In the course of his explanation of methodology and commendably full illustrations, Bynum, after delivering a critique of the major schools of folklore research, ponders the implications of his own findings. For example, in his epilogue we find the following observation: "If the stories of Creation, Adam in Eden, Moses at the burning bush, and Samson's misalliances as we have them in the Old Testament are the Word of God (whether literally or metaphorically), then the force of this book is to suggest that in fact the Word was Pentecostal from the beginning, and to an equal degree every people was chosen to receive it" (293). While his notions on the universality of fable will be too rationalistic for some, like Nagler he opens up whole new vistas of context, new principles and modes of comparison not before contemplated. One of the nagging questions in Oral Theory and generally in folklore studies has always been "What is the unit?"—that is, at what level do we seek structure, meaning, and function?

Bynum offers an intriguing answer to this continuing dilemma, one which merits application and testing by specialists in their own fields of expertise.

Bernard C. Fenik edited the papers of another conference, the volume entitled *Homer: Tradition and Invention* (1978a). As the editor explains in the preface, his aim was to join two important strands of research on Homer: that represented by Milman Parry, Albert Lord, and the Oral Theorists and that represented by those European scholars, particularly in Germany, who have not accepted the Theory because they feel it strips the poems of their artistry and imagination. Fenik's admirable goal is realized in a group of essays that illustrate various aspects of the traditional and original qualities of the epics: Albert Heubeck's "Homeric Studies Today: Results and Prospects," an excellent review of the present state of critical affairs from a Neoanalytical point of view with extensive bibliography; G. S. Kirk's "The Formal Duels in Books 3 and 7 of the *Iliad*"; J. B. Hainsworth's "Good and Bad Formulae"; Uvo Hoelscher's "The Transformation from Folk-Tale to Epic"; and Fenik's own "Stylization and Variety: Four Monologues in the *Iliad*." This last essay epitomizes the spirit of the volume, stating unambiguously the problems of unity and mode of composition and admitting straightforwardly that more work needs to be done on the apparent paradox of oral structures and the evidence for Homer's conscious control of his medium.[6]

Another collection bearing on this and other issues, *Oral Traditional Literature: A Festschrift for Albert Bates Lord* (Foley 1981a), contains, in addition to a review of formulaic studies in Old English from their inception in the nineteenth-century German Higher Criticism, nineteen papers on various aspects of Oral Theory, most of which were presented in honor of Lord at the 1978 meetings of the Medieval Institute. The contents include articles on ancient Greek, Old English, Serbo-Croatian, medieval Spanish, contemporary Hispanic, African, Old Norse, Old French, Old and Middle High German, and Russian traditions, along with studies of myth, ritual, and folklore. Many of the essays attempt extensions or modifications of the Oral Theory, with special emphasis on the issues of memorization versus recreation, the definitions of formula and formulaic system, and the individual properties of different narrative traditions.

As studies associated with the Oral Theory move forward through the 1980s, a few additional works promise to open up new methods of analysis and interpretation. For one thing, the vast resources of the Milman Parry Collection at Harvard University have not really been tapped significantly, apart from the *SCHS* series of editions and translations and scholarship by Lord, Bynum, and Foley; we need more exemplary monographs like the study by Mary P. Coote (1980) of the entire recorded repertoire of the

Parry-Lord *guslar* Ćamil Kulenović. More information about the nature of a known, well-collected oral tradition such as the South Slavic will strengthen and further validate comparative work with ancient and medieval texts now separated from their traditional contexts. Jeff Opland's contributions to African and Old English poetry have assisted greatly in building this same sort of bridge between the known and observable on the one hand and the postulated and unobservable on the other. Although Opland does not embrace the Parry-Lord orthodoxy on a number of issues, most prominently the role of memorization versus improvisation and the effects of literacy on an oral poet, his reports from the field and his careful sifting of available information on oral tradition in Anglo-Saxon should be carefully taken into account by those working in Oral Theory. In addition to his book on *Anglo-Saxon Oral Poetry* (1980a) described above, his *Xhosa Oral Poetry: Aspects of a Black South African Tradition* (1983) treats the historical and cultural backgrounds of this complex tradition, as well as assembles a typology of its genres with particular focus on the *imbongi*, or court poet, and his training and poetry.

A different sort of contextualization represents the goal of Alain Renoir's exciting series of articles during the late 1970s and afterward.[7] Renoir seeks to relate medieval and ancient texts comparatively by demonstrating their shared "oral-formulaic context"—for instance, a traditional theme that recurs in geographically widely separated literatures and which may be used, in the absence of more usual criteria such as date, authorship, and history, to establish a milieu for aesthetic criticism. In concert with current critical trends, Franz H. Bäuml has brought German Receptionalist theory to the study of oral tradition and medieval texts, inquiring into the functions of orality and literacy in the period and examining the various audiences involved.[8] Working in yet another direction, Charles Segal (1982) distinguishes the shared, oral value system of the Homeric epics from the diverse, explosively heterogeneous set of codes typical of Attic tragedy, contending that the difference extends to the variance between traditional epic diction and the new language of the drama: "La vérité de la poésie orale est plus ou moins univoque; celle de la tragédie est multiple, divisée, fragmentaire et contradictoire" (142).

While the main thrust of Richard Janko's *Homer, Hesiod, and the Hymns: Diachronic Development in Epic Diction* (1982) is the establishment of a relative chronology for ancient Greek epos, his method of linguistic dating necessarily confronts the question of Homer's orality. Pointing out that the formulaic density and enjambement tests are only negative tests, that is, that they can disprove the possibility of oral traditional provenience but are not able to affirm it beyond doubt, he believes that the evidence suggests that "writing played no part in the *composition* (as opposed to the recording) of the Homeric and Hesiodic poems" (188), and that this applies as well to some of the Hymns. He then reasons:

> In an oral or mainly oral tradition, especially one with a metre as complex as the dactylic hexameter, formulae are preserved over long periods for reasons of convenience, or even necessity, as an aid to composition. Many formulae are handed down through the generations and preserve archaic forms, some extremely ancient indeed. . . . one expects old formulae and archaisms to diminish in frequency through the generations, as innovative phraseology and language creeps in; and if this could be quantified, it might provide a yardstick useful for assigning approximate relative dates to the poems. It ought therefore to be possible to count archaisms and innovations in the poems and find out whether there is any consistent pattern of evolution in their diction. (188–89)

On the basis of certain linguistic features which he sees as appropriate for such a test, Janko finds the *Iliad* earliest, followed closely by the *Odyssey*, with a larger shift to the *Theogony* and then the *Works and Days*. And although the texts were fixed at different times, he finds it "difficult to refuse the conclusion that the texts were fixed at the time when each was composed, whether by rote memorisation or by oral dictated texts" (191). This is a book with which all Homerists, including those interested in ancient Greek oral tradition, will have to deal.

Another work which promises to open up new vistas on an important oral tradition is Werner H. Kelber's *The Oral and the Written Gospel: The Hermeneutics of Speaking and Writing in the Synoptic Tradition, Mark, Paul, and Q* (1983). Proceeding in part from the thinking of Walter J. Ong and re-shaping what Biblical studies had conceived of as oral tradition into a form that brings to the foreground the phenomenological difference between speaking and writing, Kelber emphasizes the shift from an oral to a textual reality. In place of Jesus' oral sayings and their oral reporting in the tra-ditional kerygma, Mark and the other evangelists substituted a text, a tran-scription of an oral reality that was necessarily cut off from its context in the very act of writing it down. The shift in medium amounted to a change of communicative key; but it took place only gradually, with the Gospel texts gaining true authority only more than a century after their creation. It is difficult to summarize fairly what Kelber accomplishes in this remark-able book, but it would be fair to say that he has advanced the role of oral theory in Biblical studies in important and permanent ways by recovering the orality-textuality tension that informed the composition and reception of the Gospels.[9]

One of the most crucial areas in recent studies in the field of Oral Theory has been the vexed question of the interaction between oral and written, the "gray area" in which many have argued for placement of the "transitional text."[10] New light on this poorly understood aspect of the history of literature and culture has been shed by Brian Stock's massive book, *The Implications of Literacy: Written Language and Models of Interpretation in the Eleventh and Twelfth Centuries* (1983).[11] In the midst of a reinterpretation of myriad medieval conceptions and institutions, Stock concentrates on explaining "the realignment of oral discourse within a cultural reference system based on the logical priorities of texts" (522), including chapters on "Oral and Written" and another on "Textual Communities." The first of these goes well beyond the simplistic dichotomy met elsewhere in studies related to Oral Theory and demonstrates the complex interaction between the two modes of communication and representation. Stock's concept of diglossia, which stresses the cultural role of learned Latin in the early Middle Ages as the language of the written document versus the Romance languages as much more oral media, will be of great use to medievalists struggling to explain the apparent paradox of oral structures within arguably written works. Likewise, his notions about textual communities, wherein a text (even if it is the intellectual property of a single individual) came to reform a group's thought and action, should likewise be valuable for historians seeking to explain certain movements or schools within the medieval panorama.

From the African scene, John W. Johnson has recently brought us the first linear English translation of the West African epic of Son-Jara recorded in its heartland.[12] But *The Epic of Son-Jara* (1986) is more than a fine and careful translation of an important oral text; it also provides a lengthy introductory essay on the social setting, the bard (or *griot*), and characteristics of Mande epic. Topics treated include the historical basis of the hero and his mythic extension; societal structures relevant to the understanding of epic; the role of the bard as chronicler, entertainer, preserver of customs and values, and mediator; rhythmic and melodic features of the narrative; formulaic expression and narrative structure; heroic traits; and multifunctional and multigeneric traits. Of special pertinence for Oral Theory are Johnson's demonstration that "Mande epic is not memorized verbatim. It is structured around formulas and formulaic expressions and around themes . . . " (33) and, in general, his explanation of formulaic morphology in the epic (34–38).

As works by Ong, Kelber, and Stock illustrate, in the past five to ten years more emphasis has been placed on both the interface of oral and written literature—if in fact these are still viable opposite categories—and the implications of an originative oral tradition for texts that have reached us only in manuscript. These two prevalent themes comprise the overall focus for the collection *Oral Tradition in Literature: Interpretation in Context* (Foley 1986d). Albert Lord's lead essay considers the merging of the oral and literate worlds in three specific cases in Yugoslavia; in Dalmatia, for instance, he finds that early written literature was exclusively the creation of an élite, and so there simply was no exchange between the two worlds at the start.[13] Lord also treats the phenomenon of ring-composition, long recognized as a characteristic of Homeric epic,[14] in Avdo Medjedović's *The Wedding of Smailagić Meho*. Ruth Webber confronts the meaning of the oral roots of the *Poema de Mio Cid* in her review of relevant scholarship, Gregory Nagy traces the development and generic identity of ancient Greek epic and praise poetry, Alain Renoir continues his contextual studies of medieval poetry through application of the Oral Theory, Robert Creed looks at the mnemonic system within the Anglo-Saxon oral tradition behind *Beowulf*, and Walter Ong adds a fine contribution to the emerging debate over orality and textuality in the Gospels.[15]

In 1986 a forum for continuing discussion of these and other areas was established with the founding of the journal *Oral Tradition*, edited by John Miles Foley. While this periodical takes as its province not only the Parry-Lord methodology but all approaches to oral tradition and to the influence of oral tradition on written literature,[16] many of its essays naturally bear on Oral Theory. For the sake of comparatists and specialists alike, *Oral Tradition* will devote part of each issue to surveys of scholarship on various oral traditions; among the early papers in this series are surveys of Biblical studies (Culley 1986), modern Greek (Beaton 1986), Australian Aborigines (Clunies Ross 1986), medieval Irish (J. Nagy 1986), Hispanic (Webber 1986a), Middle High German (Bäuml 1986), ancient Greek (M. Edwards 1986, 1987), Byzantine Greek (E. and M. Jeffreys 1986), Old English (Olsen 1986, 1987), Middle English (Parks 1986), and comparative perspectives (Lord 1986b).[17] Aside from analytical essays in a variety of areas, *Oral Tradition* is also publishing special issues on certain areas, such as Hispanic ballad (Webber 1987), Arabic oral traditions (Boullata 1988), and a Fest-schrift for Walter J. Ong (1987). In addition, the journal will present ex-tended responses to earlier contents in its Symposium section and an annual annotated bibliography.[18] It is hoped that *Oral Tradition* will serve as a clearinghouse for information on oral traditions all over the world, and thus as a central organ for the development of research and scholarship associated with the Oral Theory.

From the foregoing it should be clear how vital and rapidly evolving a field Oral Theory has become. It remains at this point only to record a few thoughts on some productive future directions, which I offer only as de-siderata and not as iron-clad premises. Too much still needs to be done for any investigator to speak finally and definitively about the nature of this new discipline; in fact, a caution against "final" pronouncements might well be the most general of watchwords for future scholarship.

More particularly, I see the need for an increased awareness of methodological preliminaries in studies associated with Oral Theory. Now that hundreds of books and articles have demonstrated striking similarities among ancient, medieval, and contemporary oral traditions, giving us reason to think, at least in the most general terms, of an enormous body of "oral literature" as opposed to the written texts on which most of us have cut our critical teeth, we can afford to be somewhat more careful and discerning. We can afford to set alongside the exciting similarities among literatures and individual texts a complementary account of their necessary differences, thus assembling a comparative profile that does justice to each of the comparanda in addition to furnishing a sense of the whole. To my mind, a criticism that cannot make distinctions because it is too involved in rehearsing real or apparent points of contact is not a comparative criticism. Although, as I hope is evident from the history sketched in the preceding chapters, research that led to the Oral Theory had necessarily to begin with those points of contact, it is now time to shift—or at least to redistribute—the emphasis.

I would propose that three principles be observed in formulating this kind of comparison: tradition-dependence, genre-dependence, and text-dependence.[19] By *tradition-dependence* I mean allowing each oral poetic tradition its idiosyncratic features and actively incorporating those features into one's critical model of that tradition. In practical terms, this would include aspects such as natural language characteristics, metrical and other prosodic requirements, narrative features, mythical and historical content, and any other aspect that is peculiar to the given tradition and therefore a significant part of its definition. There is, I believe, no reason to suppose that traditional units which take shape under different, tradition-dependent systems must be exactly or even closely comparable. The true picture will be the one that admits both similarities and differences concurrently, the one that places the general characteristics of oral traditional structures alongside the particular forms they may take in a given literature.

By *genre-dependence* I mean demanding as grounds for comparison among traditions nothing less than the closest generic fit available, and, further, calibrating any and all comparisons according to the exactness of that fit. It has been one of the major shortcomings of Oral Theory in the past that it has not observed this simple criterion; especially in Old English, where the variety of genres is considerable and the number of texts in any one category usually rather small, the principle has been ignored again and again—setting lyric elegy beside epic or verse hagiography or riddle, building unsupportable bridges between *Beowulf* and dissimilar genres from other traditions. Positively, on the other hand, genre-dependence encourages comparison of genres if a basic congruency can be established. More analysis needs to be done of the many non-epic forms found in different traditions, particularly where well-collected and indisputably oral material exists on one side or the other. We need to know how these other oral genres work, to what degree they conform to the laws of epic oral narrative and to what degree they have their own distinct dynamics.

The third principle of comparison, *text-dependence*, is simply the necessity to take into account the precise nature of each text: unquestionably oral or oral-derived, recorded from sung performance or dictated, audio record or manuscript, and so forth. Uncritical comparison of manuscripts and taped recordings, for example, can mislead more than inform. We should know, as far as possible, the circumstances of collection, the history of manuscript transmission, and the many other factors that would help to calibrate the comparison realistically. Where these details of contextualization are missing, we should admit the lacuna, even if it means leaving the actual oral provenance of the text in question. Finer distinctions, such as the diplomacy of an extant text or the editing process through which it might have or actually did pass, should also be made. This third principle, like its two counterparts, demands patient scrutiny of all of the problems involved before analytical research begins. And it also demands, of course, that all comparanda, even those briefly summoned, be consulted in their original languages and with philological precision, a practice unfortunately not uniformly observed in the past. This kind of rigor and the imagination characteristic of the Oral Theory to this point need not be mutually exclusive.

In addition to these three principles, I would also mention the need for more work on living oral traditions, both in collection and in analysis. Writings on dead-language traditions have, no doubt because of the academic prestige enjoyed by these literatures and the fact that the field began with the Homeric epics, always outnumbered those on more recent or still-surviving traditions. But we must have more information on unambiguously oral material, for the sake of both the living tradition itself and the comparative assistance which that information can provide for literatures whose original form and context are lost to us. It is certainly worth observing in this regard that the archive of Serbo-Croatian oral epic texts in the Milman Parry Collection offers a unique opportunity for those who would familiarize themselves with a living and well-collected tradition.

As a final desideratum, I would note the increasing interest in the aesthetics of oral traditional texts, now that many scholars have begun to recognize that formulaic and thematic structure need not preclude the possibility of verbal art. Of course, oral and oral-derived texts will not reveal precisely the same underlylng aesthetic as such fully literary works as John Milton's *Paradise Lost* or James Joyce's *Ulysses*—nor, indeed, should they. For the coming years I would emphasize the importance of defining oral traditional art sui generis, that is, of understanding its aesthetics on its own terms. Oral Theory, as it turns out, is well equipped to accomplish that goal; having adumbrated the structure of such works in terms of formula, theme, and story-pattern,[20] we need now only identify the *meaning* of these units for the given work and tradition. I submit that this meaning must be found in tradition, in the continuing, extratextual presence of which any given performance or text is but one perishable avatar. By viewing the noun-epithet formula or the "Exile" theme, for example, as metonymic of traditional meaning, so that each occurrence summons to a present reality the ongoing traditional meaning reflected in the innumerable other uses of the phrase or scene, we can begin to reconstruct the depth of signification in oral tradition.[21] Characters' special, repetitive designations are not simply convenient line-fillers or generic labels; rather, according to the traditional "shorthand," they reference the person's or the god's entire traditional identity. Likewise, a typical scene is neither a narrative stopgap nor a generically appropriate description, but a commonplace that reverberates with the associative meaning derived *pars pro toto* from its other uses in the continuing tradition. By interpreting the units given us by Oral Theory as a key to the word-hoard of tradition, by seeing them as active, dynamic entities that summon their extratextual referents by synecdoche, we shall have an opportunity to faithfully re-create the oral traditional work.[22]

In summary, I would stress the healthy variety of approaches and applications current in research on Oral Theory, a measure of its distinguished heritage in the work of Milman Parry and Albert Lord and a sure sign of the vitality of this still relatively young discipline. As the field readies itself to enter the 1990s, the possibilities for growth seem almost limitless. What I would suggest, in order to preserve the momentum so far generated, is a slight but firm tug on the reins; a calm reappraisal and commitment to greater precision in comparison will make our future efforts more meaningful and more satisfying.

NOTES

I. Philology, Anthropology, and The Homeric Question

1. Prior accounts that have some bearing on various of these antecedents include Nilsson 1933:1–55, Davison 1954, Myres 1958, Davison 1962a, Lesky 1967, Dirlmeier 1971, A. Parry 1971b, Heubeck 1974:130–52, Heubeck 1978, Latacz 1979c, Simonsuuri 1979, and Clarke 1981.

2. The translation of this passage is by Thackeray; the next translation in the text is my own. The Greek text for the two passages reads (Thackeray 1926:168–70):

11 οὐ μὴν οὐδ' ἀπ' ἐκείνου τοῦ χρόνου δύναιτό τις ἄν δεῖξαι σωζομένην
ἀναγραφὴν οὔτ' ἐν ἱεροῖς οὔτ' ἐν δημοσίοις ἀναθήμασιν, ὅπου γε καὶ
περὶ τῶν ἐπὶ Τροίαν τοσούτοις ἔτεσι στρατευσάντων ὕστερον πολλὴ
γέγονεν ἀπορία τε καὶ ζήτησις, εἰ γράμμασιν ἐχρῶντο, καὶ ταληθὲς
ἐπικρατεῖ μᾶλλον περὶ τοῦ τὴν νῦν οὖσαν τῶν γραμμάτων χρῆσιν
ἐκείνους ἀγνοεῖν.

12 ὅλως δὲ παρὰ τοῖς Ἕλλησιν οὐδὲν ὁμολογούμενον εὑρίσκεται γράμμα
τῆς Ὁμήρου ποιήσεως πρεσβύτερον, οὗτος δὲ καὶ τῶν Τρωϊκῶν ὕστερος
φαίνεται γενόμενος, καί φασιν οὐδὲ τοῦτον ἐν γράμμασι τὴν αὐτοῦ
ποίησιν καταλιπεῖν, ἀλλὰ διαμνημονευομένην ἐκ τῶν ἀσμάτων ὕστερον
συντεθῆναι καὶ διὰ τοῦτο πολλὰς ἐν αὐτˆῇ σχεῖν τὰς διαφωνίας.

3. The journey of the Homeric texts from their supposed compilation in the present form in the eighth or ninth century B.C. through their first appearance as intact wholes in the tenth century A.D. is shrouded in uncertainty and contradiction; for a survey, see Davison 1962b.

4. As Clarke notes (1981:154): "D'Aubignac's book was not published until 1715, but such was the intimacy of French literary life that his theory was known long before it appeared in print."

5. Magnien (1925:intro.,n.p.) summarizes: "Homère n'a pas existé; l'Iliade et l'Odyssée, tant vénérées par les siècles, mais qui trouvèrent aussi de sévères critiques, ont été formées par des compilateurs cousant ensemble des poésies d'esprit différent et d'époque différente: voilà la thèse soutenue en France, au XVIIe siècle. . . ."

6. To his occasional detriment; see Pope's Dunciad, Book IV:

As many quit the streams that murmuring fall
　　　　To lull the sons of Margaret and Clare Hall,
　　　　Where Bentley late tempestuous wont to sport
　　　　In troubled waters, but now sleeps in port.
　　　　(199–203)

On Bentley's discovery of the digamma, which remedied many textual and metrical problems in Homer, Pope continues:

Roman and Greek grammarians, know your better:
Author of something yet more great than letter;
While towering o'er your alphabet, like Saul,
Stands our Digamma, and o'ertops them all.
(215–18)

7. Cp. the ideas of Giambattista Vico (1668–1744; e.g., in Collingwood 1913:183–96), who, in arguing against the idea of a single "Homer" and in favor of the poems as an expression of the Greek national ethos, presaged in part the theories of Lachmann and others.

8. On the tangled web of the publication history of Wood's volume, see Lorimer 1948:13–15. Also of importance in this same period are the Scottish philosopher Adam Ferguson and classical scholar Thomas Blackwell (see Grobman 1974 and 1979, respectively), both of whom anticipated aspects of the Oral Theory; as Grobman puts it (1979:196), "it is apparent that Blackwell's Homer is an inspired bard, a manipulator of audience emotion, and a clever user of stock formulae and advanced stylistic oral techniques of composition."

9. Curiously, the *Prolegomena* was the first part of a preface to a school edition of Homer; only this initial section ever appeared in print, followed nine years later by a more serious edition (see Myres 1958:74–75).

10. "Nicht etwa, weil Parrys Theorie auf deutschen Vorarbeiten basiert (das ist bekannt und wurde von Parry selbst am wenigsten verheimlicht), sondern weil die Forschungsrichtung von Parry, Lord, und ihren Anhängern von vornherein im System der traditionellen Homerforschung angelegt war. Traditionelle Homerforschung und Oral poetry-Theorie bilden eine von vornherein durch die Sachproblematik der homerischen Frage bedingte systematische Einheit—lange bevor der Einzelforscher Milman Parry in Erscheinung trat." (Latacz 1979c:28). See further his useful reprinting of significant essays (1979a) in support of this viewpoint, as well as his "Spezialbibliographie zur Oral poetry-Theorie in der Homerforschung" (1979b).

11. Both the insight and the limitations of Hermann's research may be illustrated by his descriptions of three types of repeated phrases [*Wiederholungen*] "(1) Echte Wiederholungen (Doppelungen), geschaffen von ein und demselben Dichter in ein und demselben Gedicht, weil Substitution entweder Pedanterie oder Verschrobenheit bedeutet hätte; (2) nur scheinbare Wiederholungen, da in Wirklichkeit ein Dichter entweder die Verse eines anderen Dichters oder seine eigenen, nur aus einem anderen Gedicht, verwendet; (3) Wiederholungen, die sich zwar als Wiederholungen darstellen, die aber nicht von den Dichtern selbst stammen, sondern von denen, die Ilias und Odyssee aus verschiedenen Gedichten zusammenfügten und dabei bald etwas bewahrten, was vom einen Gedicht ins andere übertragen worden war, bald unter Verwendung von Material aus anderen Stellen eigenschöpferisch Lücken ausfüllten, um Auseinanderklaffendes zu verschmelzen" (57).

12. See Lachmann 1837–41; a brief account of his activities is available in Myres 1958 (90–93).

13. Parry refers both to this article and to a similar study by A. Shewan (1913) in his first French *thèse* (1928a:8), citing these authors and C. Rothe (e.g., 1894) as scholars who "set out to demonstrate that formulae are found everywhere in Homer, and that there must have been a common stock from which every epic poet could draw." For Shewan, concerned like Scott with the charge that the *Iliad* and *Odyssey* were not the creation of a single Homer, the main question becomes "is there reason for inferring the existence of a later poet appropriating and adapting the work of a predecessor? It is submitted . . . that there is nothing incompatible with the view that we have the same poet freely availing himself of the epic privilege of repetition" (242).

14. For a brief but cogent account of this development alongside—but separate from—Oral Theory, see Heubeck 1978.

15. It is only fair to note, too, that those who adhere to the Oral Theory have likewise almost unanimously ignored the real contributions of Neoanalysis; for an exception, see the work of Bernard C. Fenik (e.g., 1968, 1974, 1978a, b).

16. It will be noted that, however close the linguists may come to the methodology Parry used in "The Traditional Epithet in Homer" (1928a) and later studies, they nowhere attempt the thoroughgoing demonstration of traditional structure that became his trademark.

17. "Ich gebe hier nur das, was ich augenblicklich habe, glaube aber, dass durch eine *vollständige* Sammlung sich noch manches zur Aufklärung über den Gebrauch, ganze oder halbe Verse zu wiederholen, wird tun lassen" (Ellendt 1861:79).

18. Later scholars, most notably G. Nagy (esp. 1974, 1976), have called for a reassessment of the theory of metrical determination of phraseology, arguing instead for a diachronic dimension of the process in which formula first generates meter. However we envision the evolution of the diction, it is clear that formula and meter developed together, and that the proposals of Ellendt, Düntzer, and others remain important.

19. Witte also notes that, with respect to the introduction of new diction, this is the most conservative part of the line, that "nichts Neues wurde gewagt, wenn es nicht das alte Schema __ u u __ _u füllte" (1912a:115). See also Witte 1907.

20. Parry cites Hanoteau 1867 on the Berbers, Rambaud 1876 on the Russian *byliny*, Dozon 1888 on the Serbs, Darmesteter 1888–90 on the Afghans, Comparetti 1898 on the Finnish *rune*, and Krohn 1924–28 on the Finnish *Kalevala*, in addition to the works discussed in this chapter.

21. A number of the Parry-Lord *guslari* also claimed verbatim accuracy without fulfilling that claim. Further questioning, however, made it apparent that their concept of "word" was of a larger expression, usually a line or more in length, which could itself undergo substitution and modification. From their point of view, then, the claim of "word-for-word" accuracy was quite correct; see further Foley 1986c.

22. Other significant points discussed by Radlov include the problems involved with recording from oral dictation (xv–xvi), the rhyme and melody associated with narration in performance (xvi), the singer's fluency in the traditional idiom (xvii), and the role of the audience (xvii–xviii). For a sense of the influence Radlov had on contemporary classicists, consider the following remark from O. Immisch's *Die innere Entwicklung des griechischen Epos* (1904) on the Kara-Kirghiz analogy, which the author deemed helpful in assessing Homeric style: "Des Stoffes in seinen Hauptzusammenhängen Herr improvisiert er mühelos sein Lied, die herkömmlichen Motive, Reden, Gleichnisse, Übergänge, Formeln geschickt verbindend mit eignem Gut, das aber nach ihrem Muster gebildet ist" (5).

23. Thus Krauss's description of the catalogs or lists in Serbian epic: "Der Guslar, der des Lesens und Schreibens unkundig ist, schriebt natürlich keinen Katalog, doch verfasst er sich gerade so wie wir einen und, was wir wieder nicht tun, er lernt seinen auswendig" (1908:185).

24. Jousse's concepts are often on the following order: "La sensation de plaisir que le rythme cause à l'organisme a peu à peu remplacé et même fait oublier, dans notre poésie écrite, l'utilisation primitivement mnémonique des Schèmes rythmiques du Style oral, de même que le caractère esthétique de nos *ornements* sacerdotaux nous voile les qualités pratiques des *habits* romains dont ils sont dérivés par lente et insensible évolution . . ." (115–16). We find successors to this kind of approach in such scholars as Walter Ong and Eric Havelock (see chaps. 4 and 5).

25. Gesemann's references to Murko are to the *Berichte* (1912, 1913, 1915a, 1915b; perhaps 1909, 1919). I treat Gesemann before Murko because that is the

order in which Parry encountered the work of these two important ethnographers, that is, principally in Gesemann 1926 and Murko 1929.

26. To this unit should be compared Lord's "story-pattern," about which Lord remarks: "My basic assumption is that in oral tradition there exist narrative patterns that, no matter how much the stories built around them seem to vary, have great vitality and function as organizing elements in the composition and transmission of oral story texts" (1969:18).

27. Lord takes account of Gesemann 1926 (as well as Schmaus 1953; see also Schmaus 1956) in his discussion of "Songs and the Song" in *The Singer of Tales* (1960:286, n. 1).

28. Compare Parry's experiment with Avdo Medjedović (as recounted in Lord 1956a:327) and his general practice of eliciting multiple beginnings to songs in order to gain material for comparison of variant texts (described by Nikola Vujnović in the Parry Collection records).

29. Limitations of space prevent a full appreciation of the tremendous significance Murko's writings had for Parry, and so I sketch only the ethnographer's more telling findings. For a more detailed account, see Foley 1989.

30. As Murko notes (1929:8–9), his purpose was not to find or collect songs, although he often compared the songs he heard performed to their earlier published versions: "Le but essentiel de mes observations était de me rendre compte de la manière dont vit la poésie épique populaire, de voir qui sont les chanteurs, pour qui, quand et comment ils chantent, s'il naît encore des chants populaires et pourquoi la poésie populaire disparaît et meurt." Of course, as already indicated, it was just this kind of information that supplied a tangible context for oral epic tradition and so strongly suggested the comparison to Parry.

31. The exception is Parry's much less frequent citation of Murko 1919, a somewhat sketchier German edition of Murko 1929 with more attention to literary-historical context and occasionally more detail on philological matters (on the latter point, see, e.g., the treatment of dialect mixture at 1919:136). The 1929 monograph is a revision, including photographs of *guslari* with captions, of Murko 1928, which is in turn the "texte amplifié et complété des conférences faites à la Sorbonne le 23, 24 et 25 mai" (1928:321, n. 1).

32. Murko's posthumous magnum opus (1951) contains much more detailed reports on all aspects of the ethnography of oral epic in these areas, including extensive geographical surveys of epic poetry throughout contemporary Yugoslavia.

33. On the matter of "new" poems, Murko remarks (1929:25): "J'ai souvent entendu dire aussi que les chanteurs savent 'adosser' (*nasloniti*) un poème à un autre, qu'ils savent condenser plusieurs poèmes en un seul, et modifier, corriger, compléter les poèmes." Noting that singers of any value are also improvisers, he continues: "Aussi est-il superflu de débattre, comme l'ont fait les philologues classiques, la question de savoir si les aèdes préhomériques ont été suivis de rhapsodes ou simples : récitateurs, puisque des aèdes, c'est-à-dire des chanteurs qui composent eux-mêmes des poèmes, se trouvent encore aujourd'hui parmi les rhapsodes."

34. In brief, Murko managed to have some singers repeat sections about thirty lines long from the beginnings of their songs in order to produce multiple versions of the "same" material on a small scale. He was then able to demonstrate the formulaic substitution within even a single *guslar*'s phraseology. See n. 28 above.

35. Murko 1929:16–17. The English translations here take into account the frequently used historical present tense.

36. Murko also mentioned multiformity within the line as a characteristic of traditional composition (e.g., ibid.).

II. Milman Parry: From Homeric Text
to Homeric Oral Tradition

1. For other summaries of Parry's work, see esp. A. Parry 1971b and M. Edwards 1986, 1987. All citations of and references to Parry's writings are to A. Parry 1971a, although the original dates of each published or theretofore unpublished work are used in discussion.

2. Note in this connection Parry's statement (1923:421) that "the character of the diction reflects the character of the style. Its most striking feature is its traditional, almost *formulaic* quality, its regular use of certain words and phrases in a certain way" (italics added).

3. Parry's definition of *language* is "all the elements of phonetics, morphology, and vocabulary which characterize the speech of a given group of men at a given place and at a given time," while that of *diction* is "the same elements of phonetics, morphology, and vocabulary considered under another aspect: as the means by which an author expresses his thought" (1928a:6).

4. This point should be recalled when we consider Parry's analysis of other aspects of the phraseology in later studies (esp. 1930).

5. As we shall see in Parry 1928b, the demands on the composing poet are such that he will occasionally join together two formulas whose essential ideas collectively produce the desired phrase or sentence even if that conjunction results in a metrical flaw at the seam between the individual formulas.

6. It is also well to recall that noun-epithet and predicate systems are only the most obvious recurrent patterns in the diction, and that there exist myriad other phraseological patterns as well.

7. On the basis of this last distinction, Parry convincingly demonstrated that Apollonius of Rhodes and Virgil both attempted to echo what they perceived as Homer's ornate diction. While they succeeded in creating Homeric flourishes by employing a certain number of ornamental epithets, they were not employing a traditional system of diction.

8. For further, detailed information on the structure of the hexameter in relation to phraseology, see esp. O'Neill 1942 and Peabody 1975.

9. An important caveat should be added here, one which very few of those attempting to imitate Parry's analytical methods have themselves observed: "Showing the regularity with which Homer makes use of certain formulae would in no way constitute a proof that these formulae are traditional. As in the case of non-Ionic words and forms in Homeric language, metrical convenience can only explain the origin and survival of traditional elements which have already been identified by other means. The proof that we are looking for of the traditional character of Homeric formulae lies in the fact that they constitute a system distinguished at once by great extension and by great simplicity" (1928a:16).

10. Parry took some pains to emphasize that he was describing a diachronic process which epitomized ideas in metrical, and therefore useful, phrases rather than a wooden idiom composed of clumsy building blocks which the bard assembled as best he could. Consider the following passage: "The greatest danger in a study of Homeric formulae is that one may be led to assume that they follow rules which have nothing to do with the ideas denoted by the single words. We must never forget that formulary technique is designed to express the thought of epic poetry, hence varies constantly in conformity with the idea which is to be expressed" (1928a:38).

11. It will be well to recall the findings and reasoning of the supplementary thesis

(1928b) as we move on to a discussion of the narrative unit of *theme* in succeeding chapters. Just as formulas have a double identity in the tradition, combining with other phrases while at the same time maintaining lives of their own, so themes have the same kind of dual identity and are thus similarly prone to infelicities at their points of juncture with other themes. See further Lord 1936 and 1960:68–98.

12. Parry 1929:254, 256, 262. For more detailed figures, see 263–64. Note that Parry's analysis of enjambement, though questioned (Clayman and van Nortwick 1977), has been confirmed through subsequent investigation (Barnes 1979). Whether this kind of measurement is applicable to all oral traditional epics is another matter; see Lord 1960:54ff.

13. As a source for the former objection, Parry lists Shorey 1928:305 and Bassett 1930:642; for the latter, Chantraine 1929:299.

14. Thus Parry's program for the 1930 essay: "The first move in this attempt to rebuild the Homeric idea of epic poetry will be to show that the *Iliad* and the *Odyssey* are composed in a traditional style, and are composed orally, then to see just how such poetry differs from our own in style and form. When that is done, we shall have solid ground beneath us when we undertake the problem of unity in the poems, or judge a doubtful verse, or try to point out how one epic poem would differ from another, or how the greatness of a Singer would show itself. We shall find then, I think, that this failure to see the difference between written and oral verse was the greatest single obstacle to our understanding of Homer, we shall cease to be puzzled by much, we shall no longer look for much that Homer would never have thought of saying, and above all, we shall find that many, if not most of the questions we were asking, were not the right ones to ask" (269).

15. Parry was well aware both that the noun-epithet formulas provided the best proof of the systematization of Homeric diction and that "a full description of the technique [of formulaic composition] is not to be thought of, since its complexity, which is exactly that of the ideas in Homer, is altogether too great" (1930:307). He thus proposes an analysis within the realm of possibility: to examine a selection of expressions that can be considered typical (ibid).

16. See esp. 1930:304.

17. The wording of this definition may lead one to believe that Parry is advocating a memorized list of expressions as the elements that comprise a formulaic system, but in fact his examples and discussion make it quite clear that he is postulating (and demonstrating) something quite different: a category of related phrases which the poet "knows" in the same way that one "knows" a language and is therefore able to use it fluently. Note further the familiar characteristics Parry assigns to the system: "The length of a system consists very obviously in the number of formulas which make it up. The thrift of a system lies in the degree to which it is free of phrases which, having the same metrical value and expressing the same idea, could replace one another" (1930:276). We may compare the *formula type*, which consisted of expressions having the same metrical value but usually unrelated, and also observe that the features of length and thrift are less applicable to formulas and formulaic systems outside the category of noun-epithet phrases.

18. The particle *hr'* (from *hra*, full form *ara*) may be translated "then, so then," or the equivalent, but here serves primarily as an institutionalized traditional means of avoiding hiatus with the successive diphthong of *epei* and initial vowel of the verb-forms. It is of course unnecessary when the verb-form begins with a consonant.

19. In this particular case between line-beginning and the "trochaic or feminine caesura," that is, in the first half-line or hemistich, as this unit is commonly referred to.

20. These are difficult concepts for Homerists taught to seek the true and the beautiful in poetic texts according to the dictates of modern criticism. The ideas have continued to be distressing for some later scholars, especially when Parry couches them in forms like the following: "At no time is [Homer] seeking words

for an idea which has never before found expression, so that the question of originality in style means nothing to him" (1930:324).

21. One need only cite the numerous instances of medieval words no longer used in contemporary speech or of Turkicisms alongside Murko's famous example (1929:24) of the ban using a *telefon* to communicate instead of the traditionally sanctioned *pismo* or *knjiga* (letter). The dialect forms are metrically selected for the poetic language: if the formula in question needs an extra syllable to fill out the colon, for example, the poet will use the longer ijekavian form of a word (e.g., *mlijeko* in place of *mleko*), or vice versa.

22. Excerpted in A. Parry 1971a:437–64; the entire manuscript will be published in the Parry Collection series in the near future.

23. This new departure both continued Parry's former work and extended it significantly: "Here, however, we can go much further than is possible in the case of the *Iliad* and the *Odyssey*, or of any of the other early poetries of Europe: the actual practice of the poetry itself suggests the hypothesis, and the hypothesis can be verified by the observation of the actual practice of the poetry. We can learn not only how the singer puts together his words, and then his phrases, and then his verses, but also his passages and themes, and we can see how the whole poem lives from one man to another, from one age to another, and passes over plains and mountains and the barriers of speech,—more, we can see how a whole oral poetry lives and dies" (1933–35:441).

24. For the most complete accounts available of these fieldwork trips, see Lord 1948b, 1951b; *SCHS* I:3–20; and Bynum 1974a.

25. Parry 1933–35:450–51; see further Lord 1953a.

26. On this matter of genre and subgenre, see *SCHS* I:16 and Foley 1983.

27. For a numerical accounting, see Lord 1948b:41 as well as the digest of epic texts collected through 1951 in *SCHS* I (21–45).

28. See the citations in n. 24.

29. Selected texts from the Parry Collection are being published, both in the original language and in English translation, in the series *Serbo-Croatian Heroic Songs* (*SCHS*), about which more will be said in the next chapter.

30. Parry provides references to two instances of each noun-epithet complement in vol. 2 of Karadžić's *Srpske narodne pjesme*, thus sufficiently illustrating recurrence, his primary criterion for formulaic character (as in Parry 1930). Many more instances could, of course, be cited, and from other collections as well as this one.

31. Parry was careful to distinguish (as well as to compare) the two epic poetries from the start, as his discussion of differences in ornamentation illustrates (1933b:388). On the necessity of making such distinctions, see further chap. 5.

32. This study was brought to fruition in Lord 1936.

33. See, e.g., Fournier 1946, Combellack 1950, Vivante 1975 and 1982, and Nimis 1986.

III. Albert Lord: Comparative Oral Traditions

1. Printed in Lord 1948b.

2. For a bibliography of related studies through 1982, see Foley 1985; supplements to and updates of this volume will appear annually in *Oral Tradition*.

3. To attempt an exhaustive assessment of and commentary on Lord's work is beyond the scope of a single chapter. For the purpose of the present volume as a whole, I shall try instead to place some of his most important writings in the foreground and to indicate their significance for the evolution of the Oral Theory.

4. Lord 1936, "Homer and Huso I." Huso Husović was, as Lord tells us, a great

singer of a past generation: "Many of the oldest singers that we found had known and heard him, and legend pictures him riding in brilliant array with his gusle from town to town, from region to region, singing his songs—much like the Greek Homer revealed to us by the words of the *Contest of Homer and Hesiod, perierchomenos elege ta poiêmata*" (107). Cp. Foley 1978b.

5. Lord adds that "because of the progressive style of composition, the addition of theme upon theme, the singer has no difficulty in finding places to stop, and once he has made up his mind to stop, it is never necessary for him to go on for any length of time to find a convenient spot" (1936:110). Cp. Foley 1978a, where it is shown that the singer "will not resume his song at just any point. Rather he 'backtracks' to the last traditional boundary and, after a brief proem for continuance, begins anew from that boundary. This usually means reverting to the beginning of the last theme or subthematic structure and identifying it as a starting point" (7).

6. Lord 1936:113. These criteria for comparison have not been heeded by those who would discount the Yugoslav analogy on the basis of what they feel is the obvious difference in "quality" between the available samples of Homeric and South Slavic epic; see, for example, Kirk 1962:83ff. and A. Parry 1966:212–16, as against Lord 1968.

7. "In the early stages of learning the young singer learns both themes and formulas, but his attention is fixed chiefly on the latter. . . . But, even as his knowledge of formulas, which is vague in the period of absorption which precedes his first taking the accompanying instrument in his hand and opening his mouth to sing, is sharpened to precision by the act of singing his first song, so his idea of themes is given shape as he learns new songs and perhaps ultimately creates songs of his own. The real function of the theme is to be found in that phase of transmission which covers the learning of a song by a singer in the later stages of his training or by an accomplished singer and in the creation of a new song. Once a singer has command of the common themes of the tradition, he has merely to hear a song which is new to him only once to be able to perform it himself" (Lord 1951a:73–74). See further Lord 1960:13–29.

8. Lord also includes remarks on the historicity of the epic songs (e.g., Lord 1951a:74); on this topic, see further Lord 1970 and Stolz 1967.

9. On these songs, see further M. Coote 1977 and Lockwood 1983.

10. Cp. the findings of Hillers and McCall 1976.

11. For the most complete accounts available of the fieldwork trips that led to the Parry Collection, see Lord 1948b, 1951b; *SCHS* I:3–20; and Bynum 1974a. On the Lord Collection of Albanian songs, see Lord 1984 and n. 81, chap. 4, below.

A brief article from this period, "Notes on *Digenis Akritas* and Serbo-Croatian Epic" (Lord 1954), probes correspondences among the Russian, Greek, Turkish, and Serbo-Croatian traditions in order "to demonstrate how fruitful the comparative study of Byzantine Greek and Serbocroatian oral epic tradition can be" (383).

12. See Lord 1960:102–5 for a comparative analysis of these two performances.

13. Cp. Lord 1960:53-58 and, e.g., Peabody 1975:169–215.

14. Lord continues (1959:6): "Perhaps the most fundamental [of the poetic values of oral poetry] come from the myth, or myths, which first determined the themes of oral narrative poetry, which provided the story material and gave it significance. For the myths brought it into being and kept it living long after they themselves had officially been declared dead."

15. For example, more than twelve hundred of the eighteen hundred books and articles listed in Foley 1985 derive to a greater or lesser extent from *The Singer of Tales*.

16. Note Lord's further conclusions: "The metrical convenience, or even better, the metrical necessity, is probably a late phenomenon, indispensable for the growth of epic from what must have been comparatively simple narrative incantations to more complex tales intended more and more for entertainment. This was a change

concomitant with the gradual shift toward the heroic and eventually the historic. It is quite likely that the later stages could not have developed until the formula became a compositional device; yet because of its past it could never become merely a compositional device. Its symbols, its sounds, its patterns were born for magic productivity, not for aesthetic satisfaction" (1960:67).

17. See further Lord 1974c, discussed later in this chapter, on the matter of the verbal component of themes.

18. An added dimension of multiformity has to do with the provenience of the texts under examination: instances of themes from a single *guslar* will of course show more similarities than those taken from different singers in the same local tradition, and, in turn, examples drawn from different regions will show yet more variance.

19. More specialized information in this area is available in Lord 1986a.

20. See also Lord 1971c.

21. On this point, see further Lord 1986a.

22. For true comparative work, a thorough knowledge of the language, literature, and literary history of all traditions directly involved is, of course, essential; nonetheless, even this simple rule of thumb is often violated, as in the cases just cited. As Lord puts it (1967:5, n. 13), "I am constantly amazed at the ease with which scholars, meticulous in their own field, make *ex cathedra* statements about poetries of whose language they know nothing."

23. On the issue of formulaic density as a litmus test for orality, see Lord 1986b.

24. Lord does, however, caution that the size and kind of referent (the Homeric poems also formed part of the referent for the *Batrachomyomachia*) and the size of the sample may have affected his results.

25. Lord also believes that "it is important to work from line break to line break rather than with simple repetition of words and phrases by themselves, because it is in terms of parts of a line, I believe, that the singer thinks" (1968:26). Although Lord is speaking here specifically of Homer, the context of his remarks could be widened to take into account a number of oral poetries whose lines are syllabically based, including Serbo-Croatian epic. On the criteria of comparability, see further Miletich 1976 and Foley 1981c.

26. Lord's caveat speaks to the need for more of this kind of study: "Surely one of the vital questions now facing Homeric scholarship is how to understand oral poetics, how to read oral traditional poetry. Its poetics is different from that of written literature because its technique of composition is different. It cannot be treated as a flat surface. All the elements in traditional poetry have depth, and our task is to plumb their sometimes hidden recesses; for there will meaning be found" (1968:46).

27. For examples in numerous other traditions, see, e.g., M. Coote 1981 and Parks 1981.

28. See further Lord 1971a, in which he observes a possible parallel between the "Smailagić Meho" and the Odyssean Telemacheia.

29. See further Lord 1986a.

30. The comparative survey is continued in Lord 1986b.

31. Compare Lord 1978b.

32. E.g.: "Thus, even within the limited scope of the early portions of The Wedding of Smailagić Meho one can see the interweaving of ritual and mythic patterns which give a traditional depth to the modern song. For Meho is an initiatory hero, and at the same time also the dragon-slayer of divine implications with a holy crusade to bring divine order and salvation to his people, and finally he is a maiden-saving dragon-slayer" (Lord 1976a:15). For related remarks, see Lord 1980c.

33. On the oral traditional structure of Byzantine popular narratives, see E. and M. Jeffreys 1983, 1986.

34. For a history of research on oral tradition and the Bible, see Culley 1986.

35. For further comparative remarks, see Lord 1976d, which concentrates on Bulgarian epic tradition, with references to the Armenian epic *David of Sassoun* and the Finnish *Kalevala*, and 1983, which treats aspects of traditional style in the phraseology of Bulgarian narrative.

36. He continues: "Memorization requires a fixed text, and it is impossible in the oral traditional narrative poetries with which I am acquainted, because in the tradition's natural state, there are no fixed texts to memorize. The singers of the South Slavs are creators and not rhapsodes as is sometimes erroneously averred by those who do not comprehend their art" (Lord 1981a:460).

37. Cp. esp. Lord 1965a; of added interest is 1980b.

38. The thematic studies lead to this conclusion: "The reality is that singers do not remember a *text* at all from one performance to another no matter how extraordinary and memorable the circumstances of the performance itself may have been: they remember the elements of the *story*. They create the text anew each time they tell the story" (Lord 1980c:50).

39. On Bartók, see also Lord 1982.

40. On Homeric ring-composition, see esp. van Otterlo 1948 and Whitman 1958.

41. He goes on: "The non-narrative African praise poetry of the Xhosa or Zulu, for example, or the occasional or lyric poetry in Somaliland, may be helpful in studying the shorter Anglo-Saxon genres, or other true improvisations, but its usefulness for the study of epic would be very limited. For the epic, the Central Asiatic and Indian traditions, or the songs in Mali or the epics from Zaire, are much more apt and deserve further study in depth" (Lord 1986b:472).

42. Among Lord's papers in press as this volume takes its final form are studies of the characteristics of orality (1987), "Words Heard and Words Seen" (1986d), "The *Kalevala*, the South Slavic Epics, and Homer" (forthcoming a) and "Central Asiatic and Balkan Epic"(forthcoming b).

43. Even at present he is working on a book-length manuscript he describes as "a sequel to *The Singer of Tales*."

IV. The Making of a Discipline

1. For a full bibliography through 1982, see Foley 1985, updated annually in *Oral Tradition*.

2. The most recent developments in Oral Theory are the subject of chap. 5. For a full account of activity on ancient Greek, see Edwards 1986, 1987; for Old English, see Foley 1981b:51–91, 103–22 and Olsen 1986, 1987; for other literatures, see prior and forthcoming issues of *Oral Tradition* (e.g., Beaton 1986 on modern Greek, Bäuml 1986 on Middle High German, Culley 1986 on the Bible, E. and M. Jeffreys 1986 on Byzantine Greek, J. Nagy 1986 on Old Irish, Parks 1986 on Middle English, Webber 1986a on Hispanic).

3. See further Chantraine 1929, 1940–48, 1948, as well as Shorey 1928.

4. See, e.g., Fournier 1946, Combellack 1950, Vivante 1975 and 1982, Nimis 1986.

5. For example, Sheppard claims to aim at "a piece of truth, far more important than the half-truth preached by Mr. Milman Parry, who warns us that, unless we bow with him at Düntzer's shrine, intoning his new version of Kurt Witte's paradox, 'The Epic verse created Homer's style,' we run the risk of folly and extravagance in our interpretation" (1935:116). This overstatement aside, it is important to recognize that for most scholars the single most difficult tenet of the Oral Theory was from the start its alleged dismissal of Homer's (literary) art.

6. See also Bassett 1930.

7. Notopoulos's more significant articles will be treated in the appropriate chronological sections of this chapter. Lord notes (1974c:3) that Notopoulos bequeathed his taped recordings of modern Greek oral literature to the Milman Parry Collection and that he also "left a manuscript of a book on Cretan Heroic Song and Homer, which is presently being edited."

8. For a critique of parataxis in Homer, see Austin (1975, esp. chap. 1), who not surprisingly also has much to say against Parry's investigations and results.

9. In the same vein we may mention the earlier, compendious work by the Chadwicks, *The Growth of Literature* (1932–40).

10. For other work on Hesiod, see esp. G. Edwards 1971 and Peabody 1975. See also Notopoulos's extension of Oral Theory to another genre in ancient Greek, the Homeric Hymns (1962); in a related study, M. Lord 1967.

11. Cp. Notopoulos 1954, 1959a, 1960b, 1963, 1964.

12. Notopoulos 1957; see further the bibliography on this comparison in Holoka 1973:items 192–203.

13. Particularly evident in "Some Mycenaean Relics in the Iliad" (Page 1959:218–96). See also Page's other, differently focused works (esp. 1955, 1963). The approach through diachrony, relatively rare in comparison to the primarily synchronic methods of most oral-formulaic theorists, is exemplified further in, e.g., T. Webster 1958, Armstrong 1958, Pope 1960, Hoekstra 1964 and 1969, O'Nolan 1969, G. Nagy 1974 and 1979, Boedeker 1974, Peabody 1975, Shannon 1975, Clader 1976, Muellner 1976, and Frame 1978.

14. In fairness it must be added that the comparison with South Slavic epic is seriously weakened—if not actually invalidated—by Kirk's generalizations based on a few translations and a particularly uninformed treatment of the metrics of Serbo-Croatian epic. One would expect a comparative assessment to be based on firsthand scholarly acquaintance with both traditions in the original languages.

15. See esp. the works of A. Parry and Amory Parry discussed later in this chapter; cp. also the opinion of a native Yugoslav scholar in Dukat 1976, 1978.

16. For more detail, see further Kirk's remarks on Homeric prosody and syntax (1966a), the issue of formulaic density and orality (1966b), and the importance of orality for the meaning of the Homeric poems (1972), as well as his two books on myth (1970 and 1974) and two collections of articles (1964 and 1976).

17. Cp. the work of Walter J. Ong, discussed in the next chapter.

18. On related subjects and esp. on the power of the oral versus the written system of perception and expression, see Havelock's collected essays (1982) and Havelock and Hershbell 1978. For further observations on Homeric psychology and oral culture, see Russo and Simon 1968, Simon and Weiner 1966, Robb 1970 and 1974, Simon 1978, Foley 1978d; related work discussed in the next chapter includes Segal 1982 and Havelock 1983.

19. See also Hoekstra 1957, 1969, 1978, and Ruijgh 1962.

20. See further Russo 1968, 1971, 1976a and b.

21. Cp. other Hainsworth articles, esp. 1970 on critical approaches, 1976 on "phrase-clusters," and 1978 on diachrony in phraseology.

22. This seminal work led to a long series of studies of the possibility of individual characterization within the formulaic medium: Donlan 1971, Reeve 1973, Claus 1975, Hogan 1976, Friedrich and Redfield 1978, Duban 1981, Friedrich and Redfield 1981, and Messing 1981.

23. Armstrong 1958, Young 1965 and 1967 (more polemical than logical); cp. also Austin 1966 and Combellack 1959, 1965, 1976.

24. See also the recent works by Fenik treated in this chapter.

25. Cp. Peabody 1975 and, in Old English, e.g., Greenfield 1967a.

26. See further Edwards's ideas on flexibility of diction (1968), "answering" formulas (1969), speech introductions (1970), type-scenes (1975), convention and in-

dividuality (1980a), and catalogs (1980b), as well as his encyclopedic summaries of activity on Oral Theory in ancient Greek (1986, 1987).

27. See also Fenik 1974, 1978a, 1978b, 1986.

28. This volume incorporates many of Whallon's earlier articles; an exception is his treatment of Lord's theory of the oral dictated text (1969b).

29. Less directly tied to the Oral Theory is the series of contributions by W.B. Stanford (1969, 1976, 1981, and esp. 1967) on the sound of Greek, in which he attempts to reconstruct the actual oral/aural reality of early Greek and to establish its importance to formulaic diction; in this connection see also Packard 1974, 1976 and West 1981. Extensions of the Oral Theory to other texts include McLeod 1961 (the Delphic oracle) and 1966 (Panyassis); comparisons between the Homeric poems and the Irish hero tales are available in O'Nolan 1968, 1969. Among other often-cited studies from the 1960s that bear on oral theory are Pope 1963, Beye 1964 and 1966, Segal 1967, 1968 (and later 1971a, b), Lang 1969, Gaisser 1969a, b, and Heitsch 1968.

30. Cp. Gunn's work on Biblical materials, esp. 1976a, b.

31. On the similes cp. Moulton 1977, who emphasizes how a great poet may contribute "from his own genius to his traditional inheritance" (396).

32. Ingalls 1970, 1972, 1976, 1979, 1982.

33. Comparative insights on Homeric and African epic are available in Okpewho 1979 (see also 1977, 1980).

34. For histories of relevant scholarship more thorough than can be attempted here, see Foley 1981b and Olsen 1986, 1987. Some of the earliest work on oral delivery in medieval studies was done by Crosby (1936 and 1938; see further Parks 1986), and evidence for oral poets in Old English and Old Norse was offered by Norman in 1938.

35. Cp. Bredtmann 1889 on Old French, Kettner 1897 on Middle High German, Miklosich 1890 on various Slavic traditions, and Zupitza 1875–76 on Middle English romance.

36. Cp. Hermann 1877 on Homer.

37. For a complete survey of this area, see Parks 1986.

38. Cp. "A Note on Old West Germanic Poetic Unity" (Magoun 1945), in which he observes that "beyond a large common stock-in-trade of traditional story, the accumulations of parallel phrases and locations . . . afford a striking testimony to a basic, persistent community of diction" (78).

39. In which Lord performs a formulaic analysis of lines 1473–87 of the Old English *Beowulf* (see Lord 1960:199).

40. Defined by Parry as "a group of phrases which have the same metrical value and which are enough alike in thought and words to leave no doubt that the poet who knew them used them not only as a single formula, but also as formulas of a single type" (1930:275).

41. On Cædmon as an oral singer, see also Malone 1961, Blake 1962, Fritz 1969, Fry 1974 and 1981, and Opland 1977b.

42. In 1960:198–99, Lord described themes in *Beowulf* as "repeated assemblies with speeches, repetition of journeying from one place to another, and on the larger canvas the repeated multiform scenes of the slaying of monsters." See further chap. 3 above.

43. But see also Greenfield 1953a and b, which presage this piece.

44. For further studies of this narrative pattern, see Renoir 1964, 1977, 1979a, 1979b, 1981a, 1981b; Fry 1966, 1967a; C. Wolf 1970; Thormann 1970; Suzuki 1972; J.D. Johnson 1975, 1983; Olsen 1980, 1981:94–101, 1982; Dane 1982.

45. See also O'Neil's debate with Jackson Campbell over oral poetry and the Old English *Seafarer* (O'Neil 1960b, Campbell 1960), as well as O'Neil's work on Faroese oral tradition (1970).

46. Cassidy 1965; cp. 1970.

47. Cp. Rogers 1966.

48. Cp. Nagler 1967, 1974:1–63 on ancient Greek.

49. Cp. Lord 1981a and Foley 1981d, 1983.

50. See the reply by Fry (1979).

51. Initially presented in Foley 1976.

52. Also worthy of mention are Mertens-Fonck 1978, which treats formulaic structure in the introductions to direct discourse in *Beowulf*; Klinck 1983, which examines formulaic structure in ancient Greek and Old English; and Olsen 1984, which, in studying the many aspects of the "composite tradition" (Germanic and Christian Latin) behind the poems of Cynewulf, has much to contribute on the issue of formulaic structure and meaning.

53. Cp. Opland's emphasis on particular words as the thematic substrate (1976:esp. 446–53). Later on in this same essay, I commented briefly on the ritual nature and dynamics of traditional oral units of composition, noting that "echoes from one occurrence of a given theme reverberate not simply through the subsequent linear length of the given poem, but through the collective mythic knowledge of the given culture. Under these circumstances, we may have to revise our thinking about 'mistakes' and 'inconsistencies,' for example. In addition, . . . usefulness and aesthetics need no longer preclude one another's existence; they merge in the ritual unity of traditional art" (Foley 1976:232).

54. On this point cp. the similar findings of M. Coote 1980.

55. See further Foley 1980.

56. Esp. Renoir 1981a, b, 1986.

57. See Foley 1985 for more extensive bibliographical citations.

58. See also the work of Charles Hyart (e.g., 1965, 1968), who has compared the Old French *chansons de geste* and South Slavic *narodne pjesme* in some detail.

59. See also Bynum 1978, discussed in chap. 5, as well as Bynum 1974b, 1980, and 1979 (his *SCHS* editions, vols. IV, VI, and XIV), also treated in the next chapter. Of related interest is Creed's study (1981b) of sound patterning in the performances of Avdo Medjedović.

60. Exemplified in Lord and Bartók 1951.

61. See the Hispanic section of this chapter for a précis of Miletich's analytical contributions.

Given the history of Yugoslav and American research on the South Slavic area, it is hoped that the coming years will see more native scholarship translated into English and made available to a wider range of scholars working with the Oral Theory in a variety of fields. In 1987 the University of Missouri hosted a bilateral international symposium commemorating the achievements of the great Serbian ethnographer Vuk Stefanović Karadžić, who was responsible for the collection of some nine volumes of oral poetry. The proceedings, to consist of twelve essays on South Slavic oral literature (six by Yugoslavs and six by Americans) will be published both in the United States (in the journal *Southeastern Europe*) and in Yugoslavia.

62. To be discussed along with other volumes of *SCHS* in chap. 5.

63. For a review of this controversy, and of its extension in the form of Neoindividualism versus Neotraditionalism, see Faulhaber 1976; also of value in this regard are Deyermond 1977 and Miletich 1981a.

64. Unfortunately, Deyermond's comparison of medieval Spanish material with the Yugoslav songs collected by Parry and Lord is somewhat amateurish, relying as it does exclusively on translations of the South Slavic songs. For more dependable work, see studies by Miletich (e.g., 1978, 1981b).

65. See esp. Menéndez Pidal 1959; see further Faulhaber 1976.

66. Perhaps the most extensive definition of the formula in any arena: "a habitual device of style or of narrative mode: as verbal expression it is a group of words forming an identical or variable pattern which is used in the same, or similar, or dissimilar metrical conditions to express a given essential idea whose connotative

meaning is frequently determined by the extent to which it is modified by poetic context; as narrative mode, it refers to the customary but variable manner in which the verbal matter is arranged to tell a story" (de Chasca 1970: 257–58, italics deleted).

67. See esp. the *Bibliografía del romancero oral* (1980), which contains more than sixteen hundred items.

68. Geary's computerized figures of 14 percent for the *Mocedades* and 17 percent for the *Poema* are based on the method proposed and illustrated by Joseph J. Duggan (1973; see also the section on Old French in this chapter and, further, chap. 5); both figures are below Duggan's 20 percent threshold.

69. See, e.g., Miletich 1978, 1981b.

70. See Lord's response to this methodology (1986b:481–91). Also of importance are John H. McDowell's discussion of formula and theme in the Mexican ballad tradition (1972), L.P. Harvey's article on the role of oral composition in the "telling" of novels in early Spain (1974), and Kenneth Adams's consideration of the viability of the Yugoslav model for the case of the *Cid* (1976). Mention should also be made of Ruth Webber's collection of essays on the Hispanic ballad, the May 1987 issue of *Oral Tradition*.

71. Delbouille prefers to derive the surviving *chansons de geste* from the older hagiographic tradition, envisioning this new genre as the invention of cleric-minstrels who composed in writing. See further his similar arguments, together with remarks on the comparison of South Slavic and Old French works, in articles published in 1961 and 1965–66.

72. See further the discussion of Duggan's comments on the sociology of Old French epic (1986) in the next chapter.

73. On this subject, see further Zumthor 1984. An interesting extension of Oral Theory, and one similar to some of Renoir's work, is Zara P. Zaddy's article (1961) on Chrétien de Troyes's use of the Old French epic theme of arming a warrior.

74. For a complete survey and evaluation of relevant scholarship on Middle High German, see Bäuml 1986.

75. See further other, more generally focused articles by Kellogg (esp. 1974, 1977, 1979).

76. See also the earlier article on *Spielmannsepik* (Curschmann 1966, esp. 605–14).

77. Curschmann reasons that an overconcern with the formula has blinded scholars to the true nature of medieval poetry, wherein oral and written versions of texts can exist side by side. He reviews the application of Oral Theory to medieval German texts and offers as an example his view that the *Nibelungenlied* took shape in the "active interdependence of the two cultures [oral and written]" (1977:74).

78. Haymes has also written on the oral theme of arrival in the *Nibelungenlied* (1976) and the general issue of oral composition in Middle High German epic poetry (1980a, 1986).

79. For surveys in these areas, see E. and M. Jeffreys 1986 (Byzantine Greek) and Beaton 1986 (modern Greek).

80. Cp. Papacharalambous (1963), who, in describing and explaining similarities between the ancient and modern Greek traditional texts, considers the criteria of repetition and "the recasting and recomposition of the existing tradition" (41). Also of importance is the fieldwork by James Notopoulos on modern Greek oral song, already mentioned in connection with ancient Greek; see esp. 1959a and b, 1963.

81. For studies on Albanian oral narrative poetry, see Skendi 1954 and 1980, Kolsti 1968, Pipa 1978, and Lord 1984. Lord also made a collection of 100 Albanian oral texts in the northern Albanian Alps in the fall of 1937.

82. For a survey of ideas about orality and medieval Irish narrative (not restricted to the Oral Theory alone), see J. Nagy 1986.

83. See further O'Nolan 1978 on comparative formulaic structure.

84. See esp. Ó Coileáin's discussion of the possible role of oral composition in

the composition of the sagas (1978:174–78). Other important surveys and applications of theoretical models include Ó Coileáin 1977–78 and Slotkin 1978–79, 1983.

85. See also Melia's similar work on the Ulster death tales (1977–78).

86. Of related interest is J. Nagy 1983.

87. For a survey of scholarship on oral tradition and Biblical studies, see Culley 1986. Prominent examples of work in this field that have no direct connection to Oral Theory include Nielsen 1954, Widengren 1959, and Gerhardsson 1961, 1979.

88. For a continuation of this line of inquiry, see Urbrock 1976.

89. On this point cp. Watkins 1976.

90. See also the review by Culley (1976b), now superseded by Culley 1986. Of related interest is Lord 1978a, mentioned above in chap. 3.

91. See further Cross 1974, Lord 1978a, and Jacobsen 1982.

92. In 1988 *Oral Tradition* will publish a special issue on Arabic oral traditions, guest-edited by Issa Boullata.

93. See also Hamori's more general study of the *qaṣīdas* (1974).

94. It is well to note that the poems in question are short and seem to be fixed texts rather than fluid, re-created works. See further Monroe's comparative investigation of formulaic diction in the Romance and Arabic traditions (1975).

95. Zwettler's figure for the overall verbal and syntactic density of the text is 56 percent.

96. One of the strengths of Zwettler's work is his rare command of scholarship on other traditions, a feature that also characterizes McDonald 1978, who likewise champions the oral nature of the classical poetry.

97. Helpful access to the mass of published material on African oral traditions is provided, for example, by the bibliographies of Veronika Görög (1968–72, 1981).

98. See esp. Opland 1977b. His book on Xhosa oral poetry (1983) will be treated in the next chapter.

99. See also Biebuyck 1986, on "Names in Nyanga Society."

100. Although they lie outside the Oral Theory per se, we should add to Henige's study the works of Jan Vansina (e.g., 1965) and John R. Goody (e.g., 1968, 1977).

101. See further John W. Johnson 1986, treated in the next chapter.

102. See also Cross 1973 on traditional word-pairs and Semitic oral literature.

103. See also Smith's essay on "Words, Music, and Memory" (1981), and Lord's response (1986c) to Smith 1977.

104. A wider perspective on the epic tradition of Turkish peoples (Chinese Uigurs, Kazakhs, Kirghiz, Turkmen, Azeri, Uzbeks, Karakalpaks, Tatars, and other groups in Soviet Central Asia) is available in Başgöz 1978b. For more information on the Central Asian traditions, see Lord 1986b. Başgöz is editing a special issue of *Oral Tradition* on the Turkish area, scheduled to appear in 1990.

105. Less clearly in the Parry-Lord tradition is Butler 1969, which explores in part the process of oral composition as related to the Japanese *heike*.

106. Compare the oral traditions of ritual insult among inner-city black youths (Labov 1972:esp. chaps. 8 and 9) and among Turkish boys (Dundes et al. 1972). See also Harris's treatment of satire and heroic narrative pattern (1980), and related works by Jesse L. Byock (1982, 1984).

107. See further Arant 1972, 1973, as well as the survey essay on the *bylina* by Felix J. Oinas (1978b).

108. Also of interest is Treitler et al. 1981, a collection of essays on the applicability of oral theory to medieval chant and modern jazz; one of the contributions, Gushee 1981, is mentioned separately later in this chapter.

109. Cp. Titon's concept of "preforms," accompaniment units that are performed, memorized, and stored (1978), and see further Evans 1982 (esp. 315).

110. See also Conroy's 1978 collection, *Ballads and Ballad Research*, as well as Ruth Webber's special issue of *Oral Tradition* (May 1987) on Hispanic balladry.

111. In the Midwest, Elaine J. Lawless (e.g., 1983) has recorded and commented on women preachers in the Pentecostal church. See also Rosenberg's survey essay (1986) on this area of investigation.

V. Recent and Future Directions

1. It will be noted that, while some of the works covered are less clearly in the mainstream of Oral Theory than others, all of them have influenced the Theory or seem certain to do so.

2. Cp. a similar process of accretion observed within the repertoire of the Parry-Lord *guslar* Mujo Kukuruzović (Foley 1980).

3. To date two additional volumes of *SCHS* have appeared: Bynum 1979 (XIV), which includes songs from the regions of Bihać, Cazin, and Kulen Vakuf; and Bynum 1980 (VI), which presents two more songs by Avdo Medjedović, including the 13,326-line *Osmanbeg Delibegović i Pavičević Luka*.

4. See its continuation in G. Nagy 1979.

5. "The conclusion is reached that the simplest metrical unit, the colon, is essentially the same unit as the traditional single lexical element, while the single lexical element is the primary unit and essence of formula. Metrical unit, traditional lexical unit, and formula unit did not function as separate compositional features. If colon, word, and formula are all essentially the same, any composition of Greek epic formulas must also be metrical and traditional" (Peabody 1975:114).

6. See also Fenik 1986, which, while "not a book about oral poetry" (xi), treats the pattern of scenes and episodes in the *Iliad* and the *Nibelungenlied*.

7. In addition to the articles mentioned in chap. 4., Renoir has a book on "oral-formulaic context" in press.

8. See esp. Bäuml 1984.

9. On these and other points, see further Kelber 1987.

10. On this once highly controversial idea, see Lord 1986b:478–81.

11. On the advent of functional literacy in England, compare Clanchy 1979.

12. Cp. his earlier publication of epic (Johnson 1979), as well as Biebuyck 1978 and Biebuyck and Mateene 1969.

13. Of special interest for Oral Theory is Lord's examination of the case of the Montenegrin Petar II Petrović Njegoš, who learned to sing oral epic songs before acquiring writing and reading, and who later composed written epic in the traditional style.

14. See, e.g., van Otterlo 1948 and Whitman 1958.

15. Of additional interest are a translation (Foley 1989) of the major writings of Matija Murko, whose work was touched on in chap. 1, and a collection of essays on oral tradition and modern critical methods (Foley 1988).

16. The spectrum of concerns can be illustrated by citing two articles in *Oral Tradition*'s May 1986 issue: one a survey of work on Aboriginal Australian oral traditions (Clunies Ross) and the other a consideration of Alexander Pope's apparent convictions about Homer's orality and the influence of those convictions on his famous translation (Hoffman).

17. More such essays are planned over the period 1988–91. It should be noted that since these surveys do not restrict themselves to reporting on Parry-Lord scholarship alone, they focus on the Oral Theory to varying degrees.

18. To update Foley 1985. This bibliography will focus chiefly on Oral Theory, with some references to allied approaches.

19. On these principles, see further Foley 1981d, 1983.

20. This is not to say that structural studies are complete, for on the contrary much more work needs to be done on tradition-dependent properties, but rather that we have enough information on traditional structures to attempt at least some first approximations of their aesthetic significance.

21. Of course, this method has important applications for oral-derived texts as well.

22. For further thought on metonymy and the meaning of traditional elements, see Foley 1986a, c.

BIBLIOGRAPHY

Adams, Kenneth
　1976. "The Yugoslav Model and the Text of the 'Poema de Mio Cid.' " In *Medieval Hispanic Studies Presented to Rita Hamilton*. Ed. Alan D. Deyermond. London: Tamesis. Pp. 1–10.
Alexiou, Margaret
　1974. *The Ritual Lament in Greek Tradition*. Cambridge: Cambridge University Press.
　1975. "The Lament of the Virgin in Byzantine Literature and Modern Greek Folk-Song." *Byzantine and Modern Greek Studies*, 1:111–40.
Alster, Bendt
　1972. *Dumuzi's Dream: Aspects of Oral Poetry in a Sumerian Myth*. Copenhagen: Akademisk Forlag.
Alwaya, Semha
　1977. "Formulas and Themes in Contemporary Bedouin Oral Poetry." *Journal of Arabic Literature*, 8:48–76.
Amory Parry, Anne
　1963. "The Reunion of Odysseus and Penelope." In *Essays on the Odyssey: Selected Modern Criticism*. Ed. Charles H. Taylor, Jr. Bloomington: Indiana University Press. Pp. 100–121, 130–36.
　1966. "The Gates of Horn and Ivory." *Yale Classical Studies*, 20:3–57.
　1971. "Homer as Artist." *Classical Quarterly*, 65:1–15.
　1973. *Blameless Aegisthus: A Study of AMYMΩN and Other Homeric Epithets*. Mnemosyne, Bibliotheca Classica Batava, Suppl. 26. Leiden: E.J. Brill.
Arant, Patricia
　1967. "Formulaic Style and the Russian Bylina." *Indiana Slavic Studies*, 4:7–51.
　1968. "Excursus on the Theme in Russian Oral Epic Song." In *Studies Presented to Professor Roman Jakobson by His Students*. Ed. Charles E. Gribble. Cambridge, Mass.: Slavica. Pp. 9–16.
　1972. "Repetition of Prepositions in the Russian Oral Traditional Lament." *Slavonic and East European Journal*, 16:65–73.
　1973. "Alliteration and Repeated Prepositions in Russian Traditional Lament." In *Slavic Poetics: Essays in Honor of Kiril Taranovsky*. Ed. Roman Jakobson et al. The Hague: Mouton. Pp. 1–3.
　1981a. "The Intricate Web: Thematic Cohesion in Russian Oral Traditional Verse Narrative." In Foley 1981a:123–41.
　1981b. "Aspects of Oral Style: Russian Traditional Oral Lament." *Canadian-American Slavic Studies*, 15:42–51.
Arend, Walter
　1933. *Die typischen Scenen bei Homer*. Problemata: Forschungen zur Klassischen Philologie, Heft 7. Berlin: Weidmann.
Armistead, Samuel G.
　1978. "The *Mocedades de Rodrigo* and Neo-Individualist Theory." *Hispanic Review*, 46:313–27.
　1981. "Epic and Ballad: A Traditionalist Perspective." *Olifant*, 8:376–88.
　1971. With Joseph H. Silverman. *The Judeo-Spanish Chapbooks of Yacob Abraham Yoná*. Folk Literature of the Sephardic Jews, vol. 1. Berkeley: University of California Press.

1986. With Joseph H. Silverman. *Judeo-Spanish Ballads from Oral Tradition*. With musical transcriptions and studies by Israel J. Katz. Folk Literature of the Sephardic Jews, vol. 2. Berkeley: University of California Press.

Armstrong, J.I.
1958. "The Arming Motif in the *Iliad*." *American Journal of Philology*, 79:337–54.

Ashby, Genette
1979. "A Generative Model of the Formula in the *Chanson de Roland*." *Olifant*, 7, i:39–65.

Aspel, Paulène
1976. " 'I Do Thank Allah' and Other Formulas in the Fulani Poetry of Adamawa." In Stolz and Shannon 1976:177–202.

Austin, Norman
1966. "The Function of Digressions in the *Iliad*." *Greek, Roman, and Byzantine Studies*, 7:295–312.

1975. *Archery at the Dark of the Moon: Poetic Problems in Homer's Odyssey*. Berkeley: University of California Press.

Barnes, Harry R.
1979. "Enjambement and Oral Composition." *Transactions of the American Philological Association*, 109:1–10.

Barnie, John
1978. "Oral Formulas in the Country Blues." *Southern Folklore Quarterly*, 42:39–52.

Başgöz, Ilhan
1970. "Turkish *Hikaye*-Telling Tradition in Azerbaijan, Iran." *Journal of American Folklore*, 83:391–405.

1975. "The Tale Singer and His Audience: An Experiment to Determine the Effect of Different Audiences on a *hikaye* Performance." In *Folklore: Performance and Communication*. Ed. Dan Ben-Amos and Kenneth S. Goldstein. The Hague: Mouton. Pp. 153–92.

1978a. "Formula in Prose Narrative *Hikâye*." *Folklore Preprint Series* (Indiana University), 6, i:1–25.

1978b. "Epithet in a Prose Epic: The Book of My Grandfather Korkut." *Folklore Preprint Series*, 6, i, a:1–23.

1990. Ed., *Oral Traditions of the Turkic Peoples*. A special issue of *Oral Tradition*, 5.

Bassett, Samuel E.
1930. [Review of Parry 1928a, b]. *Classical Journal*, 25:641–44.

1938. *The Poetry of Homer*. Berkeley: University of California Press.

Bäuml, Franz H.
1968. "Der Übergang mündlicher zur artesbestimmten Literatur des Mittelalters: Gedanken und Bedenken." In *Fachliteratur des Mittelalters: Festschrift für Gerhard Eis*. Stuttgart: J.B. Metzler. Pp. 1–10.

1980. "Varieties and Consequences of Medieval Literacy and Illiteracy." *Speculum*, 55:237–65.

1984. "Medieval Texts and the Two Theories of Oral-Formulaic Composition: A Proposal for a Third Theory." *New Literary History*, 16:31–50.

1986. "The Oral Tradition and Middle High German Literature." *Oral Tradition*, 1:398–445.

Bayer, John G.
1980. "Narrative Techniques and the Oral Tradition in *The Scarlet Letter*." *American Literature*, 52:250–63.

Beaton, Roderick
1980. *Folk Poetry of Modern Greece*. Cambridge: Cambridge University Press.

1981. "Was *Digenes Akrites* an Oral Poem?" *Byzantine and Modern Greek Studies*, 7:7–27.

1986. "The Oral Traditions of Modern Greece: A Survey." *Oral Tradition*, 1:110–33.

Benson, Larry D.
1966. "The Literary Character of Anglo-Saxon Formulaic Poetry." *Publications of the Modern Language Association*, 81:334–41.

Bentley, Richard
1714. *Remarks Upon a Late Discourse of Free-Thinking in a Letter to F.H.D.D. by Phileleutherus Lipsiensis.* 4th ed. Cambridge: John Morphew and Cornelius Crownfield.

Beye, Charles R.
1964. "Homeric Battle Narrative and Catalogues." *Harvard Studies in Classical Philology*, 68:345–73.
1966. *The Iliad, the Odyssey, and the Epic Tradition.* London and Garden City, N.Y.: Macmillan and Doubleday.

Bibliografía
1980. *Bibliografía del romancero oral.* Ed. A. Sánchez Romeralo et al. Vol. 1. Madrid: Cátedra Seminario Menéndez Pidal.

Biebuyck, Daniel P.
1972. "The Epic as a Genre in Congo Oral Literature." In *African Folklore.* Ed. Richard M. Dorson. Garden City, N.Y.: Doubleday. Pp. 257–73.
1976. "The African Heroic Epic." *Journal of the Folklore Institute*, 13:5–36.
1978. *Hero and Chief: Epic Literature from the Banyanga Zaire Republic.* Berkeley: University of California Press.
1986. "Names in Nyanga Society." In Foley 1986b:47–71.
1969. Ed. and trans. with Kahombo C. Mateene. *The Mwindo Epic from the Banyanga.* Berkeley: University of California Press.

Blake, N.F.
1962. "Cædmon's Hymn." *Notes & Queries*, 207:243–46.

Boedeker, Deborah D.
1974. *Aphrodite's Entry into Greek Epic.* Mnemosyne, Bibliotheca Classica Batava, Suppl. 32. Leiden: E.J. Brill.

Bošković-Stulli, Maja
1971. Ed. *Usmena književnost: Izbor studija i ogleda.* Zagreb: Školska knjiga.

Boullata, Issa J.
1988. Ed., *Arabic Oral Traditions.* A special issue of *Oral Tradition*, 3, ii.

Bowra, Cecil M.
1952. *Heroic Poetry.* London: St. Martin's Press, rpt. 1966.

Braun, Maximilian
1961. *Das serbokroatische Heldenlied.* Göttingen: Vandenhoeck and Ruprecht.

Bredtmann, Hermann
1889. *Der sprachliche Ausdruck einiger der geläufigsten Gesten im altfranzösischen Karlsepos.* Marburg: Georg Schirling.

Bryan, W.F.
1929. "Epithetic Compound Folk-Names in Beowulf." In *Studies in English Philology: A Miscellany in Honor of Frederick Klaeber.* Ed. Kemp Malone and Martin B. Ruud. Minneapolis: University of Minnesota Press. Pp. 120–34.

Buchan, David W.
1972. *The Ballad and the Folk.* London: Routledge and Kegan Paul.
1977. "Oral Tradition and Literary Tradition: The Scottish Ballads." In Conroy 1978:56–68.

Butler, Kenneth D.
1969. "The Heike Monogatari and the Japanese Warrior Ethic." *Harvard Journal of Asiatic Studies*, 29:93–108.

Buttenwieser, Ellen C.
1899. *Studien über die Verfasserschaft des Andreas.* Heidelberg: E. Geisendörfer.

Bynum, David E.
1964. "Kult dvaju junaka u kulturnoj istoriji Balkana." *Anali filološkog fakulteta*, 4:65–73.
1968. "Themes of the Young Hero in Serbocroatian Oral Epic Tradition." *Publications of the Modern Language Association*, 83:1296–1303.
1969. "The Generic Nature of Oral Epic Poetry." *Genre*, 2:236–58.
1970. "Thematic Sequences and Transformation of Character in Oral Narrative Tradition." *Filološki pregled*, 8:1–21.
1974a. "Child's Legacy Enlarged: Oral Literary Studies at Harvard since 1856." *Harvard Library Bulletin*, 22:237–67. Rpt. as Documentation and Planning Series, 2. Publications of the Milman Parry Collection.
1974b. Ed. with Albert B. Lord. *Ženidba Smailagina sina*. Kazivao je Avdo Medjedović, s popratnim razgovorima s Medjedovićem i drugim. *SCHS*, IV.
1978. *The Daemon in the Wood: A Study of Oral Narrative Patterns*. Cambridge, Mass.: Center for the Study of Oral Literature.
1979. Ed., *Bihaćka krajina: Epics from Bihać, Cazin, and Kulen Vakuf. SCHS*, XIV.
1980. Ed., *Ženidba Vlahinjić Alije, Osmanbeg Delibegović i Pavičević Luka. SCHS*, VI.
1981. "Formula, Theme, and Critical Method." *Canadian-American Slavic Studies*, 15:61–77.
1986. "The Collection and Analysis of Oral Epic in South Slavic: An Instance." *Oral Tradition*, 1: 302–43.
Byock, Jesse L.
1982. *Feud in the Icelandic Saga*. Berkeley: University of California Press.
1984. "Saga Form, Oral Prehistory, and the Icelandic Social Context." *New Literary History*, 16:153–73.
Calhoun, George M.
1933. "Homeric Repetitions." *University of California Publications in Classical Philology*, 12:1–25.
1935. "The Art of Formula in Homer—ΕΠΕΑ ΠΤΕΡΟΕΝΤΑ." *Classical Philology*, 30:215–27.
Calin, William
1981a. "L'Epopée dite vivante: Réflexions sur le prétendu caractère oral des chansons de geste." *Olifant*, 8, iii:227–37.
1981b. "Littérature médiévale et hypothèse orale: Une divergence de méthode et de philosophie." *Olifant*, 8, iii:256–85.
Campbell, Jackson J.
1960. "Oral Poetry in the *Seafarer*." *Speculum*, 35:87–96.
Caraveli, Anna
1982. "The Song beyond the Song: Aesthetics and Social Interaction in Greek Folksong." *Journal of American Folklore*, 95:129–58.
Carpenter, Rhys
1946. *Folk Tale, Fiction, and Saga in the Homeric Epics*. Berkeley: University of California Press.
Cassidy, Frederic G.
1965. "How Free Was the Anglo-Saxon Scop?" In *Franciplegius: Medieval and Linguistics Studies in Honor of Francis P. Magoun, Jr.* Ed. Jess B. Bessinger, Jr., and Robert P. Creed. New York: New York University Press. Pp. 75–85.
1970. "A Symbolic Word-Group in *Beowulf*." In *Medieval Literature and Folklore Studies*. Ed. Jerome Mandel and Bruce A. Rosenberg. New Brunswick, N.J.: Rutgers University Press. Pp. 27–34.
Catalán, Diego
1969. *Siete siglos de romancero*. Madrid: Editorial Gredos.
1970–71. "Memoria e invención en el Romancero de tradición oral." *Romance Philology*, 24:1–25, 441–63.
Chadwick, H.M. and N.K.

1932–40. *The Growth of Literature*. 3 vols. Cambridge: Cambridge University Press, rpt. 1968.
Chantraine, Pierre.
1929. [Review of Parry 1928a, b]. *Revue de philologie*, 55:294–300.
1932. "Remarques sur l'emploi des formules dans le premier chant de l'Iliade." *Revue des études grecques*, 45:121–54.
1940–48. "La Langue poétique et traditionnelle d'Homère." *Conférences de l'Institut de Linguistique de l'Université de Paris*, 8:33–44.
1948. "La Langue d'Iliade." In Paul Mazon, *Introduction à l'Iliade*. Paris: Société d'Edition "Les Belles Lettres." Pp. 89–123.
Charitius, Franz
1879. "Über die angelsächsischen Gedichte vom hl. Guthlac." *Anglia*, 2:265–308.
Clader, Linda L.
1976. *Helen: The Evolution from Divine to Heroic in Greek Epic Tradition*. Leiden: E.J. Brill.
Clanchy, M.T.
1979. *From Memory to Written Record: England, 1066–1307*. Cambridge, Mass.: Harvard University Press.
Clark, George
1965a. "Beowulf's Armor." *English Literary History*, 32:409–41.
1965b. "The Traveler Recognizes His Goal: A Theme in Anglo-Saxon Poetry." *Journal of English and Germanic Philology*, 64:645–59.
Clarke, Howard
1981. *Homer's Readers: A Historical Introduction to the Iliad and the Odyssey*. Newark: University of Delaware Press.
Claus, David B.
1975. "*Aidôs* in the Language of Achilles." *Transactions of the American Philological Association*, 105:13–28.
Clayman, Dee L., and Thomas van Nortwick
1977. "Enjambement in Greek Hexameter Poetry." *Transactions of the American Philological Association*, 107:85–92.
Clunies Ross, Margaret
1986. "Australian Aboriginal Oral Traditions." *Oral Tradition*, 1:231–71.
Collingwood, R.G.
1913. Trans., *The Philosophy of Giambattista Vico*, by B. Croce. London: Macmillan.
Combellack, Frederick M.
1950. "Contemporary Unitarians and Homeric Originality." *American Journal of Philology*, 71:337–64.
1959. "Milman Parry and Homeric Artistry." *Comparative Literature*, 11:193–208.
1965. "Some Formulary Illogicalities in Homer." *Transactions of the American Philological Association*, 96:41–56.
1976. "Homer the Innovator." *Classical Philology*, 71:44–55.
Comparetti, Domenico
1898. *The Traditional Poetry of the Finns*. Trans. by Isabella M. Anderton, with intro. by Andrew Lang. London and New York: Longmans, Green, and Co.
Connelly, Bridget
1973. "The Structure of Four Bani Hilal Tales: Prolegomena to the Study of *Sira* Literature." *Journal of Arabic Literature*, 4:18–47.
1986. *Arab Folk Epic and Identity*. Berkeley: University of California Press.
Conroy, Patricia
1978. Ed., *Ballads and Ballad Research*. Seattle: University of Washington Press.
1980. "Oral Composition in Faroese Ballads." *Jahrbuch für Volksliedforschung*, 25:34–50.
Coote, Mary P.
1974. "Yugoslavia: Bibliographical Spectrum." In *The Multinational Literature of*

Yugoslavia. Ed. Albert B. Lord. New York: St. John's University [= *Review of National Literatures*, 5, i]. Pp. 127–40.

1977. "Women's Songs in Serbo-Croatian." *Journal of American Folklore*, 90:331–38.

1978. "Serbo-Croatian Heroic Songs." In Oinas 1978a:257–85.

1980. "The Singer's Themes in Serbocroatian Heroic Song." *California Slavic Studies*, 11:201–35.

1981. "Lying in Passages." *Canadian-American Slavic Studies*, 15:5–23.

Coote, Robert B.

1976. "The Application of the Oral Theory to Biblical Hebrew Literature." In Culley 1976a:51–64.

Creed, Robert P.

1955. "Studies in the Techniques of Composition of the *Beowulf* Poetry in British Museum MS. Cotton Vitellius A. xv." Ph.D. diss. (Harvard University).

1956. "*Beowulf* 2231a: *sinc-fæt (sōhte)*." *Philological Quarterly*, 35:206–8.

1957. "The *andswarode*-System in Old English Poetry." *Speculum*, 32:523–28.

1958. "*Genesis* 1316." *Modern Language Notes*, 73:321–25.

1959. "The Making of an Anglo-Saxon Poem." *English Literary History*, 26:445–54. Rpt. with "Additional Remarks" in Donald K. Fry, Jr., ed. *The Beowulf Poet.* Englewood Cliffs, N.J.:Prentice-Hall, 1968. Pp. 141–53.

1961. "On the Possibility of Criticizing Old English Poetry." *Texas Studies in Literature and Language*, 3:97–106.

1962. "The Singer Looks at His Sources." *Comparative Literature*, 14:44–52.

1981a. "The *Beowulf*-Poet: Master of Sound-Patterning." In Foley 1981a:194–216.

1981b. "Sound-Patterning in Some Sung and Dictated Performances of Avdo Medjedović." *Canadian-American Slavic Studies*, 15:116–21.

1986. "The Remaking of *Beowulf.*" In Foley 1986d:136–46.

Crosby, Ruth

1936. "Oral Delivery in the Middle Ages." *Speculum*, 11:88–110.

1938. "Chaucer and the Custom of Oral Delivery." *Speculum*, 13:413–32.

Cross, Frank M.

1973. *Canaanite Myth and Hebrew Epic: Essays in the History of the Religion of Israel.* Cambridge, Mass.: Harvard University Press.

1974. "Prose and Poetry in the Mythic and Epic Texts from Ugarit." *Harvard Theological Review*, 67:1–15.

Crowne, David K.

1960. "The Hero on the Beach: An Example of Composition by Theme in Anglo-Saxon Poetry." *Neuphilologische Mitteilungen*, 61:362–72.

Culley, Robert C.

1963. "An Approach to the Problem of Oral Tradition." *Vetus Testamentum*, 13:113–25.

1967. *Oral Formulaic Language in the Biblical Psalms.* Toronto: University of Toronto Press.

1976a. Ed., *Oral Tradition and Old Testament Studies.* A special issue of *Semeia*, 5, i.

1976b. *Studies in the Structure of Hebrew Narrative.* Missoula, Mont., and Philadelphia: Scholars Press and Fortress Press.

1986. "Oral Tradition and Biblical Studies." *Oral Tradition*, 1:30–65.

Curschmann, Michael

1966. "Spielmannsepik: Wege und Ergebnisse der Forschung von 1907–1965." *Deutsche Vierteljahresschrift für Literaturwissenschaft und Geistesgeschichte*, 40:434–78, 597–647.

1967. "Oral Poetry in Mediaeval English, French, and German Literature: Some Notes on Recent Research." *Speculum*, 42:36–52.

1968. *Spielmannsepik: Wege und Ergebnisse der Forschung von 1907–1965, mit Ergänzungen und Nachträgen bis 1967 (Überlieferung und Mündliche Kompositionsform)*. Stuttgart: J.B. Metzler.

1977. "The Concept of the Oral Formula as an Impediment to Our Understanding of Medieval Oral Poetry." *Medievalia et Humanistica*, n.s. 8:63–76.

1979. " 'Nibelungenlied' und 'Nibelungenklage': Über Mündlichkeit und Schriftlichkeit im Prozess der Episierung." In *Deutsche Literatur im Mittelalter—Kontakte und Perspektiven: Hugo Kuhn zum Gedenken*. Ed. Christoph Cormeau. Stuttgart: J.B. Metzler. Pp. 85–119.

Dane, Joseph A.

1982. "Finnsburh and *Iliad* IX: A Greek Survival of the Medieval Germanic Oral-Formulaic Theme, The Hero on the Beach." *Neophilologus*, 66:443–49.

Darmesteter, James

1888–90. *Chants populaires des Afghans*. Collection d'ouvrages orientaux, 2 sér. Paris: Ernest Leroux.

Davison, J.A.

1954. "Die homerische Gedichte und die vergleichende Literaturforschung des Abendlandes." *Gymnasium*, 61:28–36.

1962a. "The Homeric Question." In *A Companion to Homer*. Ed. Alan J.B. Wace and Frank H. Stubbings. London: Macmillan. Pp. 234–65.

1962b. "The Transmission of the Text." In *A Companion to Homer*. Pp. 215–33.

de Chasca, Edmund V.

1955. *Estructura y forma en "El Poema de Mío Cid" (hacia una explicación de la imitación poética de la historia en la epopeya castellana)*. Iowa City and Mexico: State University of Iowa Press and Editorial Patria.

1966–67. "Composición escrita y oral en el *Poema del Cid*." *Filología*, 12:77–94.

1968. *Registro de fórmulas verbales en el "Cantar de Mío Cid."* Iowa City: State University of Iowa Press.

1970. "Toward a Redefinition of Epic Formula in the Light of the *Cantar de Mio Cid*." *Hispanic Review*, 38:251–63.

1976. *The Poem of the Cid*. Boston: G.K. Hall.

De Lavan, Joanne

1981. "Feasts and Anti-Feasts in *Beowulf* and the *Odyssey*." In Foley 1981a:235–61.

Delbouille, Maurice

1959. "Les Chansons de geste et le livre." In *La Technique littéraire des chansons de geste: Actes du Colloque de Liège (septembre 1957)*. Ed. Maurice Delbouille. Paris: Société d'Edition "Les Belles Lettres." Pp. 295–407.

1961. "Chansons de geste et chants héroiques yougoslaves." In *Atti del 2° Congresso Internazionale della "Société Rencesvals."* *Cultura Neolatina*, 21:97–104.

1965–66. "Le Chant héroique serbo-croate et la genèse de la chanson de geste." *Boletín de la Real Academia de Buenas Letras de Barcelona*, 31:83–98.

Deyermond, Alan D.

1965. "The Singer of Tales and Mediaeval Spanish Epic." *Bulletin of Hispanic Studies*, 42:1–8.

1968. *Epic Poetry and the Clergy: Studies on the Mocedades de Rodrigo*. London: Tamesis.

1973. "Structural and Stylistic Patterns in the *Cantar de Mio Cid*." In *Medieval Studies in Honor of Robert White Linker*. Ed. Brian Dutton et al. Madrid: Editorial Castalia. Pp. 55–71.

1977. "Tendencies in 'Mio Cid' Scholarship, 1943–1973." In *Mio Cid Studies*. Ed. Alan D. Deyermond. London: Tamesis. Pp. 13–47.

Diamond, Robert E.

1958. "Heroic Diction in *The Dream of the Rood*." In *Studies in Honor of John Wilcox*.

Ed. A. Doyle Wallace and Woodburn O. Ross. Detroit: Wayne State University Press. Pp. 3–7.
1959. "The Diction of the Signed Poems of Cynewulf." *Philological Quarterly*, 38:228–41.
1961. "Theme as Ornament in Anglo-Saxon Poetry." *Publications of the Modern Language Association*, 76:461–68.
1963. *The Diction of the Anglo-Saxon Metrical Psalms*. The Hague: Mouton.
1975. "The Diction of the Old English *Christ*." In *Anglo-Saxon Poetry: Essays in Appreciation for John C. McGalliard*. Ed. Lewis E. Nicholson and Dolores W. Frese. Notre Dame, Ind.: University of Notre Dame Press. Pp. 301–11.

Dimock, George E.
1963. "From Homer to Novi Pazar and Back." *Arion*, 2, iv:40–57.

Dirlmeier, Franz
1971. *Das serbokroatische Heldenlied und Homer*. Heidelberg: Carl Winter.

Donlan, Walter
1971. "Homer's Agamemnon." *Classical World*, 65:109–15.

Dozon, Auguste
1888. Trans., *L'Epopée serbe: Chants populaires héroiques*. Paris: Ernest Leroux.

Duban, Jeffrey M.
1981. "Les Duels majeurs de l'Iliade et le langage d'Hector." *Les Etudes classiques*, 49:97–124.

Düntzer, Heinrich
1864. "Über den Einfluss des Metrums auf den homerischen Ausdruck." *Jahrbücher für classische Philologie*, 10:673–94. Rpt. in his *Homerische Abhandlungen*. Leipzig: Hahn'sche Verlagsbuchhandlung, 1872, pp. 517–49, and in Latacz 1979a:88–108.
1872. "Zur Beurtheilung der stehenden homerischen Beiwörter." In his *Homerische Abhandlungen*. Leipzig: Hahn'sche Verlagsbuchhandlung, pp. 507–16. [Orig. pub. in *Verhandlungen der einundzwanzigsten Philologenversammlung*, pp. 102–7].

Duggan, Joseph J.
1966. "Formulas in the *Couronnement de Louis*." *Romania*, 87:315–44.
1973. *The Song of Roland: Formulaic Style and Poetic Craft*. Berkeley: University of California Press.
1974a. Ed., A special issue of *Forum for Modern Language Studies*, 10, iii [= *Oral Literature: Seven Essays*. Edinburgh and New York: Scottish Academic Press and Barnes & Noble].
1974b. "Formulaic Diction in the *Cantar de Mio Cid* and the Old French Epic." In Duggan 1974a:74–83.
1981a "La Théorie de la composition orale des chansons de geste: Les faits et les interprétations." *Olifant*, 8, iii:238–55.
1981b. "Le Mode de composition des chansons de geste: Analyse statistique, jugement esthétique, modèles de transmission." *Olifant*, 8, iii:286–316.
1986. "Social Functions of the Medieval Epic in the Romance Literatures" [The Milman Parry Lectures on Oral Tradition for 1986]. *Oral Tradition*, 1:728–66.

Dukat, Zdeslav
1976. "Parry, Propp, and Literary Studies." *Živa antika*, 26:149–59.
1978. "Vrijednost komparativne metode u homerologiji." *Živa antika*, 28:171–78.

Dundes, Alan et al.
1972. With Jerry W. Leach and Bora Özkök. "The Strategy of Turkish Boys' Verbal Dueling Rhymes." In *Directions in Sociolinguistics: The Ethnography of Communication*. Ed. John J. Gumperz and Dell Hymes. New York: Holt, Rinehart, and Winston. Pp. 130–60.

Edwards, G. Patrick
1971. *The Language of Hesiod in Its Traditional Context.* Oxford: Basil Blackwell.
Edwards, Mark W.
1966. "Some Features of Homeric Craftsmanship." *Transactions of the American Philological Association,* 97:115–79.
1968. "Some Stylistic Notes on *Iliad* XVIII." *American Journal of Philology,* 89:257–83.
1969. "On Some 'Answering' Expressions in Homer." *Classical Philology,* 64:81–87.
1970. "Homeric Speech Introductions." *Harvard Studies in Classical Philology,* 74:1–36.
1975. "Type-Scenes and Homeric Hospitality." *Transactions of the American Philological Association,* 105:51–72.
1980a. "Convention and Individuality in *Iliad* 1." *Harvard Studies in Classical Philology,* 84:1–28.
1980b. "The Structure of Homeric Catalogues." *Transactions of the American Philological Association,* 110:81–105.
1986. "Homer and Oral Tradition: The Formula, Part I." *Oral Tradition,* 1:171–230.
1987. "Homer and Oral Tradition: The Formula, Part II." *Oral Tradition,* 2, iii: forthcoming.
Ellendt, Johann Ernst
1861. *Über den Einfluss des Metrums auf den Gebrauch von Wortformen und Wortverbindungen.* Königsberg: Programm Altstädtisches Gymnasium. Rpt. in his *Drei homerische Abhandlungen.* Leipzig: B.G. Teubner, 1864, pp. 6–34, and in Latacz 1979a:60–87.
Emeneau, Murray B.
1958. "Oral Poets of South India—The Todas." *Journal of American Folklore,* 71:312–24.
1966. "Style and Meaning in an Oral Literature." *Language,* 42:323–45.
1971. Ed., *Toda Songs.* Oxford: Clarendon Press.
1974. *Ritual Structure and Language Structure of the Todas.* Philadelphia: American Philosophical Society.
Evans, David
1982. *Big Road Blues: Tradition and Creativity in the Folk Blues.* Berkeley: University of California Press.
Faulhaber, Charles B.
1976. "Neo-traditionalism, Formulism, Individualism, and Recent Studies on the Spanish Epic." *Romance Philology,* 30:83–101.
Fenik, Bernard C.
1968. *Typical Battle Scenes in the Iliad: Studies in the Narrative Techniques of Homeric Battle Description.* Hermes Einzelschriften, 21. Wiesbaden: F. Steiner.
1974. *Studies in the Odyssey.* Hermes Einzelschriften, 30. Wiesbaden: F. Steiner.
1978a. Ed., *Homer: Tradition and Invention.* University of Cincinnati Classical Studies, n.s. 2. Leiden: E.J. Brill.
1978b. "Stylization and Variety: Four Monologues in the *Iliad.*" In Fenik 1978a:68–90.
1986. *Homer and the Nibelungenlied: Comparative Studies in Epic Style.* Cambridge, Mass.: Harvard University Press.
Finnegan, Ruth
1967. Comp. and trans., *Limba Stories and Story-Telling.* Oxford: Clarendon Press.
1970. *Oral Literature in Africa.* Oxford: Clarendon Press.
1976. "What Is Oral Literature Anyway? Comments in the Light of Some African and Other Comparative Material." In Stolz and Shannon 1976:127–66.

1977. *Oral Poetry: Its Nature, Significance, and Social Context.* Cambridge: Cambridge University Press.

Firestone, Ruth H.

1975. *Elements of Traditional Structure in the Couplet Epics of the Late Middle High German Dietrich Cycle.* Göppingen: A. Kümmerle.

Foley, John Miles

1976. "Formula and Theme in Old English Poetry." In Stolz and Shannon 1976:207–32.

1977a. "The Traditional Oral Audience." *Balkan Studies,* 18:145–54.

1977b. "Research on Oral Traditional Expression in Šumadija and Its Relevance to the Study of Other Oral Traditions." In *Selected Papers on a Serbian Village.* Ed. Barbara Kerewsky-Halpern and Joel M. Halpern. Amherst: University of Massachusetts Anthropology Department. Pp. 199–236.

1978a. "The Traditional Structure of Ibro Bašić's 'Alagić Alija and Velagić Selim'." *Slavic and East European Journal,* 22:1–14.

1978b. "The Oral Singer in Context: Halil Bajgorić, *Guslar.*" *Canadian-American Slavic Studies,* 12:230–46.

1978c. "A Computer Analysis of Metrical Patterns in *Beowulf.*" *Computers and the Humanities,* 12:71–80.

1978d. "Education before Letters: Oral Epic Paideia." *Denver Quarterly,* 13:94–117.

1979. "Epic and Charm in Old English and Serbo-Croatian Oral Poetry." *Comparative Criticism,* 2:71–92.

1980. "*Beowulf* and Traditional Narrative Song: The Potential and Limits of Comparison." In *Old English Literature in Context: Ten Essays.* Ed. John D. Niles. London and Totowa, N.J.: D.S. Brewer and Rowman & Littlefield. Pp. 117–36, 173–78.

1981a. Ed., *Oral Traditional Literature: A Festschrift for Albert Bates Lord.* Columbus, Ohio: Slavica, rpt. 1983.

1981b. "Introduction: The Oral Theory in Context." In Foley 1981a:27–122.

1981c. "Tradition-dependent and -independent Features in Oral Literature: A Comparative View of the Formula." In Foley 1981a:262–81.

1981d. "Oral Texts, Traditional Texts: Poetics and Critical Methods." *Canadian-American Slavic Studies,* 15:122–45.

1982. "Field Research on Oral Literature and Culture in Serbia." In *Oral and Traditional Literature,* a special issue of *Pacific Quarterly Moana,* 7, ii:47–59.

1983. "Literary Art and Oral Tradition in Old English and Serbian Poetry." *Anglo-Saxon England,* 12:183–214.

1985. *Oral-Formulaic Theory and Research: An Introduction and Annotated Bibliography.* New York: Garland, rpt. 1986.

1986a. "Tradition and the Collective Talent: Oral Epic, Textual Meaning, and Receptionalist Theory." *Cultural Anthropology,* 1:203–22.

1986b. Ed., *Current Issues in Oral Literature Research: A Memorial for Milman Parry.* Columbus, Ohio: Slavica.

1986c. "Reading the Oral Traditional Text: Aesthetics of Creation and Response." In Foley 1986b:185–212.

1986d. Ed., *Oral Tradition in Literature: Interpretation in Context.* Columbia: University of Missouri Press.

1988. Ed., *Orality and Literacy: Modern Critical Methods.* Hamden, Conn.: Archon Books.

1989. *Matija Murko and South Slavic Oral Epic Tradition: A Translation of His Major Writings with Commentary.* Irvine, Calif.: Charles Schlacks.

Fournier, H.

1946. "Formules homériques de références avec verbe 'dire'." *Revue de philologie, de littérature, et d'histoire anciennes,* 3 sér., 22:29–68.

Frame, Douglas
  1978. *The Myth of Return in Early Greek Epic.* New Haven, Conn.: Yale University
    Press.
Friedman, Albert B.
  1961. "The Formulaic Improvisation Theory of Ballad Tradition—A Counter-
    statement." *Journal of American Folklore,* 74:113–15.
  1983. "The Oral-Formulaic Theory of Balladry—A Re-rebuttal." In *The Ballad
    Image: Essays Presented to Bertrand Harris Bronson.* Ed. James Porter. Los An-
    geles: Center for the Study of Comparative Folklore and Mythology, Uni-
    versity of California Los Angeles. Pp. 215–40.
Friedrich, Paul, and James Redfield
  1978. "Speech as Personality Symbol: The Case of Achilles." *Language,* 54:263–
    88.
  1981. "Contra Messing." *Language,* 57:901–3.
Fritz, Donald W.
  1969. "Cædmon: A Traditional Christian Poet." *Mediaeval Studies,* 31:334–37.
Fry, Donald K., Jr.
  1966. "The Hero on the Beach in *Finnsburh.*" *Neuphilologische Mitteilungen,* 67:27–
    31.
  1967a. "The Heroine on the Beach in *Judith.*" *Neuphilologische Mitteilungen,*
    68:168–84.
  1967b. "Old English Formulas and Systems." *English Studies,* 48:193–204.
  1968. "Old English Formulaic Themes and Type-Scenes." *Neophilologus,* 52:48–
    54.
  1974. "Cædmon as a Formulaic Poet." *Forum for Modern Language Studies* [=
    Oral Literature: Seven Essays, ed. Joseph J. Duggan. Edinburgh and Totowa,
    N.J.: Scottish Academic Press and Rowman & Littlefield, 1975]. Pp. 41–61.
  1979. "Old English Formulaic Statistics." *In Geardagum,* 3:1–6.
  1981. "The Memory of Cædmon." In Foley 1981a:282–93.
Gaisser, Julia H.
  1969a. "Adaptation of Traditional Material in the Glaucus-Diomedes Episode."
    Transactions of the American Philological Association, 100:165–76.
  1969b. "A Structural Analysis of the Digressions in the *Iliad* and the *Odyssey.*"
    Harvard Studies in Classical Philology, 73:1–43.
Gardner, Thomas
  1973. "How Free Was the *Beowulf* Poet?" *Modern Philology,* 71:111–27.
Gattiker, Godfrey
  1962. "The Syntactic Basis of the Poetic Formula in *Beowulf.*" Ph.D. diss. (Uni-
    versity of Wisconsin).
Geary, John S.
  1980. *Formulaic Diction in the* Poema de Fernán González *and the* Mocedades de
    Rodrigo: *A Computer-Aided Analysis.* Madrid: José Porrúa Turanzas.
Gerhardsson, Birger
  1961. *Memory and Manuscript: Oral Tradition and Written Transmission in Rabbinic
    Judaism and Early Christianity.* Lund: C.W.K. Gleerup.
  1979. *[Evangeliernas förhistoria] The Origins of the Gospel Tradition.* Philadelphia:
    Fortress Press.
Gesemann, Gerhard
  1926. *Studien zur südslavischen Volksepik.* Veröffentlichungen der Slavistischen Ar-
    beitsgemeinschaft (Prague), I. Reihe: Untersuchungen, Heft 3. Reichen-
    berg: Verlag Gebrüder Stiepel.
Goody, John R.
  1968. Ed., *Literacy in Traditional Societies.* Cambridge: Cambridge University Press.
  1977. *The Domestication of the Savage Mind.* Cambridge: Cambridge University
    Press.

Görög, Veronika
1968–72. "Bibliographie analytique sélective sur la littérature orale d'Afrique noire." *Cahiers d'études africaines*, 8:453–501, 9:641–66, 10:583–631, 12:174–92.
1981. *Littérature orale d'Afrique noire: Bibliographie analytique*. Paris: G.-P. Maisonneuve et Larose.
Green, Donald C.
1971. "Formulas and Syntax in Old English Poetry: A Computer Study." *Computers and the Humanities*, 6:85–93.
Greenfield, Stanley B.
1953a. "The Theme of Spiritual Exile in *Christ I.*" *Philological Quarterly*, 32:321–28.
1953b. *"The Wife's Lament* Reconsidered." *Publications of the Modern Language Association*, 68:907–12.
1955. "The Formulaic Expression of the Theme of 'Exile' in Anglo-Saxon Poetry." *Speculum*, 30:200–206.
1963. "Syntactic Analysis and Old English Poetry." *Neuphilologische Mitteilungen*, 64:373–78.
1967a. "The Canons of Old English Criticism." *English Literary History*, 34:141–55.
1967b. "Grendel's Approach to Heorot: Syntax and Poetry." In *Old English Poetry: Fifteen Essays*. Ed. Robert P. Creed. Providence, R.I.: Brown University Press. Pp. 275–84.
Grobman, Neil R.
1974. "Adam Ferguson's Influence on Folklore Research: The Analysis of Mythology and the Oral Epic." *Southern Folklore Quarterly*, 38:11–22.
1979. "Thomas Blackwell's Commentary on the Oral Nature of Epic." *Western Folklore*, 38:186–98.
Gunn, David M.
1970. "Narrative Inconsistency and the Oral Dictated Text in the Homeric Epic." *American Journal of Philology*, 91:192–203.
1971. "Thematic Composition and Homeric Authorship." *Harvard Studies in Classical Philology*, 75:1–31.
1974a. "Narrative Patterns and Oral Tradition in Judges and Samuel." *Vetus Testamentum*, 24:286–317.
1974b. "The 'Battle Report': Oral or Scribal Convention?" *Journal of Biblical Literature*, 93:513–18.
1976a. "Traditional Composition in the 'Succession Narrative'." *Vetus Testamentum*, 26:214–29.
1976b. "On Oral Tradition: A Response to John Van Seters." In Culley 1976a:155–63.
Gushee, Lawrence
1981. "Lester Young's 'Shoeshine Boy'." In Treitler et al. 1981:151–69.
Hainsworth, J.B.
1964. "Structure and Content in Epic Formulae: The Question of the Unique Expression." *Classical Quarterly*, 14:155–64.
1968. *The Flexibility of the Homeric Formula*. Oxford: Clarendon Press.
1970. "The Criticism of an Oral Homer." *Journal of Hellenic Studies*, 90:90–98.
1976. "Phrase-Clusters in Homer." In *Studies in Greek, Italic, and Indo-European Linguistics Offered to Leonard R. Palmer on the Occasion of His Seventieth Birthday, June 5, 1976*. Ed. Anna M. Davies and Wolfgang Meid. Vienna: Ernst Becvar. Pp. 83–86.
1978. "Good and Bad Formulae." In Fenik 1978a:41–50.
Hamori, Andras

1969. "Examples of Convention in the Poetry of Abū Nuwās."*Studia Islamica*, 30:5–26.

1974. *On the Art of Medieval Arabic Literature*. Princeton, N.J.: Princeton University Press.

Hanoteau, Adolphe

1867. *Poésies populaires de la Kabylie du Jurjura: Texte Kabyle et traductions*. Paris: Imprimerie Impériale.

Hansen, William F.

1972. *The Conference Sequence: Patterned Narration and Narrative Inconsistency in the Odyssey*. Berkeley: University of California Press.

Harris, Joseph

1979. "The *senna*: From Description to Literary Theory."*Michigan Germanic Studies*, 5:65–74.

1980. "Satire and the Heroic Life: Two Studies (*Helgakviða Hundingsbana*, I, 18 and Bjorn Hítdoelakappi's *Grámagaflím*). In Foley 1981a:322–40.

1983. "Eddic Poetry as Oral Poetry: The Evidence of Parallel Passages in the Helgi Poems for Questions of Composition and Performance." In *Edda: A Collection of Essays*. Ed. Robert J. Glendinning and Haraldur Bessason. Manitoba: University of Manitoba Press. Pp. 210–42.

1986. "Eddic Poetry." In *Old Norse-Icelandic Literature: A Critical Guide*. Ed. Carol J. Clover and John Lindow. Ithaca, N.Y.: Cornell University Press. Pp. 68–156.

Harvey, L.P.

1974. "Oral Composition and the Performance of Novels of Chivalry in Spain." In Duggan 1974a:84–100.

Havelock, Eric A.

1963. *Preface to Plato*. Cambridge, Mass.: Harvard University Press, rpt. 1982.

1982. *The Literate Revolution in Greece and Its Cultural Consequences*. Princeton, N.J.: Princeton University Press.

1983. "The Linguistic Task of the Presocratics." In *Language and Thought in Early Greek Philosophy*. Ed. Kevin Robb. La Salle, Ill.: The Hegeler Institute. Pp. 7–82.

1986. "The Alphabetic Mind: A Gift of Greece to the Modern World." *Oral Tradition*, 1:134–50.

1987. "The Cosmic Myths of Homer and Hesiod." In *A Festschrift for Walter J. Ong, S.J.*, a special issue of *Oral Tradition*, 2, i:31–53.

1978. Ed. with Jackson P. Hershbell. *Communication Arts in the Ancient World*. New York: Hastings House.

Haymes, Edward R.

1970. *Mündliches Epos in mittelhochdeutscher Zeit*. Erlangen: Palm und Ecke. Reissued with new foreword, Göppingen: A. Kümmerle, 1975.

1976. "Oral Poetry and the Germanic *Heldenlied*." *Rice University Studies*, 62, ii:47–54.

1977. *Das mündliche Epos: Eine Einführung in die "Oral Poetry" Forschung*. Stuttgart: J.B. Metzler.

1980a. "Oral Composition in Middle High German Epic Poetry." In Foley 1981a:341–46.

1980b. "Formulaic Density and Bishop Njegoš." *Comparative Literature*, 32:390–401.

1986. *The Nibelungenlied: History and Interpretation*. Urbana: University of Illinois Press.

Heitsch, Ernst

1968. *Epische Kunstsprache und homerische Chronologie*. Heidelberg: Carl Winter.

Henige, David P.

1974. *The Chronology of Oral Tradition: Quest for a Chimera.* Oxford: Clarendon Press.

Hermann, Gottfried
1840 (1877). "De Iteratis apud Homerum." In *Godofredi Hermanni Opuscula,* vol. 8. Ed. Theodorus Fritzsche. Lipsia: E. Fleischer and Theodorus Fritzsche, 1877. Pp. 11–23. [Orig. pub. as Leipzig dissertation, 1840.] Trans. into German in Latacz 1979a:47–59.

Heubeck, Alfred
1974. *Die homerische Frage: Ein Bericht über die Forschung der letzten Jahrzehnte.* Erträge der Forschung, 27. Darmstadt: Wissenschaftliche Buchgesellschaft.
1978. "Homeric Studies Today: Results and Prospects." In Fenik 1978a:1–17.

Hillers, Delbert R., and Marsh H. McCall, Jr.
1976. "Homeric Dictated Texts: A Reexamination of Some Near Eastern Evidence." *Harvard Studies in Classical Philology,* 80:19–23.

Hoekstra, A.
1957. "Hésiode et la tradition orale: Contribution à l'étude du style formulaire." *Mnemosyne,* 4th ser., 10:193–225.
1964. *Homeric Modifications of Formulaic Prototypes: Studies in the Development of Greek Epic Diction.* Amsterdam: Noord-Hollandsche Uitgevers Maatschappij, rpt. 1969.
1969. *The Sub-Epic Stage of the Formulaic Tradition: Studies in the Homeric Hymns to Apollo, to Aphrodite, and to Demeter.* Amsterdam: Noord-Hollandsche Uitgevers Maatschappij.
1978. "Metrical Lengthening and Epic Diction." *Mnemosyne,* 4th ser., 31:1–26.

Hoelscher, Uvo
1978. "The Transformation from Folk-Tale to Epic." In Fenik 1978a:51–67.

Hoenigswald, Henry
1976. "Summary." In Stolz and Shannon 1976:273–78.

Hoffman, Elizabeth A.
1986. "Exploring the Literate Blindspot: Alexander Pope's *Homer* in Light of Milman Parry." *Oral Tradition,* 1:381–97.

Hogan, James C.
1976. "Double πρίν and the Language of Achilles." *Classical Journal,* 71:305–10.

Holoka, James P.
1973. "Homeric Originality: A Survey." *Classical World,* 66:257–93.
1976. "The Oral Formula and Anglo-Saxon Elegy: Some Misgivings." *Neophilologus,* 60:570–76.

Hyart, Charles
1965. "Srpske narodne pesme i chansons de geste." *Narodno stvaralaštvo folklor,* 13–14:1008–16.
1968. "Les Groupements de vers dans les pesme yougoslaves et les chansons de geste françaises." In *Communications présentées par les slavisants de Belgique au VIe Congrès International de Slavistique (Prague—Août 1968).* Brussels: Ministère de l'Education Nationale et de la Culture. Pp. 21–65.

Immisch, O.
1904. *Die innere Entwicklung des griechischen Epos.* Leipzig: B.G. Teubner.

Ingalls, Wayne B.
1970. "The Structure of the Homeric Hexameter: A Review." *Phoenix,* 24:1–12.
1972. "Another Dimension of the Homeric Formula." *Phoenix,* 26:111–22.
1976. "The Analogical Formula in Homer." *Transactions of the American Philological Association,* 106:211–26.
1979. "Formular Density in the Similes of the *Iliad.*" *Transactions of the American Philological Association,* 109:87–109.
1982. "Linguistic and Formular Innovation in the Mythological Digressions in the *Iliad.*" *Phoenix,* 36:201–8.

Jacobsen, Thorkild
  1982. "Oral to Written." In *Societies and Languages of the Ancient Near East: Studies in Honor of I.M. Diakonoff.* Ed. M.A. Dandamayev et al. Warminster: Aris and Phillips. Pp. 129–37.
Janko, Richard
  1982. *Homer, Hesiod, and the Hymns: Diachronic Development in Epic Diction.* Cambridge: Cambridge University Press.
Jeffreys, Elizabeth and Michael
  1971. "*Imberios* and *Margarona*: The Manuscripts, Sources, and Edition of a Byzantine Verse Romance." *Byzantion*, 41:122–60.
  1979. "The Traditional Style of Early Demotic Verse." *Byzantine and Modern Greek Studies*, 5:115–39.
  1983. *Popular Literature in Late Byzantium.* London: Variorum Reprints.
  1986. "The Oral Background of Byzantine Popular Poetry." *Oral Tradition*, 1:504–47.
Jeffreys, Michael
  1973. "Formulas in the Chronicle of the Morea." *Dumbarton Oaks Papers*, 27:163–95.
Johnson, James D.
  1975. "The 'Hero on the Beach' in the Alliterative *Morte Arthure*." *Neuphilologische Mitteilungen*, 76:271–81.
  1983. "A Note on the Substitution of 'Door' for 'Beach' in a Formulaic Theme." *Neophilologus*, 67:596–98.
Johnson, John W.
  1979. Coll., trans., ed. with the assistance of Cheick Omar Mara et al. *The Epic of Sun-Jata according to Magan Sisòkò.* 2 vols. Bloomington: Indiana University Folklore Publications Group.
  1980. "Yes, Virginia, There Is an Epic in Africa." *Review of African Literatures*, 11:308–26.
  1986. *The Epic of Son-Jara: A West African Tradition.* Bloomington: Indiana University Press.
Jones, James H.
  1961. "Commonplace and Memorization in the Oral Tradition of the English and Scottish Popular Ballads." *Journal of American Folklore*, 74:97–112.
Jousse, Marcel
  1925. *Le Style oral rythmique et mnémotechnique chez les Verbo-moteurs.* Paris: Gabriel Beauchesne. [Orig. pub. in *Archives de philosophie*, 2 (1924): cahier IV.]
Kail, Johannes
  1889. "Über die Parallelstellen in der angelsächsischen Poesie." *Anglia*, 12:21–40.
Kailasapathy, K.
  1968. *Tamil Heroic Poetry.* Oxford: Clarendon Press.
Kavros, Harry E.
  1981. "*Swefan æfter symble*: The Feast-Sleep Theme in *Beowulf*." *Neophilologus*, 65:120–28.
Kelber, Werner H.
  1980. "Mark and Oral Tradition." *Semeia*, 16:7–55.
  1983. *The Oral and the Written Gospel: The Hermeneutics of Speaking and Writing in the Synoptic Tradition, Mark, Paul, and Q.* Philadelphia: Fortress Press.
  1987. "The Authority of the Word in St. John's Gospel." In *A Festschrift for Walter J. Ong, S.J.,* a special issue of *Oral Tradition*, 2, i:108–31.
Kellogg, Robert L.
  1965. "The South Germanic Oral Tradition." In *Franciplegius: Medieval and Linguistics Studies in Honor of Francis P. Magoun, Jr.* Ed. Jess B. Bessinger, Jr., and Robert P. Creed. New York: New York University Press. Pp. 66–74.

1974. "Oral Literature." *New Literary History*, 5:55–66.

1977. "Oral Narrative, Written Books." *Genre*, 10:655–65.

1979. "Varieties of Tradition in Medieval Literature." In *Medieval Narrative: A Symposium*. Ed. Hans Bekker-Nielsen et al. Odense: Odense University Press. Pp. 120–29.

Kerewsky-Halpern, Barbara

1981a. "Text and Context in Serbian Ritual Lament." *Canadian-American Slavic Studies*, 15:52–60.

1981b. "Genealogy as Genre in a Serbian Village." In Foley 1981a:301–21.

Kerewsky-Halpern, Barbara, and John Miles Foley

1978a. "The Power of the Word: Healing Charms as an Oral Genre." *Journal of American Folklore*, 91:903–24.

1978b. "*Bajanje*: Healing Magic in Rural Serbia." In *Culture and Curing*. Ed. Peter Morley and Roy Wallis. London and Pittsburgh: Peter Owen and University of Pittsburgh Press. Pp. 40–56.

Kettner, Emil

1897. *Die österreichische Nibelungendichtung: Untersuchungen über die Verfasser des Nibelungenliedes*. Berlin: Weidmann.

Kilson, Marion

1971. *Kpele Lala: Ga Religious Songs and Symbols*. Cambridge, Mass.: Harvard University Press.

Kiparsky, Paul

1976. "Oral Poetry: Some Linguistic and Typological Considerations." In Stolz and Shannon 1976:73–106.

Kirk, Geoffrey S.

1960. "Homer and Modern Oral Poetry: Some Confusions." *Classical Quarterly*, n.s. 10:271–81.

1962. *The Songs of Homer*. Cambridge: Cambridge University Press. Rpt. in abridged form as *Homer and the Epic*, 1965.

1964. Ed., *The Language and Background of Homer: Some Recent Studies and Controversies*. Cambridge and New York: Heffer and Barnes & Noble.

1966a. "Studies in Some Technical Aspects of Homeric Style." *Yale Classical Studies*, 20:76–152.

1966b. "Formular Language and Oral Quality." *Yale Classical Studies*, 20:155–74.

1970. *Myth: Its Meaning and Functions in Ancient and Other Cultures*. Cambridge and Berkeley: Cambridge University Press and University of California Press.

1972. "Homer: The Meaning of an Oral Tradition." Chapter 6 in *Literature and Western Civilization: The Classical World*. Ed. David Daiches and Anthony Thorlby. London: Aldus Books. Pp. 155–71.

1974. *The Nature of Greek Myths*. Harmondsworth: Penguin.

1976. *Homer and the Oral Tradition*. Cambridge: Cambridge University Press.

1978. "The Formal Duels in Books 3 and 7 of the *Iliad*." In Fenik 1978a:18–40.

Klinck, Anne L.

1983. "*Folces Hyrde* and ποιμένα/-ι λαῶν: A Generic Epithet in Old English and Homeric Verse." *Papers on Language and Literature*, 19:117–23.

Kolar, Walter W.

1976. Ed., *The Folk Arts of Yugoslavia*. Pittsburgh: Duquesne University Tamburitzans Institute of Folk Arts.

Koljević, Svetozar

1980. *The Epic in the Making*. Oxford: Clarendon Press.

Kolsti, John

1968. "Albanian Oral Epic Poetry." In *Studies Presented to Professor Roman Jakobson by His Students*. Ed. Charles E. Gribble. Cambridge, Mass.: Slavica. Pp. 165–67.

Krauss, Friedrich S.

1908. "Vom wunderbaren Guslarengedächtnis." In *Slavische Volksforschungen: Abhandlungen über Glauben, Gewohnheitrechte, Sitten, Bräuche und die Guslarenlieder der Südslaven.* Leipzig: Wilhelm Heims. Pp. 183–89.

Krischer, Tilman
1971. *Formale Konventionen der homerischen Epik.* Munich: C.H. Beck.

Krohn, Kaarle L.
1924–28. *Kalevalastudien.* 6 vols. Folklore Fellows Communications 53, 67, 71, 72, 75, 76. Helsinki: Suomalainen Tiedeakatemia.

Labov, William
1972. *Language in the Inner City: Studies in the Black English Vernacular.* Philadelphia: University of Pennsylvania Press. Rpt. Oxford: Basil Blackwell, 1977.

Lachmann, Karl
1837–41. *Betrachtungen über Homers Ilias.* Rpt. Berlin: G. Reimer, 1847.

Lang, Mabel L.
1969. "Homer and Oral Techniques." *Hesperia,* 38:159–68.
1984. *Herodotean Narrative and Discourse.* Cambridge, Mass.: Harvard University Press.

La Pin, Deirdre
1981. "Narrative as Precedent in Yorùbá Oral Tradition." In Foley 1981a:347–74.

Latacz, Joachim
1979a. Ed., *Homer: Tradition und Neuerung.* Wege der Forschung, 463. Darmstadt: Wissenschaftliche Buchgesellschaft.
1979b. "Spezialbibliographie zur Oral poetry-Theorie in der Homerforschung." In Latacz 1979a:573–618.
1979c. "Tradition und Neuerung in der Homerforschung: Zur Geschichte der Oral poetry-Theorie." In Latacz 1979a:25–44.

Lattimore, Richmond
1951. Introduction to his trans., *The Iliad of Homer.* Chicago: University of Chicago Press. Pp. 11–55.

Lawless, Elaine J.
1983. "Shouting for the Lord: The Power of Women's Speech in the Pentecostal Religious Service." *Journal of American Folklore,* 96:434–59.

Lawrence, R.F.
1966. "The Formulaic Theory and Its Application to English Alliterative Poetry." In *Essays on Style and Language.* Ed. Roger Fowler. London: Routledge and Kegan Paul. Pp. 166–83.

Lejeune, Rita
1954. "Technique formulaire et chansons de geste." *Le Moyen âge,* 60:311–34.

Lesky, Albin
1967. "Oral Poetry als Voraussetzung der homerischen Epen." In his *Homeros* (Sonderausgabe der Paulyschen Realencyclopädie der classischen Altertumswissenschaft). Stuttgart: Alfred Druckenmüller. Pp. 7–18.

Lockwood, Yvonne R.
1983. *Text and Context: Folksong in a Bosnian Muslim Village.* Columbus, Ohio: Slavica.

Lönnroth, Lars
1971. "Hjálmar's Death-Song and the Delivery of Eddic Poetry." *Speculum,* 46:1–20.
1979. "The Double Scene of Arrow-Odd's Drinking Contest." In *Medieval Narrative: A Symposium.* Ed. Hans Bekker-Nielsen et al. Odense: Odense University Press. Pp. 94–119.
1981. " Iorð fannz æva né upphiminn. A Formula Analysis." In *Speculum Norroenum: Norse Studies in Memory of Gabriel Turville-Petre.* Ed. Ursula Dronke et al. Odense: Odense University Press. Pp. 310–27.

Lohr, Charles H.
1961. "Oral Techniques in the Gospel of Matthew." *Catholic Biblical Quarterly*, 23:403–35.
Long, Eleanor R.
1973. "Ballad Singers, Ballad Makers, and Ballad Etiology." *Western Folklore*, 32:225–36.
Lord, Albert Bates
1936. "Homer and Huso I: The Singer's Rests in Greek and Southslavic Heroic Song." *Transactions of the American Philological Association*, 67:106–13.
1938. "Homer and Huso II: Narrative Inconsistencies in Homer and Oral Poetry." *Transactions of the American Philological Association*, 69:439–45.
1948a. "Homer and Huso III: Enjambement in Greek and Southslavic Heroic Song." *Transactions of the American Philological Association*, 79:113–24.
1948b. "Homer, Parry, and Huso." *American Journal of Archaeology*, 52:34–44.
1951a. "Composition by Theme in Homer and Southslavic Epos." *Transactions of the American Philological Association*, 82:71–80.
1951b. "Yugoslav Epic Folk Poetry." *International Folk Music Journal*, 3:57–61.
1953a. "Homer's Originality: Oral Dictated Texts." *Transactions of the American Philological Association*, 84:124–34.
1953b. "Opening Statement, Symposium IV, Fourth Session." In *Four Symposia on Folklore*. Ed. Stith Thompson. Bloomington: Indiana University Press. Pp. 305–11; discussion, pp. 311–23.
1954. "Notes on *Digenis Akritas* and Serbo-Croatian Epic." *Harvard Slavic Studies*, 2:375–83.
1956a. "Avdo Medjedović, Guslar." *Journal of American Folklore*, 69:320–30.
1956b. "The Role of Sound Patterns in Serbo-Croatian Epic." In *For Roman Jakobson*. The Hague: Mouton. Pp. 301–5.
1959. "The Poetics of Oral Creation." In *Comparative Literature: Proceedings of the Second Congress of the International Comparative Literature Association*. Ed. Werner P. Friedrich. Chapel Hill: University of North Carolina Press. Pp. 1–6.
1960. *The Singer of Tales*. Harvard Studies in Comparative Literature, 24. Cambridge, Mass.: Harvard University Press. Rpt. New York: Atheneum, 1968 et seq.
1962a. "Homeric Echoes in Bihać." *Zbornik za narodni život i običaje južnih slavena*, 40:313–20.
1962b. "Homer and Other Epic Poetry." In *A Companion to Homer*. Ed. Alan J.B. Wace and Frank H. Stubbings. London: Macmillan. Pp. 179–214.
1962c. "The Epic Singers." *Atlantic*, 210:126–27.
1965a. "Beowulf and Odysseus." In *Franciplegius: Medieval and Linguistics Studies in Honor of Francis P. Magoun, Jr*. Ed. Jess B. Bessinger, Jr., and Robert P. Creed. New York: New York University Press. Pp. 86–91.
1965b. "Oral Poetry." In *Princeton Encyclopedia of Poetry and Poetics*. Ed. A. Preminger. Princeton, N.J.: Princeton University Press. Pp. 591–93.
1967. "The Influence of a Fixed Text." In *To Honor Roman Jakobson: Essays on the Occasion of His Seventieth Birthday (11 October 1966)*. The Hague and Paris: Mouton. Vol. 2:1199–1206.
1968. "Homer as Oral Poet." *Harvard Studies in Classical Philology*, 72:1–46.
1969. "The Theme of the Withdrawn Hero in Serbo-Croatian Oral Epic." *Prilozi za književnost, jezik, istoriju i folklor*, 35:18–30.
1970. "Tradition and the Oral Poet: Homer, Huso, and Avdo Medjedović." In *Atti del Convegno Internazionale sul Tema: La Poesia epica e la sua formazione*. Ed. Enrico Cerulli et al. Rome: Accademia Nazionale dei Lincei. Pp. 29–30.
1971a. "An Example of Homeric Qualities of Repetition in Medjedović's 'Smailagić Meho'." In *Serta Slavica Aloisii Schmaus: Gedenkschrift für Alois Schmaus*. Ed. Wolfgang Gesemann et al. Munich: Rudolf Trofenik. Pp. 458–64.

1971b. "Homer, the Trojan War, and History." *Journal of the Folklore Institute*, 8:85–92.

1971c. "Some Common Themes in Balkan Slavic Epic." In *Actes du premier congrès international des études balkaniques et sud-est européennes*. Sofia: Editions de l'Académie Bulgare des Sciences. Pp. 653–62.

1972a. "The Effect of the Turkish Conquest on Balkan Epic Tradition." In *Aspects of the Balkans: Continuity and Change*. Ed. Henrik Birnbaum and Speros Vryonis, Jr. The Hague and Paris: Mouton. Pp. 298–318.

1972b. "History and Tradition in Balkan Oral Epic and Ballad." *Western Folklore*, 31:53–60.

1974a. Ed., *The Multinational Literature of Yugoslavia*. New York: St. John's University [= *Review of National Literatures*, 5, i].

1974b. "The Nineteenth-Century Revival of National Literatures: Karadžić, Njegoš, Radičević, the Illyrians, and Prešeren." In Lord 1974a:101–11.

1974c. "Perspectives on Recent Work on Oral Literature." In Duggan 1974a:1–24.

1976a. "The Traditional Song." In Stolz and Shannon 1976:1–15.

1976b. "Formula and Non-Narrative Theme in South Slavic Oral Epic and the OT." In Culley 1976a:93–105.

1976c. "The Heroic Tradition of Greek Epic and Ballad: Continuity and Change." In *Hellenism and the First Greek War of Liberation (1821–30): Continuity and Change*. Thessaloniki: Institute for Balkan Studies. Pp. 79–94.

1976d. "Studies in the Bulgarian Epic Tradition: Thematic Parallels." In *Bulgaria Past and Present: Studies in History, Literature, Economics, Music, Sociology, Folklore, and Linguistics*. Ed. Thomas Butler. Columbus, Ohio: American Association for the Advancement of Slavic Studies. Pp. 349–58.

1977. "Parallel Culture Traits in Ancient and Modern Greece." *Byzantine and Modern Greek Studies*, 3:71–80.

1978a. "The Gospels as Oral Traditional Literature." In *The Relationships among the Gospels: An Interdisciplinary Dialogue*. Ed. William O. Walker, Jr. San Antonio, Tex.: Trinity University Press. Pp. 33–91.

1978b. "Folklore, 'Folklorism,' and National Identity." *Balkanistica*, 3:63–73.

1979–80. "The Opening Scenes of the *Dumy* on Holota and Andyber: A Study in the Technique of Oral Traditional Narrative." *Harvard Ukrainian Studies*, 3–4:569–94.

1980a. "Interlocking Mythic Patterns in *Beowulf*." In *Old English Literature in Context: Ten Essays*. Ed. John D. Niles. London and Totowa, N.J.: D.S. Brewer and Rowman & Littlefield. Pp. 137–42, 178.

1980b. "The Mythic Component in Oral Traditional Epic: Its Origins and Significance." *Proceedings of the Comparative Literature Symposium*, 11:145–61.

1980c. "Memory, Meaning, and Myth in Homer and Other Oral Epic Traditions." In *Oralità*. Rome: Edizioni dell'Ateneo. Pp. 37–67.

1981a. "Memory, Fixity, and Genre in Oral Traditional Poetries." In Foley 1981a:451–61.

1981b. "Comparative Slavic Epic." *Harvard Ukrainian Studies*, 5:415–29.

1982. "Béla Bartók as a Collector of Folk Music." *Cross Currents*, 1:295–304.

1983. "Aspects of the Poetics of Bulgarian Oral Traditional Narrative Song." In *Literaturoznanie i folkloristika v čest na 70-godišninata na akademik Pet'r Dinekov*. Sofia: Bulgarska Akademija na Naukite. Pp. 353–59.

1984. "The Battle of Kosovo in Albanian and Serbocroatian Oral Epic Songs." In *Studies on Kosova*. Ed. Arshi Pipa and Sami Repishti. New York: Columbia University Press. Pp. 65–83.

1985. "Béla Bartók and Text Stanzas in Yugoslav Folk Music." In *Music and Context: Essays for John M. Ward*. Ed. Anne D. Shapiro. Cambridge, Mass.: Harvard University Department of Music. Pp. 385–403.

1986a. "The Merging of Two Worlds: Oral and Written Poetry as Carriers of Ancient Values." In Foley 1986d:19–64.

1986b. "Perspectives on Recent Work on the Oral Traditional Formula." *Oral Tradition*, 1:467–503.

1986c. "The Nature of Oral Poetry." In Foley 1986b:313–49.

1986d. "Words Heard and Words Seen." In *Oral Tradition and Literacy: Changing Visions of the World*. Ed. R.A. Whitaker and E.R. Sienaert. Durban, South Africa: Natal University Oral Documentation and Research Centre. Pp. 1–17.

1987. "Characteristics of Orality." In *A Festschrift for Walter J. Ong, S.J.*, a special issue of *Oral Tradition*, 2, i:54–72.

Forthcoming a. "The *Kalevala*, the South Slavic Epics, and Homer." *Béaloideas*.

Forthcoming b. "Central Asiatic and Balkan Epic." In the proceedings of a conference on "Central Asiatic Epic" in Bonn, West Germany, September 1985.

Forthcoming c. "Text, Tone, Tune, Rhythm, and Performance in South Slavic Sung Narrative." In the proceedings of a conference on "Text, Tune, and Tone" in New Delhi, India, December 29, 1986–January 1, 1987.

Lord, Albert Bates, and Béla Bartók

1951. *Serbo-Croatian Folk Songs*. New York: Columbia University Press.

Lord, Albert Bates, and David E. Bynum

1974. Eds. and trans., *The Wedding of Smailagić Meho*. SCHS, III.

Lord, Mary Louise

1967. "Withdrawal and Return: An Epic Story Pattern in the Homeric Hymn to Demeter and in the Homeric Poems." *Classical Journal*, 62:241–48.

Lorimer, H.L.

1948. "Homer and the Art of Writing: A Sketch of Opinion between 1713 and 1939." *American Journal of Archaeology*, 52:11–23.

Lutz, Dieter

1974. "Zur Formelhaftigkeit mittelhochdeutscher Texte und zur 'theory of oral-formulaic composition.'" *Deutsche Vierteljahresschrift für Literaturwissenschaft und Geistesgeschichte*, 48:432–47.

Magnien, Victor (Hédelin 1715)

1925. *Conjectures académiques ou Dissertation sur l'Iliade*, by François Hédelin. Paris: Librarie Hachette.

Magoun, Francis P., Jr.

1929. "Recurring First Elements in Different Nominal Compounds in *Beowulf* and in the *Elder Edda*." In *Studies in English Philology: A Miscellany in Honor of Frederick Klaeber*. Ed. Kemp Malone and Martin B. Ruud. Minneapolis: University of Minnesota Press. Pp. 73–78.

1945. "A Note on Old West Germanic Poetic Unity." *Modern Philology*, 43:77–82.

1953. "The Oral-Formulaic Character of Anglo-Saxon Narrative Poetry." *Speculum*, 28:446–67.

1955a. "Bede's Story of Cædman: The Case History of an Anglo-Saxon Oral Singer." *Speculum*, 30:49–63.

1955b. "The Theme of the Beasts of Battle in Anglo-Saxon Poetry." *Neuphilologische Mitteilungen*, 56:81–90.

Malone, Kemp

1960. Review of Godfrid Storms' *Compounded Names of Peoples in Beowulf*. *English Studies*, 41:200–205.

1961. "Cædmon and English Poetry." *Modern Language Notes*, 76:193–95.

McDonald, M.V.

1978. "Orally Transmitted Poetry in Pre-Islamic Arabia and Other Pre-literate Societies." *Journal of Arabic Literature*, 9:14–31.

McDowell, John H.

1972. "The Mexican *Corrido*: Formula and Theme in a Ballad Tradition." *Journal of American Folklore*, 85:205–20.

McLeod, Wallace
1961. "Oral Bards at Delphi." *Transactions of the American Philological Association*, 92:317–25.
1966. "Studies on Panyassis—An Heroic Poet of the Fifth Century." *Phoenix*, 20:95–110.

McNeill, I.
1963. "The Metre of the Hittite Epic." *Anatolian Studies*, 13:237–42.

Meillet, Antoine
1923. *Les Origines indo-européennes des mètres grecs.* Paris: Presses Universitaires de France.

Melia, Daniel F.
1974. "Parallel Versions of 'The Boyhood Deeds of Cuchulainn.'" In Duggan 1974a:25–40.
1977–78. "Remarks on the Structure and Composition of the Ulster Death Tales." *Studia Hibernica*, 17–18:36–57.

Menéndez Pidal, Ramón
1959. *La Chanson de Roland y el neotradicionalismo (orígenes de la épica románica).* Madrid: Espasa-Calpe. 2d ed., *La Chanson de Roland et la tradition épique des Francs.* Trans. I.-M. Cluzel and rev. with René Louis. Paris: A. and J. Picard, 1960.
1965–66. "Los cantores épicos yugoeslavos y los occidentales. El *Mío Cid* y dos refundidores primitivos." *Boletín de la Real Academia de Buenas Letras de Barcelona*, 31:195–225.

Mertens-Fonck, Paula
1978. "Structure des passages introduisant le discours direct dans *Beowulf*." In *Mélanges de philologie et de littératures romanes offerts à Jeanne Wathelet-Willem.* Liège: Marché Romane. Pp. 433–45.

Messing, Gordon M.
1981. "On Weighing Achilles' 'Winged Words'." *Language*, 57:888–900.

Meyer, Richard M.
1889. *Die altgermanische Poesie nach ihren formelhaften Elementen beschrieben.* Berlin: W. Hertz.

Miklosich, Franz
1890. "Die Darstellung im slavischen Volksepos." *Denkschriften der Wiener Akademie der Wissenschaften*, 38, Abh. 3:1–51.

Miletich, John S.
1974. "Narrative Style in Spanish and Slavic Traditional Narrative Poetry: Implications for the Study of the Romance Epic." *Olifant*, 2:109–28.
1976. "The Quest for the 'Formula': A Comparative Reappraisal." *Modern Philology*, 74:111–23.
1978. "Oral-Traditional Style and Learned Literature: A New Perspective." *Poetics and the Theory of Literature*, 3:345–56.
1981a. "Hispanic and South Slavic Traditional Narrative Poetry and Related Forms: A Survey of Comparative Studies." In Foley 1981a:375–89.
1981b. "Repetition and Aesthetic Function in the *Poema de Mio Cid* and South-Slavic Oral and Literary Epic." *Bulletin of Hispanic Studies*, 58:189–96.

Minton, William W.
1965. "The Fallacy of the Structural Formula." *Transactions of the American Philological Association*, 96:241–53.

Mohay, András
1974–75. "Schriftlichkeit und Mündlichkeit in der byzantinischen Literatur." *Acta Classica*, 10–11:175–81.

Monroe, James T.

1972. "Oral Composition in Pre-Islamic Poetry." *Journal of Arabic Literature*, 3:1–53.
1975. "Formulaic Diction and the Common Origins of Romance Lyric Traditions." *Hispanic Review*, 43:341–50.

Morgan, Gareth
1960. "Cretan Poetry: Sources and Inspiration." *Kretika Chronika*, 14:7–68.

Moulton, Carroll
1977. *Similes in the Homeric Poems*. Göttingen: Vandenhoeck and Ruprecht.

Muellner, Leonard C.
1976. *The Meaning of Homeric* eukhomai *through Its Formulas*. Innsbruck: Institut für Sprachwissenschaft, Universität Innsbruck.

Murko, Matija
1909. "Die Volksepik der bosnischen Mohammedaner." *Zeitschrift des Vereins für Volkskunde*, 19:13–30.
1912. *Bericht über phonografische Aufnahmen epischer, meist mohammedanischer Volkslieder im nordwestlichen Bosnien im Sommer 1912*. Berichte der Phonogramm-Archivs-Kommission der Kaiserlichen Akademie der Wissenschaften in Wien, 30. Vienna: Alfred Hölder.
1913. *Bericht über eine Bereisung von Nordwestbosnien und der angrenzenden Gebiete von Kroatien und Dalmatien behufs Erforschung der Volksepik der bosnischen Mohammedaner*. Sitzungsberichte der Kaiserlichen Akademie der Wissenschaften in Wien, philosophisch-historische Klasse, Band 173, Abhandlung 3. Vienna: Alfred Hölder.
1915a. *Bericht über eine Reise zum Studium der Volksepik in Bosnien und Herzegowina im Jahre 1913*. Sitzungsberichte der Kaiserlichen Akademie der Wissenschaften in Wien, philosophisch-historische Klasse, Band 176, Abhandlung 2. Vienna: Alfred Hölder.
1915b. *Bericht über phonografische Aufnahmen epischer Volkslieder im mittleren Bosnien und in der Herzegowina im Sommer 1913*. Mitteilung der Phonogramm-Archivs-Kommission, 37. Sitzungsberichte der Kaiserlichen Akademie der Wissenschaften in Wien, philosophisch-historische Klasse, Band 179, Abhandlung 1. Vienna: Alfred Hölder.
1919. "Neues über südslavische Volksepik." *Neue Jahrbücher für das klassische Altertum, Geschichte und deutsche Literatur*, 22:273–96.
1928. "L'Etat actuel de la poésie populaire épique yougoslave." *Le Monde slave*, 5:321–51.
1929. *La Poésie populaire épique en Yougoslavie au début du XXe siècle*. Travaux publiés par l'Institut d'Etudes Slaves, 10. Paris: Librairie Ancienne Honoré Champion.
1931. "Auf den Spuren der Volksepik durch Jugoslavien." *Slavische Rundschau*, 3:173–83.
1933. "Nouvelles observations sur l'état actuel de la poésie épique en Yougoslavie." *Revue des études slaves*, 13:16–50.
1938a. "Nekoliko zadaća u proučavanju narodne epike." *Prilozi proučavanja narodne poezije*, 5:2–5.
1938b. "Za narodnom epikom na Kosovu." *Prilozi za književnost, jezik, istoriju i folklor*, 18:565–76.
1951. *Tragom srpsko-hrvatske narodne epike: Putovanja u godinama 1930–32*. 2 vols. Djela Jugoslavenske Akademije Znanosti i Umjetnosti, knj. 41–42. Zagreb: Jugoslavenska Akademija Znanosti i Umjetnosti.

Myres, J.L.
1958. *Homer and His Critics*. Ed. D.F. Gray. London: Routledge and Kegan Paul.

Nagler, Michael N.
1967. "Towards a Generative View of the Oral Formula." *Transactions of the American Philological Association*, 98:269–311.

1974. *Spontaneity and Tradition: A Study in the Oral Art of Homer.* Berkeley: University of California Press.

Nagy, Gregory
1974. *Comparative Studies in Greek and Indic Meter.* Cambridge, Mass.: Harvard University Press.
1976. "Formula and Meter." In Stolz and Shannon 1976:239–60.
1979. *The Best of the Achaeans: Concepts of the Hero in Archaic Greek Poetry.* Baltimore: Johns Hopkins University Press.
1986. "Ancient Greek Epic and Praise Poetry: Some Typological Considerations." In Foley 1986d:89–102.

Nagy, Joseph Falaky
1983. "Close Encounters of the Traditional Kind in Medieval Irish Literature." In *Celtic Folklore and Christianity: Studies in Memory of William W. Heist.* Ed. Patrick K. Ford. Santa Barbara, Calif.: McNally and Loftin. Pp. 129–49.
1985. *The Wisdom of the Outlaw: The Boyhood Deeds of Finn in Gaelic Narrative Tradition.* Berkeley: University of California Press.
1986. "Orality in Medieval Irish Narrative: An Overview." *Oral Tradition,* 1:272–301.

Nichols, Stephen G.
1961. *Formulaic Diction and Thematic Composition in the Chanson de Roland.* Chapel Hill: University of North Carolina Press.

Niditch, Susan
1985. *Chaos to Cosmos: Studies in Biblical Patterns of Creation.* Chico, Calif.: Scholars Press.

Nielsen, Eduard
1954. *Oral Tradition: A Modern Problem in Old Testament Introduction.* London: SCM Press.

Niles, John D.
1981a. "Formula and Formulaic System in *Beowulf.*" In Foley 1981a:394–415. Rpt. in Niles 1983:121–37.
1981b. "Compound Diction and the Style of *Beowulf.*" *English Studies,* 62:489–503.
1983. *Beowulf: The Poem and Its Tradition.* Cambridge, Mass.: Harvard University Press.

Nilsson, Martin P.
1933. *Homer and Mycenae.* Rpt. New York: Cooper Square, 1968, and Philadelphia: University of Pennsylvania Press, 1972.

Nimis, Steve
1986. "The Language of Achilles." *Classical World,* 79:217–25.

Norman, Frederick
1938. "The Germanic Heroic Poet and His Art." In *German Studies Presented to Professor H.G. Fiedler, M.V.O. by Pupils, Colleagues, and Friends on His Seventy-Fifth Birthday 28 April 1937.* Oxford: Clarendon Press. Pp. 293–322.

Notopoulos, James A.
1938. "Mnemosyne in Oral Literature." *Transactions of the American Philological Association,* 69:465–93.
1949. "Parataxis in Homer." *Transactions of the American Philological Association,* 80:1–23.
1950. "The Generic and Oral Composition in Homer." *Transactions of the American Philological Association,* 81:28–36.
1951. "Continuity and Interconnexion in Homeric Oral Composition." *Transactions of the American Philological Association,* 82:81–101.
1952. "Homer and Cretan Heroic Poetry: A Study in Comparative Oral Poetry." *American Journal of Philology,* 73:225–50.
1954. "Homer as an Oral Poet in the Light of Modern Greek Heroic Oral Poetry."

Yearbook of the American Philosophical Society [for 1953]. Philadelphia: American Philosophical Society. Pp. 249–53.

1957. "Homer and Geometric Art: A Comparative Study in the Formulaic Technique of Composition." *Athena*, 61:65–93.

1959a. "Originality in Homeric and Akritan Formulae." *Laographia*, 18:423–31.

1959b. "Modern Greek Heroic Oral Poetry and Its Relevance to Homer." Text accompanying Folkways Record FE 4468, *Modern Greek Heroic Oral Poetry*. New York: Folkways.

1960a. "Homer, Hesiod, and the Achaean Heritage of Oral Poetry." *Hesperia*, 29:177–97.

1960b. "The Genesis of an Oral Heroic Poem." *Greek, Roman, and Byzantine Studies*, 3:135–44.

1962. "The Homeric Hymns as Oral Poetry: A Study of the Post-Homeric Oral Tradition." *American Journal of Philology*, 83:337–68.

1963. "The Influence of the Klephtic Ballads on the Heroic Oral Songs of Crete" [in Greek]. *Kretika Chronika*, 15–16:77–91.

1964. "Studies in Early Greek Oral Poetry." *Harvard Studies in Classical Philology*, 68:1–77.

Ochrymowycz, Orest R.

1975. *Aspects of Oral Style in the Romances Juglarescos of the Carolingian Cycle*. Iowa City: State University of Iowa Press.

Ó Coileáin, Seán

1977–78. "Oral or Literary? Some Strands of the Argument." *Studia Hibernica*, 17–18:7–35.

1978. "Irish Saga Literature." In Oinas 1978a:172–92.

Oinas, Felix J.

1978a. Ed., *Heroic Epic and Saga: An Introduction to the World's Great Folk-Epics*. Bloomington: Indiana University Press.

1978b. "Russian Byliny." In Oinas 1978a:236–56.

Okpewho, Isidore

1977. "Does the Epic Exist in Africa? Some Formal Considerations." *Research in African Literatures*, 8:171–200.

1979. *The Epic in Africa: Toward a Poetics of the Oral Performance*. New York: Columbia University Press.

1980. "The Anthropologist Looks at Epic." *Research in African Literatures*, 11:429–48.

Olsen, Alexandra Hennessey

1980. "Guthlac on the Beach." *Neophilologus*, 64:290–96.

1981. *Guthlac of Croyland: A Study of Heroic Hagiography*. Washington, D.C.: University Press of America.

1982. "Inversion and Political Purpose in the Old English *Judith*." *English Studies*, 63:289–93.

1984. *Speech, Song, and Poetic Craft: The Artistry of the Cynewulf Canon*. New York and Berne: Peter Lang.

1986. "Oral-Formulaic Research in Old English Studies: I." *Oral Tradition*, 1: 548–606.

1987. "Oral-Formulaic Research in Old English Studies: II." *Oral Tradition*, 2:forthcoming.

O'Neil, Wayne

1960a. "Oral-Formulaic Structure in Old English Elegiac Poetry." Ph.D. diss. (University of Wisconsin).

1960b. "Another Look at Oral Poetry in *The Seafarer*." *Speculum*, 35:596–600.

1970. "The Oral-Formulaic Structure of the Faroese *kvæði*." *Fróðskaparrit*, 18:59–68.

O'Neill, Eugene, Jr.
  1942. "The Localization of Metrical Word-Types in the Greek Hexameter." *Yale Classical Studies*, 8:105–78.
Ong, Walter J., S.J.
  1965. "Oral Residue in Tudor Prose Style." *Publications of the Modern Language Association*, 80:145–54.
  1967. *The Presence of the Word: Some Prolegomena for Cultural and Religious History.* New Haven, Conn.: Yale University Press. Rpt. New York: Simon and Schuster, 1970, and Minneapolis: University of Minnesota Press, 1981.
  1975. "The Writer's Audience Is Always a Fiction." *Publications of the Modern Language Association*, 90: 9–22.
  1977. *Interfaces of the Word: Studies in the Evolution of Consciousness and Culture.* Ithaca, N.Y.: Cornell University Press.
  1982. *Orality and Literacy: The Technologizing of the Word.* London: Methuen.
  1986. "Text as Interpretation: Mark and After." In Foley 1986d:147–69.
O'Nolan, Kevin
  1968. "Homer and the Irish Hero Tale." *Studia Hibernica*, 8:7–20.
  1969. "Homer and Irish Heroic Narrative." *Classical Quarterly*, n.s. 19:1–19.
  1975. "The Use of Formula in Storytelling." In *Hereditas: Essays and Studies Presented to Professor Séamus Ó Duilearga.* Ed. Bo Almqvist et al. Dublin: Folklore of Ireland Society. Pp. 233–50.
  1978. "Formula in Oral Tradition." In *Approaches to Oral Tradition.* Ed. Robin Thelwall. Coleraine: The New University of Ulster. Pp. 24–34.
Opland, Jeff
  1970. "The Oral Origins of Early English Poetry." *University of Cape Town Studies in English*, 1:40–54.
  1971. "*Scop* and *Imbongi*: Anglo-Saxon and Bantu Oral Poets." *English Studies in Africa*, 14:161–78.
  1975. "*Imbongi Nezibongo*: The Xhosa Tribal Poet and the Contemporary Poetic Tradition." *Publications of the Modern Language Association*, 90:185–208.
  1976. "*Beowulf* on the Poet." *Mediaeval Studies*, 38:442–67.
  1977a. "On Anglo-Saxon Poetry and the Comparative Study of Oral Poetic Traditions." *Acta Germanica*, 10:49–62.
  1977b. "Cædmon and Ntkisana: Anglo-Saxon and Xhosa Traditional Poets." *Annals of the Grahamstown Historical Society* [for 1977]: 56–65.
  1980a. *Anglo-Saxon Oral Poetry: A Study of the Traditions.* New Haven, Conn.: Yale University Press.
  1980b. "Southeastern Bantu Eulogy and Early Indo-European Poetry." *Research in African Literatures*, 11:295–307.
  1983. *Xhosa Oral Poetry: Aspects of a Black South African Tradition.* Cambridge: Cambridge University Press.
Packard, David W.
  1974. "Sound-Patterns in Homer." *Transactions of the American Philological Association*, 104:239–60.
  1976. "Metrical and Grammatical Patterns in the Greek Hexameter." In *The Computer in Literary and Linguistic Studies: Proceedings of the Third International Symposium.* Ed. Alan Jones and R.F. Churchhouse. Cardiff: University of Wales Press. Pp. 85–91.
Page, Denys L.
  1955. *The Homeric Odyssey.* Oxford: Clarendon Press, rpt. 1966, 1976.
  1959. *History and the Homeric Iliad.* Berkeley: University of California Press, rpt. 1966 et seq.
  1963. "Archilochus and the Oral Tradition." Chapter 4 in *Archiloque.* Geneva: Vandoeuvres. Pp. 117–63.
Papacharalambous, G.

1963. "Akritic and Homeric Poetry." *Kupriakai Spoudai,* 27:23–65.

Parks, Walter Ward

1981. "Generic Identity and the Guest-Host Exchange: A Study of Return Songs in the Homeric and Serbo-Croatian Traditions." *Canadian-American Slavic Studies,* 15:24–41.

1986. "The Oral-Formulaic Theory in Middle English Studies." *Oral Tradition,* 1:636–94.

Parry, Adam

1956. "The Language of Achilles." *Transactions of the American Philological Association,* 87:1–7.

1966. "Have We Homer's *Iliad?*" *Yale Classical Studies,* 20:177–216.

1971a. Ed., *The Making of Homeric Verse: The Collected Papers of Milman Parry.* Oxford: Clarendon Press.

1971b. Introduction to A. Parry 1971a:ix–lxii.

1972. "Language and Characterization in Homer." *Harvard Studies in Classical Philology,* 76:1–22.

Parry, Milman

1923. "A Comparative Study of Diction as One of the Elements of Style in Early Greek Epic Poetry." M.A. thesis, University of California, Berkeley. Rpt. in A. Parry 1971a:421–36.

1928a. *L'Epithète traditionnelle dans Homère: Essai sur un problème de style homérique.* Paris: Société Editrice "Les Belles Lettres." Trans. into English in A. Parry 1971a:1–190.

1928b. *Les Formules et la métrique d'Homère.* Paris: Société Editrice "Les Belles Lettres." Trans. into English in A. Parry 1971a:191–239.

1929. "The Distinctive Character of Enjambement in Homeric Verse." *Transactions of the American Philological Association,* 60:200–220. Rpt. in A. Parry 1971a:251–65.

1930. "Studies in the Epic Technique of Oral Verse-Making. I. Homer and Homeric Style." *Harvard Studies in Classical Philology,* 41:73–147. Rpt. in A. Parry 1971a:266–324.

1931. "The Homeric Metaphor as a Traditional Poetic Device" (abstract). *Transactions of the American Philological Association,* 62:xxiv. Rpt. in A. Parry 1971a:419.

1932. "Studies in the Epic Technique of Oral Verse-Making. II. The Homeric Language as the Language of an Oral Poetry." *Harvard Studies in Classical Philology,* 43:1–50. Rpt. in A. Parry 1971a:325–64.

1933a. "The Traditional Metaphor in Homer." *Classical Philology,* 28:30–43. Rpt. in A. Parry 1971a:365–75.

1933b. "Whole Formulaic Verses in Greek and Southslavic Heroic Song." *Transactions of the American Philological Association,* 64:179–97. Rpt. in A. Parry 1971a:376–90.

1933–35. "Ćor Huso: A Study of South Slavic Songs. Extracts." Printed in part in A. Parry 1971a:437–64.

1934. "The Traces of the Digamma in Ionic and Lesbian Greek." *Language,* 10:130–44. Rpt. in A. Parry 1971a:391–403.

1935. "Homer and Huso I. The Singer's Rests in Greek and Southslavic Heroic Song" (abstract). *Transactions of the American Philological Association,* 66:xlvii. Rpt. in A. Parry 1971a:420.

1936a. "On Typical Scenes in Homer." *Classical Philology,* 31:357–60. Rpt. in A. Parry 1971a:404–7.

1936b. "The Historical Method in Literary Criticism." *Harvard Alumni Bulletin,* 38:778–82. Rpt. in A. Parry 1971a:408–13.

1937. "About Winged Words." *Classical Philology,* 32:59–63. Rpt. in A. Parry 1971a:414–18.

Patzer, Harald
1972. *Dichterische Kunst und poetisches Handwerk im homerischen Epos*. Wiesbaden:
F. Steiner.
Peabody, Berkley
1975. *The Winged Word: A Study in the Technique of Ancient Greek Oral Composition
as Seen Principally through Hesiod's* Works and Days. Albany: State University
of New York Press.
Pipa, Arshi
1978. *Albanian Folk Verse: Structure and Genre*. Munich: Rudolf Trofenik.
Pope, M.W.M.
1960. "Athena's Development in Homeric Epic." *American Journal of Philology*,
81:113–35.
1963. "The Parry-Lord Theory of Homeric Composition." *Acta Classica*, 6:1–21.
Postlethwaite, N.
1979. "Formula and Formulaic: Some Evidence from the Homeric Hymns." *Phoenix*, 33:1–18.
1981. "The Continuation of the *Odyssey*: Some Formulaic Evidence." *Classical
Philology*, 76:177–87.
Quirk, Randolph
1963. "Poetic Language and Old English Metre." In *Early English and Norse Studies
Presented to Hugh Smith in Honor of His Sixtieth Birthday*. Ed. Arthur Brown
and Peter Foote. London: Methuen. Pp. 150–71.
Radlov, Vasilii V.
1885. *Proben der Volkslitteratur der nördlichen türkischen Stämme*, vol. 5: *Der Dialect
der Kara-Kirgisen*. St. Petersburg: Commissionäre der Kaiserlichen Akademie
der Wissenschaften.
Rambaud, Alfred
1876. *La Russie épique: Etudes sur les chansons héroiques de la Russie*. Paris: Maisonneuve.
Reeve, M.D.
1973. "The Language of Achilles." *Classical Quarterly*, n.s. 23:193–95.
Renoir, Alain
1962a. "*Judith* and the Limits of Poetry." *English Studies*, 43:145–55.
1962b. "Point of View and Design for Terror in *Beowulf*." *Neuphilologische Mitteilungen*, 63:154–67.
1963. "The Heroic Oath in *Beowulf*, the *Chanson de Roland*, and the *Nibelungenlied*." In *Studies in Old English Literature in Honor of Arthur G. Brodeur*. Ed.
Stanley B. Greenfield. Eugene: University of Oregon Press. Rpt. New York:
Russell and Russell, 1973. Pp. 237–66.
1964. "Oral-Formulaic Theme Survival: A Possible Instance in the *Nibelungenlied*." *Neuphilologische Mitteilungen*, 65:70–75.
1976a. "Oral Theme and Written Texts." *Neuphilologische Mitteilungen*, 77:337–
46.
1976b. "Crist Ihesu's Beasts of Battle: A Note on Oral-Formulaic Theme Survival." *Neophilologus*, 60:455–59.
1977. "The Armor of the *Hildebrandslied*: An Oral-Formulaic Point of View."
Neuphilologische Mitteilungen, 78:389–95.
1979a. "The English Connection Revisited: A Reading Context for the *Hildebrandslied*." *Neophilologus*, 63:84–87.
1979b. "Germanic Quintessence: The Theme of Isolation in the *Hildebrandslied*."
In *Saints, Scholars, and Heroes: Studies in Medieval Culture in Honour of Charles
W. Jones*. Ed. Margot King and Wesley M. Stevens. Collegeville, Minn.: Hill
Monastic Manuscript Library and St. John's Abbey and University. Vol.
2:143–78.

1981a. "Oral-Formulaic Context: Implications for the Comparative Criticism of Mediaeval Texts." In Foley 1981a:416–39.

1981b. "The Least Elegiac of the Elegies: A Contextual Glance at *The Husband's Message*." *Studia Neophilologica*, 53:69–76.

1986. "Oral-Formulaic Rhetoric and the Interpretation of Literary Texts." In Foley 1986d:103–35.

Richmond, W. Edson

1963. " '*Den utrue egtemann*': A Norwegian Ballad and Formulaic Composition." *Norveg*, 10:59–88.

Riedinger, Anita

1985. "The Old English Formula in Context." *Speculum*, 294–317.

Ritzke-Rutherford, Jean

1981a. "Formulaic Microstructure: The Cluster." In *The Alliterative Morte Arthure: A Reassessment of the Poem*. Ed. Karl H. Göller. London and Totowa, N.J.: D.S. Brewer and Rowman & Littlefield. Pp. 70–82, 167–69.

1981b. "Formulaic Macrostructure: The Theme of Battle." In *The Alliterative Morte Arthure*. Pp. 83–95, 169–71.

Robb, Kevin

1970. "Greek Oral Memory and the Origins of Philosophy." *The Personalist*, 51:5–45.

1974. "Oral Bards at Mycenae: A Speculation." *Coranto*, 9, ii:8–16.

Rogers, H.L.

1966. "The Crypto-Psychological Character of the Oral Formula." *English Studies*, 47:89–102.

Rosenberg, Bruce A.

1970a. *The Art of the American Folk Preacher*. New York: Oxford University Press.

1970b. "The Formulaic Quality of Spontaneous Sermons." *Journal of American Folklore*, 83:3–20.

1974. "The Psychology of the Spiritual Sermon." In *Religious Movements in Contemporary America*. Ed. Irving I. Zaretsky and Mark P. Leone. Princeton, N.J.: Princeton University Press. Pp. 135–49.

1986. "The Message of the American Folk Sermon." *Oral Tradition*, 1:695–727.

Rosenmeyer, Thomas G.

1965. "The Formula in Early Greek Poetry." *Arion*, 4:295–311.

Ross, James

1959. "Formulaic Composition in Gaelic Oral Literature." *Modern Philology*, 57:1–12.

Rothe, C.

1894. *Die Bedeutung der Widersprüche für die homerische Frage*. Berlin: A. Haack.

Ruijgh, C.J.

1962. *L'Elément achéen dans la langue épique*. Assen: Koninklijke Drukkerij Van Gorcum and Comp., rpt. 1962.

Russo, Joseph A.

1963. "A Closer Look at Homeric Formulas." *Transactions of the American Philological Association*, 94:235–47.

1966. "The Structural Formula in Homeric Verse." *Yale Classical Studies*, 20:219–40.

1968. "Homer against His Tradition." *Arion*, 7:275–95.

1971. "The Meaning of Oral Poetry. The Collected Papers of Milman Parry: A Critical Re-assessment." *Quaderni Urbinati di Cultura Classica*, 12:27–39.

1976a. "Is 'Oral' or 'Aural' Composition the Cause of Homer's Formulaic Style?" In Stolz and Shannon 1976:31–71.

1976b. "How, and What, Does Homer Communicate? The Medium and Message of Homeric Verse." *Classical Journal*, 71:289–99.

Russo, Joseph A., and Bennett Simon

1968. "Homeric Psychology and the Oral Epic Tradition." *Journal of the History of Ideas*, 29:483–98.

Russom, Geoffrey R.
1978. "Artful Avoidance of the Useful Phrase in *Beowulf, The Battle of Maldon,* and *Fates of the Apostles.*" *Studies in Philology*, 75:371–90.

Rychner, Jean
1955. *La Chanson de geste: Essai sur l'art épique des jongleurs.* Geneva and Lille: E. Droz and Giard.

Sarrazin, Gregor
1886. "Beowulf und Kynewulf." *Anglia*, 9:515–50.
1888. *Beowulf-Studien: Ein Beitrag zur Geschichte altgermanischer Sage und Dichtung.* Berlin: Mayer and Müller.

Schaar, Claes
1956. "On a New Theory of Old English Poetic Diction." *Neophilologus*, 40:301–5.

Scheub, Harold
1975. *The Xhosa "Ntsomi."* Oxford: Clarendon Press.

Schmaus, Alois
1953. *Studije o krajinskoj epici.* Rad Jugoslavenske Akademije Znanosti i Umjetnosti, knj. 297. Zagreb: Jugoslavenska Akademija Znanosti i Umjetnosti. Pp. 89–247.
1956. "Ein epenkundliches Experiment." *Die Welt der Slaven*, 1:322–33.

SCHS
1953–. *Serbo-Croatian Heroic Songs (Srpskohrvatske junačke pjesme).* Coll., ed., and trans. by Milman Parry, Albert B. Lord, and David E. Bynum. Cambridge, Mass.: Harvard University Press [vols. I and II co-published by the Serbian Academy of Sciences, Belgrade].

Schwarz, Werner
1965. "Notes on Formulaic Expressions in Middle High German Poetry." In *Mediaeval German Studies Presented to Frederick Norman.* London: Institute for Germanic Studies, University of London. Pp. 60–70.

Scott, John A.
1911. "Repeated Verses in Homer." *American Journal of Philology*, 32:313–21.

Scott, William C.
1974. *The Oral Nature of the Homeric Simile.* Leiden: E.J. Brill.

Segal, Charles P.
1967. "Transition and Ritual in Odysseus' Return." *La Parola del passato*, 22:321–42.
1968. "The Embassy and Duals of *Iliad* 9.182–98." *Greek, Roman, and Byzantine Studies*, 9:101–14.
1971a. *The Theme of the Mutilation of the Corpse in the Iliad.* Leiden: E.J. Brill.
1971b. "Andromache's Anagnorisis: Formulaic Artistry in *Iliad* 22.437–476." *Harvard Studies in Classical Philology*, 75:33–57.
1982. "Tragédie, oralité, écriture." Trans. Vincent Giroud. In *Généalogies de l'écriture*, a special issue of *Poétique*, 50:131–54.

Shannon, Richard S.
1975. *The Arms of Achilles and Homeric Compositional Technique.* Leiden: E.J. Brill.

Sheppard, J.T.
1935. "Zeus-Loved Achilles: A Contribution to the Study of Stock Epithets in Homer's *Iliad.*" *Journal of Hellenic Studies*, 55:113–23.
1936. "Great-Hearted Odysseus: A Contribution to the Study of Stock Epithets in Homer's *Odyssey.*" *Journal of Hellenic Studies*, 56:36–47.

Shewan, A.
1913. "Does the *Odyssey* Imitate the *Iliad*?" *Classical Philology*, 7:234–42.

Shorey, Paul
1928. [Review of Parry 1928a, b]. *Classical Philology*, 23:305–6.

Sievers, Eduard
　1878. "Formelverzeichnis." In his ed., *Heliand*. Halle: Buchhandlung des Wai-
　　senhauses. Pp. 391–496.
Simon, Bennett
　1978. *Mind and Madness in Ancient Greece: The Classical Roots of Modern Psychiatry*.
　　Ithaca, N.Y.: Cornell University Press.
　1966. With Herbert Weiner. "Models of Mind and Mental Illness in Ancient
　　Greece: I. The Homeric Model of Mind." *Journal of the History of the Behavioral
　　Sciences*, 2:303–15.
Simonsuuri, Kirsti
　1979. *Homer's Original Genius: Eighteenth-Century Notions of the Early Greek Epic*.
　　Cambridge: Cambridge University Press.
Sioud, Hèdi
　1976. "La Poésie orale tunisienne: Structure formulo-orale." *Revue tunisienne de
　　sciences sociales*, 46:153–92.
　1978. "Rapports structuro-thématiques entre la poésie orale tunisienne et la poé-
　　sie pré-islamique." *Les Cahiers de Tunisie*, 26:191–218.
Skendi, Stavro
　1954. *Albanian and South Slavic Oral Epic Poetry*. Philadelphia: American Folklore
　　Society.
　1980. *Balkan Cultural Studies*. New York: Columbia University Press.
Slotkin, Edgar M.
　1978–79. "Medieval Irish Scribes and Fixed Texts." *Eigse*, 17:437–50.
　1983. "Folkloristics and Medieval Celtic Philology: A Theoretical Model." In *Celtic
　　Folklore and Christianity: Studies in Memory of William W. Heist*. Ed. Patrick K.
　　Ford. Santa Barbara, Calif.: McNally and Loftin. Pp. 213–25.
Smith, John D.
　1977. "The Singer or the Song? A Reassessment of Lord's 'Oral Theory'." *Man*,
　　n.s. 12:141–53.
　1981. "Words, Music, and Memory." In *Memory and Poetic Structure*. London:
　　Middlesex Polytechnic. Pp. 50–65.
Sowayan, Saad Abdullah.
　1985. *Nabaṭi Poetry: The Oral Poetry of Arabia*. Berkeley: University of California
　　Press.
Spraycar, Rudy S.
　1976. "*La Chanson de Roland*: An Oral Poem?" *Olifant*, 4:63–74.
Stanford, W.B.
　1967. *The Sound of Greek: Studies in the Greek Theory and Practice of Euphony*. Berke-
　　ley: University of California Press.
　1969. "Euphonic Reasons for the Choice of Homeric Formulae?" *Hermathena*,
　　108:14–17.
　1976. "Varieties of Sound-Effects in the Homeric Poems." *College Literature*,
　　3:219–27.
　1981. "Sound, Sense, and Music in Greek Poetry." *Greece & Rome*, 2 ser., 28:127–
　　40.
Stevick, Robert D.
　1962. "The Oral-Formulaic Analyses of Old English Verse." *Speculum*, 37:382–
　　89.
Stock, Brian
　1983. *The Implications of Literacy: Written Language and Models of Interpretation in
　　the Eleventh and Twelfth Centuries*. Princeton, N.J.: Princeton University Press.
Stolz, Benjamin A.
　1967. "Historicity in the Serbo-Croatian Heroic Epic: Salih Ugljanin's 'Grčki rat'."
　　Slavic and East European Journal, 11:423–32.
　1969. "On Two Serbo-Croatian Oral Epic Verses: The *Bugarštica* and the *Dese*-

terac." In *Poetic Theory/Poetic Practice.* Ed. Robert Scholes. Iowa City: Midwest Modern Language Association. Pp. 153–64.

1970. "Nikac and Hamza: Multiformity in the Serbo-Croatian Heroic Epic." *Journal of the Folklore Institute,* 7:60–79.

1976. With Richard S. Shannon, eds. *Oral Literature and the Formula.* Ann Arbor, Mich.: Center for Coordination of Ancient and Modern Studies.

Suzuki, Eiichi

1972. "Oral-Formulaic Theme Survival: Two Possible Instances and Their Significance in *Sir Gawain and the Green Knight.*" *Studies in English Literature* [for 1972, English no.]:15–31.

Tatlock, John S.P.

1923a. "Epic Formulas, Especially in Layamon." *Publications of the Modern Language Association,* 38:494–529.

1923b. "Layamon's Poetic Style and Its Relations." In *The Manly Anniversary Studies in Language and Literature.* Chicago: University of Chicago Press. Rpt. Freeport, N.Y.: Books for Libraries Press, 1968. Pp. 3–11.

Taylor, Paul B.

1963. "The Structure of *Völundarkviða.*" *Neophilologus,* 47:228–36.

Thackeray, H. St. J.

1926. Ed. and trans. *Josephus, I. The Life, Against Apion.* London and New York: Loeb Classical Library.

Thormann, Janet

1970. "Variations on the Theme of 'The Hero on the Beach' in *The Phoenix.*" *Neuphilologische Mitteilungen,* 71:187–90.

Titon, Jeff Todd

1977a. *Early Downhome Blues: A Musical and Cultural Analysis.* Urbana: University of Illinois Press.

1977b. "Thematic Pattern in Downhome Blues Lyrics: The Evidence on Commercial Phonograph Records Since World War II." *Journal of American Folklore,* 90:316–30.

1978. "Every Day I Have the Blues: Improvisation and Daily Life." *Southern Folklore Quarterly,* 42:85–98.

Treitler, Leo

1974. "Homer and Gregory: The Transmission of Epic Poetry and Plainchant." *The Musical Quarterly,* 60:333–72.

1975. " 'Centonate Chant': *Übles Flickwerk* or *E pluribus unus?*" *Journal of the American Musicological Society,* 28:1–23.

1981. Et al., eds. *Transmission and Form in Oral Traditions.* Kassel: Bärenreiter.

Trousdale, Marion

1981. "Shakespeare's Oral Text." *Renaissance Drama,* 12:95–115.

Trypanis, C.A.

1963. "Byzantine Oral Poetry." *Byzantinische Zeitschrift,* 56:1–3.

Urbrock, William J.

1972. "Formula and Theme in the Song-Cycle of Job." In *Society of Biblical Literature, 1972 Proceedings (September 1–5).* Missoula, Mont.: Scholars Press. Vol. 2:459–87.

1976. "Oral Antecedents to Job: A Survey of Formulas and Formulaic Systems." In Culley 1976a:111–37.

van Gennep, Arnold

1909. *La Question d'Homère: Les Poèmes homériques, l'archéologie et la poésie populaire.* Paris: Mercure de France.

van Otterlo, Willem A.A.

1948. *De Ringcompositie als Opbouwprincipe in de epische Gedichten van Homerus.* Amsterdam: Noord-Hollandsche Uitgevers Maatschappij.

Van Seters, John
1972. "The Conquest of Sihon's Kingdom: A Literary Examination." *Journal of Biblical Literature*, 91:182–97.
1976. "Oral Patterns or Literary Conventions in Biblical Narrative." In Culley 1976a:139–54.
Vansina, Jan
1965. *Oral Tradition: A Study in Historical Methodology*. Trans. H.M. Wright. Chicago and London: Aldine and Routledge & Kegan Paul.
Vikis-Freibergs, Vaira, and Imants Freibergs
1978. "Formulaic Analysis of the Computer-Accessible Corpus of Latvian Sun-Songs." *Computers and the Humanities*, 12:329–39.
Vilmar, August F.C.
1862. *Deutsche Altertümer im Heliand als Einkleidung der evangelischen Geschichte*, 2d ed. Marburg: N.G. Elwert'sche Universitäts-Buchhandlung.
Vivante, Paolo
1975. "On Homer's Winged Words." *Classical Quarterly*, n.s. 25:1–12.
1982. *The Epithets in Homer: A Study in Poetic Values*. New Haven, Conn.: Yale University Press.
Walker, Warren S.
1981. "Cooper's Use of the Oral Tradition." In *James Fenimore Cooper: His Country and His Art*. Ed. George A. Test. Oneonta: Department of English, State University of New York. Pp. 24–39.
Waltman, Franklin M.
1973. "Formulaic Expression and Unity of Authorship in the *Poema de Mio Cid*." *Hispania*, 56:569–78.
1976–78. "Divided Heroic Vision or Dual-Authorship in the *Poema de Mio Cid*?" *Romance Notes*, 17:84–88.
Wang, Ching-Hsien
1974. *The Bell and the Drum*: Shih Ching *as Formulaic Poetry in an Oral Tradition*. Berkeley: University of California Press.
Warner, Elizabeth A.
1974. "Pushkin in the Russian Folk-Plays." In Duggan 1974a:101–7.
Watkins, Calvert
1976. "Response" to Kiparsky 1976. In Stolz and Shannon 1976:107–11.
Watters, William R.
1976. *Formula Criticism and the Poetry of the Old Testament*. Berlin: Walter de Gruyter.
Watts, Ann C.
1969. *The Lyre and the Harp: A Comparative Reconsideration of Oral Tradition in Homer and Old English Epic Poetry*. New Haven, Conn.: Yale University Press.
Webber, Ruth House
1951. *Formulistic Diction in the Spanish Ballad*. *University of California Publications in Modern Philology*, 34, ii:175–277.
1966. "The Diction of the *Roncesvalles* Fragment." In *Homenaje a Rodríguez-Moñino: Estudios de erudición que le ofrecen sus amigos o discípulos hispanistas norteamericanos*. Madrid: Editorial Castalia. Vol. 2:311–21.
1973. "Narrative Organization of the *Cantar de Mio Cid*." *Olifant*, 1, ii:21-34.
1986a. "Hispanic Oral Literature: Accomplishments and Perspectives." *Oral Tradition*, 1:344–80.
1986b. "The *Cantar de Mio Cid*: Problems of Interpretation." In Foley 1986d:65–88.
1987. Ed., *Oral Tradition and the Hispanic Ballad*. A special issue of *Oral Tradition*, 2, ii.
Webster, John

1976. "Oral Form and Written Craft in Spenser's *Faerie Queene.*" *Studies in English Literature*, 16:75–93.

Webster, T.B.L.
1958. *From Mycenae to Homer.* London: Methuen, 2d ed. with corrs. 1964.
1963. [Review of Kirk 1962]. *Journal of Hellenic Studies*, 83:157.

West, Martin L.
1981. "The Singing of Homer and the Modes of Early Greek Music." *Journal of Hellenic Studies*, 101:113–29.

Whallon, William
1969a. *Formula, Character, and Context: Studies in Homeric, Old English, and Old Testament Poetry.* Cambridge, Mass.: Harvard University Press.
1969b. "Who Wrote Down the Formulaic Poem?" In *Actes du Ve Congrès de l'Association Internationale de Littérature Comparée.* Ed. Nikola Banašević. Belgrade and Amsterdam: Beogradski Grafički Zavod and Swets & Zeitlinger. Pp. 469–72.

Whitaker, Richard E.
1972. *A Concordance of the Ugaritic Literature.* Cambridge, Mass.: Harvard University Press.

Whitman, Cedric H.
1958. *Homer and the Heroic Tradition.* Cambridge, Mass.: Harvard University Press. Rpt. New York: Norton, 1965.

Widengren, G.
1959. "Oral Tradition and Written Literature among the Hebrews in Light of Arabic Evidence, with Special Regard to Prose Narratives." *Acta Orientalia*, 23:201–62.

Wilamowitz-Moellendorff, Ulrich von
1884. *Homerische Untersuchungen.* Berlin: Weidmann.

Wilgus, D.K.
1983. "A Tension of Essences in Murdered-Sweetheart Ballads." In *The Ballad Image: Essays Presented to Bertrand Harris Bronson.* Ed. James Porter. Los Angeles: Center for the Study of Comparative Folklore and Mythology, University of California, Los Angeles. Pp. 241–56.

Windelberg, Marjorie L., and D. Gary Miller
1980. "How (Not) to Define the Epic Formula." *Olifant*, 8:29–50.

Witte, Kurt
1907. *Singular und Plural: Forschungen über Form und Geschichte der griechischen Poesie.* Leipzig: B.G. Teubner.
1912a. "Zur Flexion homerischer Formeln." *Glotta*, 3:110–17. Rpt. in his *Zur homerischen Sprache.* Darmstadt: Wissenschaftliche Buchgesellschaft, 1972, pp. 34–41, and in Latacz 1979a:109–17.
1912b. "Der Einfluss des Verses auf die Bildung von Komposita." *Glotta*, 3:120–29. Rpt. in his *Zur homerischen Sprache.* Darmstadt: Wissenschaftliche Buchgesellschaft, 1972, Pp. 44–53.

Wolf, Carol J.
1970. "Christ as Hero in *The Dream of the Rood.*" *Neuphilologische Mitteilungen*, 71:202–10.

Wolf, Friedrich August
1795. *Prolegomena ad Homerum sive (de) Operum Homericorum Prisca et Genuina Forma Variisque Mutationibus et Probabili Ratione Emendandi.* Halle: Saxonum. Rpt. ed. Rudolf Peppmüller, Hildesheim: Georg Olms Verlag, 1963.

Wood, Robert
1767. *An Essay on the Original Genius of Homer (1769 and 1775).* Anglistica and Americana, 174. Hildesheim and New York: Georg Olms Verlag, 1976.

Yoder, Perry B.

1971. "A-B Pairs and Oral Composition in Hebrew Poetry." *Vetus Testamentum*, 21:470–89.

Young, Douglas C.
1965. "Was Homer an Illiterate Improvisor?" *Minnesota Review*, 5:65–75.
1967. "Never Blotted a Line? Formula and Premeditation in Homer and Hesiod." *Arion*, 6:279–324.

Zaddy, Zara P.
1961. "Chrétien de Troyes and the Epic Tradition." In *Atti del 2° Congresso Internazionale della "Société Rencesvals." Cultura Neolatina*, 21:71–82.

Zumthor, Paul
1973. "La Chanson de geste: Etat de la question." In *Mélanges . . . Teruo Sato*. Nagoya: Centre d'Etudes Mediévales et Romanes. Pp. 97–112.
1982. "Le Discours de la poésie orale." In *Le Discours de la poésie*, a special issue of *Poétique*, 52:387–401.
1983. *Introduction à la poésie orale*. Paris: Editions du Seuil.
1984. "The Text and the Voice." Trans. Marilyn C. Engelhardt. *New Literary History*, 16:67–92.

Zupitza, Julius
1875–76. Ed., *Guy of Warwick*. Early English Text Society, Extra Series 25–26. London: Oxford University Press.

Zwettler, Michael J.
1976. "Classical Arabic Poetry between Folk and Oral Tradition." *Journal of the American Oriental Society*, 96:198–212.
1978. *The Oral Tradition of Classical Arabic Poetry: Its Character and Implications*. Columbus: Ohio State University Press.

INDEX